Obsessive Compulsive Cycling Disorder

First Published in 2012 by **Phased Publications**

www.phased.co.uk

Phased Publications
19 Greywethers Avenue
Swindon
Wiltshire
SN3 1QG

Web: www.phased.co.uk
Email: dave@phased.co.uk
Twitter: @citizenfishy

Local: The Steam Railway, Newport Street, Swindon

Preface

About this Book

Obsessive Compulsive Cycling Disorder is an anthology of thirty articles written by an amateur cyclist over a period of ten years. The collection exhibits the madness that engulfs those who descend into cycling obsession, celebrating the average cyclist living in a world defined by the pros. The writings range from fanciful musings concerning the Tao of singlespeeding to lengthy descriptions of end-to-end rides in Britain and Ireland. Mountain biking, road cycling and all sorts of other cycling events are chronicled along the way. Each is written in a lighthearted style designed to bring the reader into the author's world which is often littered with incident and humour. Within the pages the reader will find a loose ticklist of events to ride, bikes to own and challenges to take on. Each described in the author's own inimitable style.

About the Author

Dave Barter is a British cyclist. Excellent we've got that out of the way. A non-cycling author of a series of bicycle based reflections would have a hint of incongruity about it. He likes to think of himself as an all rounder having tried many two wheeled disciplines and fallen off most of them. In 2001 he chucked in his job and went cycling. In 2010 he did exactly the same thing again. In between times he's written a few articles about cycling and a few of them have even made it into print.

Dave was born in Ely Hospital in 1966 after his Dad raced floodwater to get his Mum to the ward before the river Ouse burst. This explains why he is always in a rush. Dave lives in deepest Wiltshire with his wife Helen and his children Jake and Holly. Wembley the cat used to reside within the family as well but sadly snuffed it a few years ago. Dave's fiscal profession is Information Technology. He writes articles to fund bike parts and is currently attempting to finish a number of books. Once he has read them, he'll turn his attention to his half completed writing projects. Like all good IT practitioners he rarely finishes anything. Obsessive Compulsive Cycling Disorder is the rare exception.

Table of Contents

Before You Begin

Let me begin with a huge "Thank You" for either buying this stream of consciousness, rescuing it from the depths of a charity shop or illegally downloading it from a file sharing site. If it is the latter I must warn you that I've learnt a thing or two in twenty years of IT and that while you are reading this document it is quietly informing Scotland Yard of your whereabouts. The next knock at the door will be the police. Anyway, here's a few things that I wanted to say to the legal readers before they dive into the book.

Firstly, a lot of the content has been published before. Some of it in paper magazines, some of it on cycling websites and most of the articles on my own personal site at www.phased.co.uk. However, there is also a load of new stuff. I have written an introductory article for each piece just for you. So please be reassured that this isn't just a great big cut-and-paste job. Some value really has been added, did I really just write that?

I have thought long and hard about the arrangement of the articles and a logical order. Then I threw order in the bin and decided upon the first and last pieces, with the bits in the middle just slotting in wherever they felt right. I've attempted to mix it all up a bit to keep the reading experience fresh. You'll be the judge of that.

Then we come onto content. I hope you realise by the title that this book covers articles concerning cycling. If not then I suggest you skip right to the end and read the section on "Thanks" as there might not be a lot else in here that interests you. However, if you are curious as to the psyche of a mediocre British cyclist driven by a strange obsession then have a dip in and see if there is something that you can identify with. I've not written specifically about a single cycling genre. I've mixed up the off and on road experiences and also thrown in a few pieces of general cycling reflection.

The quality and depth of articles may vary as well. This is down to the fact that the book has not been consciously written as a single entity. The articles and my style have evolved over a ten year period. But if you've bought this as an eBook then you will have paid less than the price of a pint which I hope is reasonable value for ten years worth of keyboard hammering. Again, I'll let you be the judge of that.

Finally, I am afraid there is some swearing. I'm sorry about that but sometimes I write as I speak, and often cycling has driven me to the extremes of the English language in search of a suitable profanity. I considered editing it all out but then thought, fuck it, nobody will care. I've even heard swearing on Radio Four, if it's good enough for them it'll do for me.

Obsessive Compulsive Cycling Disorder

I can remember the moment clearly. At the age of twenty eight stepping into a mirror panelled lift in a Birmingham hotel. I was wearing a tight fitting white T-shirt and was treated to a 360 degree view of my midriff. It was huge, bulging out all over the place. It looked like a stirrup pump had been connected to my upper half and pumped vigorously until the skin was about to tear.

Who was this portly fellow? Surely it couldn't be me? I was supposed to be a skinny wisp of a thing whose waist size always lagged behind my age. I felt for the label in my jeans and was reminded that it was at least 6 numbers ahead of my current longevity. Another glance at the mirrors confirmed that I'd officially joined the ranks of the wobbly. To make matters worse I was slightly late and had to jog to the bar for an evening social with work colleagues. Fleshy saddle bags battered my sides as I puffed my way towards Ronnie Scotts. It was as if my trunk was attempting to rotate the entire way around my spine.

Something had to be done. I was about to leave my twenties, waist size heading for the forties with most of the excess hanging off my hips and arse. Help was close at hand in my work colleagues. As soon as I'd "come out" as a tubby they were happy to help by taking me running.

The Post Office Research Centre had a decent compliment of runners and some of them were pretty handy. I fell in with this crowd and so began the ritual of a lunchtime jog. This replaced the previous ritual of the lunchtime "jug" (of ale) which was probably the single greatest reason why I ended up in this state in the first place. After a few weeks of severe oxygen debt the jog morphed into a run. Mile became miles. Stopwatch replaced wrist watch, running shoes ousted the daps and an obsession was born.

Six months later the waistline was all but gone. I'd shaken it off all over Wiltshire pounding pavements, paths, tracks and byways in my quest to push it a little bit more. Then it happened, as it does to all who turn to running with a crowd. I was taken aside and quietly advised that it would be a good idea if I entered a race. This is the sport equivalent of the drug dealer upping the stakes from a sneaky lump of dope to full on heroin injection.

The race was a 10k held in the village of Highworth. My dealer advised that under 40 minutes would be an adequate time and so the training stepped up to ensure that I wouldn't disappoint. 39 minutes 47 seconds, figures etched permanently into my memory as it was the first time my body had done anything to make me remotely proud. I entered many other races and ran faster 10k's, longer distances and harder events.

I was probably the only cinema goer who cheered at the words "Run Forrest, Run!". It's what happened to me in the nineties. Three stone of excess weight drove me to an obsession with sport that only increased as the weight disappeared. But Pete was waiting in the wings, a deadly weapon encased within his football boot. A weapon that would kill the obsession with running only to resurrect it into something with a far greater price tag.

Pete unwittingly turned me into a cyclist.

Whilst running was my true love, she wasn't the first. I'd had a messy encounter with squash that ended badly when a school mate duffed me up for beating him fairly on the court. I sought solace in football convincing myself that she'd not do me over as there were 21 others who would probably get her attention first. I played five aside for the works team. To qualify that further, I played five aside for the works reserve of reserves team, I was pretty crap. But being crap at something has never killed my enthusiasm for it. I still play guitar, bring up children, attempt to cook proper food and turn my hand to DIY.

The works team played Thursday evenings on an astroturf pitch. That was where Pete was waiting for me, his deadly weapon hidden deep within his shoe. I did my usual running-around-like-a-pillock-whilst-shouting-football-type-things and my team did the usual letting in loads of goals due to lack of defence, passing or any semblance of talent within its players.

Then a fluke pass saw me heading towards goal with Pete the only obstacle in front. I cunningly faked to the left whilst deftly dragging the ball to the right. It didn't fool Pete. His repost was to aim squarely at both legs with his secret weapon, his size ten foot. This was connected to a leg of reasonable girth and a body of even more reasonable girth. Pete's foot based haymaker connected squarely with my right lower leg, which in turn pivoted in a manner that it isn't supposed to around the knee.

I fell to the ground in pain, just managing to get the "penalty" claim out before hitting the deck. My teammates rushed to the centre circle full of concern..that I might get up and take it. A collective sigh of relief was heard as it became clear that I wasn't getting up. I was dragged off the pitch with some mumblings about "putting some ice on it". The game continued without me.

Two weeks later a strange lump appeared on the knee. I'd continued to run but things on the right hand side just weren't right. All sorts of grating sensations were present with each run and the lump moved around the place constantly varying in size. My doctor looked at it quizzically then prescribed Aspirin. I refused to leave his surgery until he'd written the word "Physiotherapist" upon a referral note. In hindsight, the Aspirin would have been a better choice.

Physiotherapist number one was an out and out quack. First he hooked me up to a device that mildly electrocuted me for twenty minutes whilst he had a cup of tea and a fag. When this failed to show results he stuck me full of needles. I walked out after spotting his rubber gloves and lube. Physiotherapist number two was even worse. He prescribed "not running" along with "not doing anything else either", that should sort it. I squeezed past his belly in the hallway on the way out and went private the very next day.

Doctor Williams was in a different class. He had proper machines that could look inside my leg and take very clever pictures that stimulated him to sit and stroke his chin. Many pictures later a lightbulb went off above his head. He called the electrician and then told me that I was suffering from a Cystic Meniscus. Hatchet Pete had ripped the cartilage in my knee and the synovial fluid was flowing out making the lump.

Within days I was under his knife and the offending cartilage removed. Mistakenly they handed it to me in recovery whilst I was still under the influence of their wonderful drugs. Even more mistakenly they had parked my trolley next to a young boy who'd also been under the knife. Seconds later they wheeled me away from a teenager scared for life by a manic idiot who'd pressed knee tissue into his face whilst chanting "That was in me it was, they took it out, see that white thing, that was in me..."

Doctor Williams had done a good job, but things in the knee were never quite the same. Running is a high impact sport and even though he'd only robbed me of a third of my cartilage I felt it every stride. And so I compensated with my left and things went wrong. The left knee started to hurt, foot pronation got worse, back problems appeared and my timings were crap.

My love affair with running was over. It had been a mad passionate affair carried out in the dirtiest of locations and in the company of some of the strangest people I will ever meet. Running robbed me of my waist whilst introducing me to my physical self once again. She'd dragged me outside and stuffed the four seasons into my face. I'd loved her throughout all of the pain but now she was leaving me for somebody else.

I sought solace in swimming but an incident with an old man who dried his wiggly bits for far too long in front of me convinced me to look elsewhere. Climbing made a brief appearance and still does, but only on sunny days with friends who know how to properly tie knots and arrest my frequent falls. Then I got a call from Steve.

He told me about a cycling event in a woods near Oxford. Riding around looking for checkpoints on a map with a barbecue at the end. We stuffed our entirely unsuitable bikes into his car and made ourselves known at the start. Two hours later we laughed ourselves to the finish.

Scooting through trees on dry mud singletrack we'd made many mistakes and were probably last. But everyone else had wide tyres and some even had bouncy forks.

In the car we planned our next assault. Steve drove home entirely unaware that the man sat next to him was falling in love. A love that would cost him dearly both in time and money. A love that would drag him round the world in search of new adventures. A love that would come with new friends and a whole bastion of motorised enemies. A love that would cost him his job, twice. And worst of all, a love that would cause him to write copiously in vain attempt to describe to others just what this love was and why he'd never give her up.

I'd found cycling again, reunited with a childhood sweetheart. As a youth cycling had liberated me from my house. It had taken me fishing, whisked me off to far flung friends, raced the bus into school and instigated numerous adventures that usually ended in holed trousers and a telling off.

Cycling was ripe for an obsessive like me and what's more it had much more gear than running. There are only so many performance enhancing trainers you can buy but cycling had all sorts of shiny stuff just waiting to make me go faster or longer. What's more, it seemed to work ok even with a dodgy right knee.

Cycling slowly took over my life. I rode on and off road, purchased all manner of bicycles, upgraded them, broke them and crashed them in equal measure. I raced, rode with clubs, time trialled, took part in sportives/audaxes/twenty four hour events, rode countries end to end and even climbed Snowdon on a mountain bike dressed as a gorilla. If a two wheeled challenge presented itself, then I'd be prepared to have a go.

The situation was further polarised by my Mum and her cancer. "Oh no! not another cycling/cancer tale", I hear you cry, "We've only recently got over Lance!". Please read on though, it's not what you think.

"Yes" Mum did get cancer and "Yes" she kicked it's arse but not before going through a long and painful fight with radiotherapy and hospital waiting rooms. Mum's cancer was Ovarian, difficult to spot and hard to treat as it usually pops up once the real damage is done. Mum threw herself into supporting others via the charity Ovacome. So I thought I'd raise a bit of money to help as well.

Most people would have ridden a few miles and held out the hat. Not me, I'm an obsessive. I needed a proper challenge, Land's End to John O'Groats was beckoning. You'll find the story later in the book and I won't spoil it for you. But let's just summarise that it was bloody hard and I learnt a huge amount about myself in the process.

Mum kept asking about the ride, unsatisfied by the terse "It was all-right" that I'd attempt to fob her off with. Eventually I decided to write the whole thing down and so my first cycling article was born. It was aimed at Mum along with a wider audience who I'd hoped might be interested in the "warts and all" version of events. I sat down and wrote it in a few days, words seemed to come easily when writing about cycling and so I wrote a few more.

Next thing I knew, I'd grown another obsession. Not only was I fixated upon farting around on two wheels, I had to tell everyone about it as well. Articles sprang up at the end of every eventful ride, some of them even made it into magazines, others sat mournfully upon my website waiting for bored passers by to take an interest.

Ten years later I sat down and reviewed what I'd done. In cycling terms my achievements are relatively modest, a few miles here and there, a few reasonable performances, but nothing that hasn't been done before. The writing is along the same lines. It's not Shakespeare, but it is hopefully mildly entertaining providing an interesting snapshot as to how a cyclist is rapidly born and drawn into "the cult".

That's what you're reading now. A collection of thirty articles that I've written over the years covering my many cycling misdemeanours. Like my cycling club it's a ragged bunch, varying in style and sometimes meandering into places they probably shouldn't. Each comes with a brief introductory text that sets the scene and attempts to explain just what I was trying to do. They have all been published before in various places but only by bringing them together does the full picture emerge of a man obsessed by cycling, even though he has no particular talent for it. But cycling's like that. Once it draws you in, you'll never get out.

Hopefully you'll enjoy the journey as much as I have. If not, drop me a line and tell me why? The best bit about writing is the feedback, no matter what form it takes. It's the feedback that drives the next article or says to the author "Dave..I think enough is enough!".

Dave Barter, Obsessive Compulsive Cyclist
January 2012

Chapter 1

Beginnings

This is where my writing started in earnest after a few previous dabbles with the word processor. It was written nearly ten years ago but I can still feel the excitement as the words sped from my fingers into the computer. I felt I had something genuinely new and exciting to tell my fellow riders. Mountain biking in Wiltshire isn't always rubbish, there are ways of spicing it up.

I'd been riding mountain bikes for a while, across dry trails bathed in summer sunshine, when suddenly it got cold and dark and wet. Winter had arrived and in my cycling naivety I was poorly prepared for the effort required to ride when the light disappears and the weather turns sour. I started riding at night as the perfect antidote to a stressful job in the day. I discovered the Tao of the night ride along with the preparation required to actually get out on the bike. Once out it's a glorious experience.

This article was the first that I wrote inspired by my emotions rather than the magnitude of the event. I showed it to my wife who informed me that it was "quite good" whilst quietly seething at another large washing machine repair bill caused by my cycling filth. Buoyed by this feedback I emailed it to every magazine I could find that had anything remotely to do with cycling. Tumbleweed flowed through my in-box, I cancelled plans to become a Booker prize winner and went out for a night ride instead.

It must have been a year later that Dan Joyce, editor of the Cyclist Touring Club's "Cycle" magazine got in touch. He'd kept hold of the article and wanted to run it in the mag. This was my big break (or so I thought), all Dan needed were some pictures. Cue Trev "the Sparky" who also moonlighted as a photographer (apt for a night ride article). A long night on the Wiltshire downs followed, attempting to capture some atmospheric pictures. I looked in horror as Trev dropped his £2000 camera whilst vaulting a gate. Fortunately it bounced.

One of the photographs had me riding in the dark past a fire. Nothing to do with Trev or me I hasten to add. It was simply a random fire that some farmer or hooligan had lit in the middle of nowhere and subsequently abandoned. Trev wanted me to ride through it for extra drama, his camera nearly bounced again as I made clear my intention to do exactly the opposite.

I've still got the magazine. The feeling of seeing my words in print for the first time will never leave. "Somebody's actually going to read this stuff" ran through my mind over and over again. Hopefully they did. The following month's letters page covered cycle clips, beard hygiene and penny farthings. No mention of my article at all. I took that as "silent approval" Reading the text over ten years later, I find it still wholeheartedly applies. The ritual's the same, the kids still laugh and I'm convinced that some sort of panther lurks on the hill down to Rockley.

Anatomy of a West Country Night Ride

We all have our rituals, from the priest laying out his altar on a Sunday to the driving test examiner carefully outlining test procedure to a nervous candidate. Preparation for my mid-winter night rides exceeds the time and intricacies of both. The requisite clothing must be rounded up. A cycling jersey will spring with glee from a mountain of cycling clothes stuffed into my corner of the bedroom wardrobe, the waterproof jacket hangs dripping next to the bib longs and, reliable as ever, my shoes are sat warming upon the boiler.

The ritual then moves on to the pre-ride wail. Helen, my wife, turns the volume of the TV up a notch as I cry "Have you seen my gloves anywhere ?". She usually ignores the first incantation, but knows it's unlikely that I'll replace whingeing with actually looking for them. With a heavy sigh she rises, walks a short distance and plucks my gloves from a half empty radiator. "I'm sure I looked there ?" I offer … she gives me that knowing look.

I'm starting to gear up. I open the overloaded bathroom cabinet and a contact lens box flies out along with the detritus of numerous other holidays. Lenses are stuffed into unwelcoming eyes and spasms of blinking eventually settle them into place. A three minute rummage liberates my energy powder from the pan cupboard and scientifically I stuff a load of it into my Camelback, swamping it with a random volume of water. Helen stares in resignation as I prise all of the TV controllers apart for AAA batteries for my rear lights, furiously glancing at the battery recharger I never manage to use.

I attempt to attach a moth eaten set of overshoes and notice that "over"shoes is becoming an "over"statement due to the number of holes they sport. My car toolkit is raided for cable ties and lights are attached to my full suspension bike. I take a long look at my nice clean, well maintained hardtail, but yet again fall victim to the comfort and predictability of full suspension. The Camelback is pulled over the waterproof, helmet located and jammed onto my head, gloves pulled on, then off, speedo attached, gloves pulled on, then off, drinking tube pulled over my back and into position, gloves pulled on, then off, rear light attached, gloves pulled on, then off, Camelback removed, pump and CO2 canister shoved in, gloves pulled on, then off, garage door opened, bike wheeled outside, door shut, gloves pulled on, bike mounted and I'm off.

This has taken nearly half an hour: Holy Communions are finished in this time period, you're over halfway through your driving test in half an hour. I do this nearly twice a week, but it still takes me half an hour every time. As you can see, night riding needs ritual and careful preparation.

I'm now half a mile down the road and heading for the Ridgeway, it's still light. I've learnt to leave home 40 minutes before dark thus ensuring that I get to glimpse sunset at the highest point of the ride. Sunset is an essential ingredient of a West Country night ride, whilst our landscape may be bettered, our sunsets are just as good as anybody else's.

I'm doing my post departure checklist:-

- Drink in Camelback (slurp) Ugh ! too concentrated - check,
- Creaking pedals – check
- Poorly lubed chain – check
- Worn brake pads, part functioning rear brake – check
- Poor shifting at the front – check
- Forgotten camera – check
- Twisted Camelback straps – check
- Inadequate and over thin tyres for the conditions - check

I usually survive, so I pootle along the road and over the motorway. I often pause and look down sanctimoniously at the drivers trapped within the confines of a carriageway with little choice of line or technical challenge. My journey will be harder then theirs, it's going to have variety and difficulty and sometimes an element of sheer beauty. If they're unlucky their journey may be punctuated with an accident, otherwise white lines and featureless signposts await them.

I'm climbing steeply on a winding singletrack road, past the radio mast and swooping down and up again. I greet the "Calley Arms" and write myself a mental note to carry the "price of a pint" next ride. I've written this mental note every week for two years, one day I'll go in. The road gives up to bridleway, tyres sink into mud, but are below the surface by the remains of the summer grass, my heart rate soars. This section is the worst of the ride, over a mile of waterlogged bridleway shredded by horses hooves and still suffering from the light ploughing. I'm really breathing now as tyres fail to bite and the rear wheel spins in the sodden clay, I stray close to the barbed wire fence and glance nervously at the shredded right glove, testament to a recent entanglement. But tonight I'm going to make it, I've cleared the most strenuous section and smile as I join the gritty doubletrack and climb towards the Ridgeway escarpment.

Light is fading, I'm sweating into my three layers as I grind my way up the steep road climb to Barbury Castle. It's quiet up here and I can hear every pimple on the tyre make contact then part company with the tarmac below. Pushing on the middle ring, the devil on my shoulder tells me that "it's time for granny", however, my fitness angel prevails and I persevere, my reward being another dose of sanctimony as I crest the hill and head towards "Four Mile Clump".

I've timed it well tonight and admire the wild tapestry of colours. The sun is dragged below the Marlborough Downs leaving me encircled in the cold darkness. I clip in and follow my breath down a wide chalky descent and into the "water section". This section of the Ridgeway is often frequented by our cousins in 4x4's. They have created a series of narrow lakes, two feet wide and almost as deep. Once I took the time to find a line above, tonight I throw caution, a bottom bracket and two hubs to the wind as I drive ankle deep through each "puddle". My waterproof socks fill with freezing puddle water and my arse ambient temperature is lowered by several degrees as the water seeps down my back and into my welcoming underpants.

Giggling, I meet the road again and turn sharp left past some old country houses and onto a steep climb. On a previous ride I followed something large, black and "cat like" down this section. The recent memory accelerates my climb towards the rolling downs surrounding Avebury. It's a full moon and I catch an owl in my headlamps as it sweeps effortlessly up into the shadows.

A dirt track road accompanies me through a herd of restless sheep who herald my efforts with bleating and general melee. I push hard up a steep stony climb, cross a smooth grassy field and rejoin the Ridgeway. I'm alone, sweaty and very reflective.

I do a lot of thinking on solo night rides. The solitude, remoteness and contrasting environment allow me to line up the day's thoughts and make some sort of sense of them. My latest programming problem is solved as I navigate a muddy bridleway, a long rut gives me the concentration necessary to decide how to deal with a particularly obnoxious client, a breathless climb allows me to reach a decision concerning a family problem. Tonight I simply exult in my surroundings, it's dark, silent and I'm following the tracks of Neolithic Man. Scattered stones tell the story of part completed tombs or sites of worship. A representative of every one of the local species have taken the trouble to cross my path at least once this evening and I've managed to ride 15 miles without a puncture.

I hit a section of ruts. I haven't got my light mountings quite right and am jostled off line by mud ridges, the odd boulder and a tinge of less than confident riding. However, I'm still enjoying it and let out a muted "whoop" as I leave the ruts and crank down the wide open descent that skirts an ancient hill fort and leads me back home.

I'm tired now and spin the last few miles at a leisurely pace. I've survived another solo night ride, I've been out there even though its cold, wet and the riding conditions are atrocious.

Back home the ritual continues. I push the garage door and divest the bike of all electrical gadgets. A liberal dose of water from the hose transfers all the mud from my bike to my driveway, car and garden wall. My neighbours' curtain twitches in time with the "What's that bloody idiot doing now ?" conversation.

My muddy sweaty apparel is parted from my body and dumped "expectantly" close to the washing machine my wife gives out another long deep sigh.

Sweaty panted, I stride into the house and the kids fall about laughing at the muddy apparition that was once their father. I look longingly at the kids fish fingers which are rapidly snatched from my grasp and presented to the children. The computer signals 15 new emails and my mobile phone tells me that I have 7 missed calls, I couldn't care less as I drag myself up to my bedroom and fall into the embrace of warm dry clothes.

So, to reflect upon the title of this article, what is the anatomy of a West Country Night Ride ?

It's made of mud, water, hills, valleys, roads and a bit more mud thrown in for good measure. A liberal sprinkling of sunset adds colour and cold often gives it that defining edge. It wouldn't exist without a bike, some lights and a few pieces of rudimentary equipment. Ritual defines mine and it often produces thought, reflection and exhilaration. I'm sure that West Country night rides have a very similar anatomy to those elsewhere, they don't need a recipe book, why not cook one up for yourself?

Chapter 2

A Mountain Biker Strays

L'Etape du Tour was a defining moment for me as a cyclist. Or to be a little more precise, a defining moment for me as a road cyclist given that before I rode it I had clearly stuck my colours to the mountain biking mast. My first foray into proper cycling had been as a mountain biker and I'd quickly upgraded both my bike and myself turning into a fairly competent mountain bike orienteer.

Mountain bike orienteering basically involves cycling to as many checkpoints as possible in a given time. Each checkpoint has a points value and those who return with the most points within the time limit are declared the winner. The race is usually won by a combination of fitness, strategic and tactical planning. Which checkpoints to aim for and which to avoid? What is the best route to gather the maximum points? I developed a very clever strategy indeed, I entered the men's pairs event and left the clever bit to my race partner Russ.

Russ had a keen eye for the points and I had keen legs for the hills. Sometimes this worked, sometimes it didn't. There was the infamous occasion when I rode beside a walking Russ up Dunkery Beacon (17% average over 2 miles in length). I was chiding him on, he was muttering a mixture of swear words and "Dave". But many times we won mostly down to Russ's tactics.

Russ suffered a nasty accident whilst riding his bike breaking his back and losing the use of his legs. Our racing partnership was over, but strong friendship remained. A bunch of us asked Russ if we could help in any way. Magnanimously he requested that we raise funds for the Air Ambulance that had lifted him away from the accident and saved his life in the process. As a result we formed the "RUSS Appeal" and raised over £40,000 for the charity. Russ and I still run it today (www.russ-appeal.org. uk). If you've enjoyed reading thus far, maybe you could spare us a quid or two?

For my part I decided to attempt L'Etape du Tour and gain sponsorship as a result. As part of my publicity campaign I contacted the local paper and told them I was going to ride a stage of the tour. Bless the Swindon Evening Advertiser, they wrote a piece implying I was about to ride the Tour de France omitting the fact that I was only doing a stage that thousands of amateurs do each year.

I wrote this piece after the event in a small bed and breakfast halfway up the Tourmalet. I speculatively emailed it to Chipps Chippendale at Singletrack magazine who stuck it up on their website that same day. The feedback was great as the mountain bike community identified with one of their own who had strayed over to the "dark side".

L'Etape had a profound affect on me as a cyclist as well. Within a year the hair from my legs was gone.

An Impostor Rides L'Etape du Tour

Every year thousands of amateur cyclists are given the chance to compete across a stage of the Tour de France. This race is called L'Etape du Tour and is run during the middle of the Tour, usually on a rest day. This year an impostor sneaked in with the shaven legged road cyclists. I was the hairy mountain biker within their midst. This is my account of what happened next. L'Etape du Tour 2003 ran for 125 miles from Pau to Bayonne, up and down 11000 feet of Pyrenees mountains and across a few river valleys for good measure. 8500 entries for the race had been accepted including 1000 British riders.

The roads along the route were closed and it followed exactly the same course as the professionals would ride one week later. Medals are awarded to riders who complete the course within certain time bands. This year a gold medal required a time of 7 hours 30 and a silver 8 hours 46. A group of five of us left our hotel at 5am on the morning of the race in order to make the start time of 7am. Don't ask why, but I had booked accommodation almost 40 miles from the start of the race, luckily they had laid on a mini-bus for us brave riders. The journey to the start was punctuated with nervous silence, hardly a word was said as we each pondered our fate whist ticking off a list of regrets (I should have ridden more, packed different tools, tweaked my gears, bought better food, not had that second glass of wine last night....).

I wondered whether I was really up to the challenge of the Etape. I had never ridden in a road race, my training had been unstructured, my bike handling skills pertained to off road riding not road racing, I'd never climbed 12,000 feet in a single ride and I had hairy legs. Hope lay in my food preparation. One of the other riders, Peter, had advised me that I probably needed to eat 60g of carbohydrate per hour in order to survive the race.

This led to a frantic shopping session with detailed nutritional content label reading, followed by an incredibly complex spreadsheet. The spreadsheet estimated my time between feed stops and the amount of food to be ingested on the move. To summarise, I was to start the race with 14 fig rolls, 3 energy bars, 2 carbohydrate gels, 1 banana and 3 bags of carefully measured energy powered to be added to my water. The spreadsheet told me when to eat it all and what to pickup at each feeding station. According to my sheet I would finish the ride in 8 hours 29 minutes and consume 498g of carbohydrate, or 62 fig rolls!

I was now inducted within a feeding program similar to that of a goose destined for the fois gras factory. Mountain biking seemed so much simpler with my own personal rule of thumb being "sling some stuff in my Camelback, ride for 3 hours and forget to eat any of it, return home and leave it festering on the bench in my garage until the mice take pity and cart it away". Anyway, back to the race. Our van made good time to Pau and as we came within ½ a mile of the start the Lycra to cotton ratio took a serious escalation. Thousands of riders milled about the streets, twiddling gears, adjusting bits both personal and on the bike and pissing.

Riders were pissing everywhere, up walls, on trees, against cars and into the street as pre-ride hydration took its toll. We hurled our bikes out of the van, pissed up a wall, stuffed our pockets with food, muttered hasty "Good Lucks" at each other and strode round the block to the start line. Setting 8500 riders off at once from a race that begins in a town centre is impossible. Therefore, each rider is allocated a pen according to their race number where they must wait until the race starts. Each pen holds 1000 riders and they're released in number order. I had number 6092, which meant that I would have to wait for about 20 minutes before it was my turn to start.

Migual Indurin had number 1 and Alan Prost number 2, they both twitched nervously knowing that Dave Barter was due to start 20 minutes after them. They were the ones under pressure, desperate to avoid the humiliation of being overtaken by a hairy mountain biker. I'd even brought my road bike along so no advantage for them on that front either. I found my pen and sized up the riders that surrounded me.

Almost without exception they fell into the following genus:-

- About 40 years old
- Holding a very very expensive bike
- Looking tanned and fit
- Appearing relaxed and confident
- Dressed in clean, neat colour co-ordinated clothes
- Speaking French too fast
- Punctuating their sentences with "Migual Migual"

After an eternity the commentator's speed-French reached a frenzied peak and I think he announced that "They're Off!". The start had to be the biggest anti-climax of the day as we simply stood and waited for our turn to go. Finally an orchestra of cleats clicked into pedals and our section started to move, then stopped, then moved, then stopped, then walked a bit, then got on, wobbled stopped again and walked some more. It took nearly five minutes for us to reach the start line and be able to cycle freely.

I jabbed my digital watch and the seconds started to tick away. A transponder strapped to my ankle informed the Etape computer that Dave Barter was on his way, but not to panic as it probably wouldn't hear from him for a while. It was then that I realised that the organisers had cleverly created a bottleneck to ensure that riders were not bunched after the start line.

My pack of riders hared through the streets of Pau at close to 40 km/h. I joined a mini-peleton ate a fig roll (according to schedule) and for a while felt like a proper bike racer. The next 10 kilometres disappeared frighteningly quickly as a combination of flat roads, cool conditions and adrenaline sped us on. We reached the town of Gan and veered right towards the first real climb of the day. My drinking strategy was working a treat and an overflowing bladder forced me to the side of the road for a moment of relief.

It struck me that female cyclists must have an interesting time during these long events and I kept a close eye out for rustling bushes. The road went up, and my first surprise of the day, most of the riders went backwards. Gears clicked, deep breaths were sucked and spat out and a sea of grunts flowed up a not too difficult climb. I realised that I was not the only impostor within the Etape as many of the riders around me faded at a very early stage. Having said that, there were also those who shot up the incline at race speed shouting "Attention! au gauche" at those riders in their way. I took it relatively easy, I knew that this was a mere pimple in comparison to the mountains we faced 40 kilometres later.

More undulations took us on to Oloron. I was eating well and hiding behind other riders negating the slight headwind that nagged at me. As the road flattened out into a long river valley I decided that I felt pretty good and allowed myself a few moments of overtaking and generally pretty fast cycling. This bit of the ride was there to enjoy. The first feeding station was located at the 57 kilometre point. I needed to refill my bottles and pick up a couple of bananas. I imagined some sort of slick manoeuvre whereby I could accomplish all of this without dismounting. As I reached it I realised that I had scored a perfect 10 on the scale of wrongness. The feeding station was besieged with riders clamouring for water and food. It was physically impossible to reach the table that held the bottled water as riders queued three deep.

I raised my hand and was spotted by an eagle eyed attendant, a plastic bottle of Evian sailed through the air and landed perfectly within my outstretched palm.

A perfect throw and catch. This was repeated three times and I then had enough to fill my bottles. I nodded a "thank you" at my pitcher and made a mental note to have a word with the scouts for Wiltshire Cricket Club. I then moved on to the banana section and raised the hand again. Fully stocked, I was ready to move off until I spotted Gordon. He was one of our other riders and was not looking too well. In a fit of feeding enthusiasm he had downed four bananas on the trot. They were not having that and rapidly reappeared along with various other residents of Gordon's stomach. The two of us set off and headed towards the incline known as the Col du Soudet. When I say incline, what I really mean is 14 kilometres of road that ascends at a gradient averaging 8% over 2000 metres. The climb was packed with riders, grunting and sweating their way to the top. Gordon and I seemed to be climbing well and made good progress through the pack.

I even took time to take a photo of him, much to the disgust of the grunters and heavy breathers. Halfway up the climb we came across people walking their bikes. I felt sorry for them as this was the easier mountain pass and they had a long way to go yet. I maintained a steady pace and ground away at the gradient, nearly one hour after the start of the climb we reached the top.

Another scene of total chaos presented itself as a feeding station was located upon the summit. My cricket skills were tested once again as I refuelled and picked my way through the mass of riders towards the steep descent. Gordon had already left the top so I sped down on my own. Sped being a relative term as I realised that most riders were catching and passing me, on the way down I was slow. The dormant sexism within my brain was reawakened as two women cruised past.

I wasn't going to have that and decided to let off the brakes and pick up a little more speed A long straight section saw me exceed 70 kmh and I started to gain confidence which was rudely shattered by the sounds of a bike disintegrating behind me. I was travelling too fast to look back and see what had happened. Later I read that a British rider had crashed seriously on the Soudet descent, I'll never know whether that clash of metal I heard was him. The descent carried on and on and on.

A rough road surface required total concentration and my arms began to ache from the effort of constant braking. Eventually the gradient began to ease and I was required to turn my cold legs once more in order to maintain momentum. I'd done the first mountain of the day, I felt good, I'd eaten well and my spirits were up. Onwards to the next mountain. At this point I noticed a slight headwind and made more of an effort to hide behind other riders as we climbed up towards Larrau.

The climb was steady, but long enough to cause many riders some pain. Gordon and I were still going well and fought our way through the pack. However, I was starting to have a slight problem .. total food aversion. I had consumed over 10 fig rolls, 2 energy bars, 1 carbohydrate gel, 2 bananas and some horrible biscuit type thing picked up at a feed station. All of this was washed down with sickly sweet energy drink and few passing French flies. My schedule said "eat more" but my stomach said "please Dave can I have something a little more savoury?", unfortunately the schedule won and I forced more energy bar down my reluctant gullet.

Climb over, we descended for a short while and prepared ourselves for the Col de Bargagui. This climb was not as long as the Col de Soudet, but it was much steeper, reaching 13-15% at certain sections. Additionally the road was very narrow and riders started to bunch up and block traffic as they regretted the decision to leave the low gears off the back of their bikes. Me, I'm mountain biker, so my bike was well equipped with a triple chainset and a 25 tooth cog at the rear. I simply sat back and spun gently up the climb smiling cheerfully at my road riding brethren as their legs pumped and their lungs put in a planning application for a large extension.

The steep sections at the top became quite frustrating as riders dismounted and blocked the path of others. It was very hard to gain a rhythm as I dodged from left to right in an effort to avoid the walkers. As we gained height, so we gained spectators. Many second winds were obtained from the shrieks of "Allez allez" shouted with enthusiasm by the French, a far cry from the gentle clapping in between cups of tea that we would probably get were the event to run in England.

Climbing the col I passed some real heroes. A man on the back of a tandem pedalling with prosthetic lower legs overtaking many fully able riders, older riders who can't have been shy of 65 years, tired riders still grinding away determined to make the top and many ladies out-climbing their male counterparts. After endless switchbacks a large noisy crowd signalled the summit of the col. I'd not been working that hard as the triple had helped and the roads were congested with riders. I saw a gap and sprinted to the top. This drew a large cheer from the crowd "Bravo Monsieur" they shouted, thinking that I had ridden like that from the bottom. I was happy to leave them with that illusion. I stopped briefly at the feed station, refilled and refuelled, donned my jacket and chased off down the descent.

The Col de Burdincurutcheta briefly interrupted proceedings by being harder to pronounce than climb. On the long descent that followed I scared myself silly with the speed attained. The roads were in better condition and there seemed to be fewer hairpins. I haven't checked the maximum speed I gained on my cycle computer as it would probably frighten me to death. No girlies passed me on this section either. At the bottom I looked at my watch and noted that the ride had taken me nearly 6 hours. I had another 70-80 kilometres to go and if I wanted a medal I'd have to be back within 8 hours 46 minutes.

A further calculation highlighted that I needed to average 18 miles an hour to do this, including stops. It was going to be tight. However, salvation was in sight as I spotted a large group of riders in front of me moving at pace. A determined effort saw me join the group and I sat on their tail spinning comfortably at about 23 miles per hour. The course profile showed the final section as mostly downhill with one slight climb at the end.

So I relaxed as it looked like I would be well within the silver medal band with time to spare. Our group sped towards St Jean Pied-de-Port where I spurned the feed station and chased the silver instead. But soon disaster struck, we went up hill. The climb destroyed my peleton as riders became strung out and I soon found myself pedalling on my own at about 15 mph, too slow! I stepped up the effort and joined another group, which also became fragmented as we went up hill.

Something was wrong here, it was supposed to be an easy final 50 miles but a combination of hills and a headwind were making life difficult. I jumped from group to group for the next 40 kilometres desperately searching for a bunch of riders with the same objective as me. It wasn't to be and I became progressively more tired and dehydrated, my silver medal was starting to slip away. Desperate measures were called for and I reached into my back pocket and pulled out another carbohydrate energy gel. Somehow I forced it down myself and kept it down, this very act seemed to spur my legs into action again and I stepped up my pace. 20 kilometres from the finish and I had about 45 minutes to go.

I screamed "du l'eau, du l'eau" at every spectator until a young lad thrust a 2 litre bottle of Evian into my pleading hand. I filled my water bottle, poured water over my head ('cos the pros do it and it looks cool) and upped the pace a little bit more. With 10 kilometres to go I'd exhausted my mental arithmetic and we were climbing up hills as well. I had no idea whether it was feasible to still make silver, but I tried anyway. My leg muscles signed all sorts of loan agreements with other parts of my body and borrowed heavily to gain more energy. I surprised myself with my speed up the final climb and turned to visualisation to get me to the finish.

My thoughts : I WAS a Tour de France rider, this was going to be MY stage win and I'm going to out lead a breakaway and steal the stage from Lance Armstrong. Spectators saw: Some scruffy British rider on a dirty bike huffing and puffing like a mad thing when hundreds of riders have finished already in front of him. It worked. Seven minutes remaining and I found myself in Bayonne with only 2 kilometres to go.

Other riders were now picking up the pace and we sprinted along the river front towards the finish. A right hand bend and we came into the final straight, we were out of the saddles doing nearly 25 mph each determined to gain our own personal victory. Two riders came down in front of me after one of them hit a barrier and crashed into the other. I narrowly avoided the tangle of flesh and metal, too scared to look back at the scene they had presented. Finally it was done, I crossed the line with 3 minutes to spare.

My transponder was yanked off me and I was presented with a silver medal. I still find it hard to portray the sense of elation I felt at that point. I had strayed into road bike territory and performed reasonably well, I had completed a stage of the Tour de France and could talk with conviction as to how hard it really is. I'd felt good for most of the ride, I'd actually enjoyed it. I'm convinced that this was down to the detailed feeding strategy.

And finally I'd finished only 2 hours and 2 minutes behind the winner ... he had to be worried about that. I queued for a while for a food bag and was then reunited with some of the other riders from our hotel. Peter had finished very quickly in just over 8 hours and Gordon wasn't far behind him. Gordon turned to me and said "Even if they do take drugs I can't argue with the professional riders finishing that in 6 hours after 2 weeks of riding"

He's right. I left the race with a new respect for professional and amateur road racers alike. The training, dedication skill and stamina required to perform at a reasonable level in a road race is phenomenal. The enjoyment factor really is there as well both in terms of executing a race strategy and also riding at speed both up and down. I'm going back next year, though not as an impostor. I now feel I've been "blooded" into road racing and am already considering taking the razor to my legs.

Chapter 3

The Arms Race

When you buy a packet of cigarettes there are warnings all over them telling you that if you smoke one you'll probably die. These days most alcohol is advertised along with text advising you to "drink responsibly". The roads are littered with signage warning the traveller of imminent danger, but cycling lacks any form of counsel to prepare entrants for the hazards they may face.

I'm not talking about accidents or fashion faux pas or long term health problems. I'm talking about real fiscal damage that can happen to the wallet over time. The unwary cyclist enters a dangerous arms race as soon as they purchase their first bike. It is physically impossible to buy one that cannot be upgraded in some fashion or that does not have a better model further up the range.

No matter how hard you try you'll covet another machine, a lighter component or an alternative genre for which you don't currently have a bike. At the last count I've got nine, covering road cycling, mountain biking, track riding, cyclocross and one that I'm not even really sure what it's for, but it's shiny.

The advent of a new bicycle into the house is akin to a birth. A brand new shiny bundle of expectation. All the things you'll do with it, all the places it will take you and let's not forget all of the money it will inevitably cost you when bits of it fall off (fortunately we've only had bruises with our children).

When I got into cycling the bike arms race kicked off with a vengeance. Rigid mountain bikes morphed into hardtails, which mysteriously disappeared to be replaced with full suspension rigs. Within a couple of years of taking up mountain biking I reckon I had owned four brand new bikes, each promising to make me a better rider than the last.

The same occurred with clothing and accessories. I started out with a basic pump and a puncture repair kit, football shorts a T-shirt and a coke can stuffed in the bottle cage. These days I have the latest lightweight "pocket rocket" pump, space age lycra clothing, sophisticated pieces of plastic engineering that pin me to pedals and a lightweight bidon filled with scientifically proven electrolytes. I doubt they've made any difference at all.

It got out of hand with "The Russian Bride", I'll let the article explain it in depth, but hope that you see that the analogy stands. I'm sure my wife empathises with the content as well given that she's lost me on many occasions to my two wheeled harem. The piece has sat on my website for a number of years without many reads. Google statistics show me that only a certain "demographic" finds it from the search engine. You can guess what they were looking for and understand their disappointment upon arrival. Searching for "sex" and finding a bike, only those with obsessive compulsive cycling disorder would be delighted.

The Russian Bride

If a friend of yours informed you that he had just bought a Russian bride from a mail order catalogue, you'd probably be quite disgusted. "That's nice," you'd reply, whilst secretly wondering how on earth he could decide to spend the rest of his life with a woman he had never met, flesh that had not been pressed and a character that had only been described within marketing literature. Figuratively speaking, I bought a Russian bride last week. I wrestled my credit card from my wallet and paid for a bike that I had never ridden, a bike that I'd only ever read about, a bike possessed by nobody I know, a bike made of titanium.

An Airborne Lancaster. It would be easy to claim that I have become a victim of marketing hype, however, that would only be partly true. I've been overcome by something much worse than that, I've been egged on. An innocent question posted upon an internet forum led to recommendations, followed by a pointer to a specific bike shop along with a name and a phone number. Out of courtesy I made the phone call. "Of course we could ship it to your locality, Mr Barter." A well baited bike-shop hook snatches another innocent fish from the pond.

I'm committed now and it's time to tell my wife. Six months previously I spent a month's wages upon the latest full-suspension technology and now I have to justify another bike. Like a child in the Headmaster's office I begin my preamble. I paint a picture of the hardworking husband and father diligently slaving away for the good of his family and needing "that" outlet to keep himself sane. I don't know why I bother; Helen gives me that "You've bought another bike" look and gently smiles at me. She cuts me short. "You've worked hard enough, it's your money, and it's not as if it won't be used," she muses. I'm elevated from wayward schoolboy to lottery winner in an instant, new bike AND attractive understanding wife? best check the lottery numbers as well. For the next two days I'm playing a game of "1-2-3 in!" with my telephone.

I daren't stray too far from it just in case the voice on the other end has news of my shiny new baby. Every other call is treated with impatience or disdain, I cut friends and family off short, I précis complex work issues, anything to clear the line for the bike shop. In true bike-shop fashion the call never comes.

I swear they do this for entertainment. I can picture them all sat their hugging their mugs of Tetley and looking at my new frame. "He'll be wondering if it's in yet, shall we call him?" the apprentice queries. Silence, followed by giggling from the mechanics. "What's so funny ?" the apprentice asks nervously. The head mechanic stands, rubs a greasy finger down his trousers and turns to face the apprentice direct, a wry grin slowly growing across his face.

"You have a lot to learn sonny, but picture this scene in your mind. That bloke wants this bike, he wants it bad, he's started chewing his nails over that bike and he's even cleared a little space in his shed for it. He's sat at home now waiting for us to call, he won't leave the phone, he's tied to it, it's his toilet during a bout of dysentery, all that guy wants is for us to phone, and every minute that we don't he becomes a little more insane. His wife has started to worry a bit, she thinks he's having an affair. So, young man, are we going to phone him, or shall we push him that little bit further? Shall we see just what sort of state we can get him worked up into?"

He sits down satisfied that he has passed on an important bike-shop commandment to the junior. "Thou shalt not ring the punter when the goods come in, they'll call, and it'll save us the ten pence." Finally, my bough breaks and I call them; of course it's in, and before the handset hits the cradle I'm in the car and up the road, shirt hanging out but credit card firmly grasped in hand. And at the counter we meet. A gorgeous piece of titanium floats across towards me as I meet my Russian bride for the first time. Subtle curves accentuate her rear end, my fingers trace the CNC'd makeup on the heat tube and her shiny body is delicately encased in colour co-ordinated decals. The shop assistant could have charged my card for five times the value of the frame and I wouldn't have noticed.

My Russian bride is love at first sight. I'm sure there are better quality, lighter, more attractive shinier frames than mine but I immediately know that this is the right one for me. It is small, light and simple. It screams at me to build it up, this frame wants me on top of it, it wants to get down and dirty, it wants me to fall off every now and then and it will say "sorry," scoop me back up and carry on; it wasn't made for a hanger, it was made for ruts, roots, rocks, ridges and, most importantly, it was made to be ridden.

The next few days were the most testing of my cycling career, as in order to do the frame justice I had to learn a completely new skill, patience. All of my other bikes were assembled by bike shops, using middle-of-the-range components specified by my naivety rather than informed choice. However, I was determined to get it right. I wanted a light bike, one that looked good but could take a fall. It had to have discs, it had to be low maintenance and it was to be the first bike I'd ever owned with something "pimpy" hanging from it.

I wanted to have that one component that made fellow bikers point and ask "Is that a? How do you find she rides?" Curiously I'd never yet heard "Ohhh, is that a Deore front mech. on there, mate? I've been wanting one of those for ages" even though I've been out cycling for many years now. So, I patiently waited for my supply of components to trickle in. The Chris King Headset arrived, and went straight back as they'd sent me the wrong size. Forks, cranks, chainset and shifters were lifted from my existing bikes and buffed to military standards.

The new bike shop round the corner battled with their distributors to bring me bottom bracket, seatpost and saddle and finally pushed my credit card balance up to GDP levels by selling me Goodridge brake hoses (my "point-and-ask" component). Several days later I had all of the ingredients for my new bike recipe and locked myself within the garage to begin cooking. I could write another ten thousand words describing the building of the bike; however, it can be summarised in a few simple images:

- Blood dripping from a finger sliced by passing brake disc
- Teeth clenched, face grimaced as cable cutters fail to cleave
- The déjà vu of dropping the seatpost saddle-clamp components again and again
- Floor spattered with brake fluid that drips from handlebars and the amateur mechanic's nose.
- Inserting the same combination of shims between the disc calliper and the mount that you had tried two hours previously, and the disc rotating freely without rub
- The desperate search for the bolt/washer/nut/spring/clip, the resigned slump in a heap, the subsequent reuniting with said component that was on the bench all along
- Tools that aren't quite the right size, or are too old, or are completely inappropriate
- The stress of bottom bracket insertion

All of these happened to me and more. Finally the bike was finished, but if I'm honest I was close to hating it. In a bike shop half a mile away a group of mechanics began to giggle again. To make matters worse I finished it at 11.29 pm and my lights weren't charged. I sulked in front of the TV with a bottle of wine. Morning came and with it a new enthusiasm for my new bike. The day's work disappeared in a childish haze of excitement and at 3 pm I could take it no more. Trails were dry, the sun had made an appearance and it was time to demand my conjugal rights from my new bride. I rushed myself into lycra, shouted an incomprehensible farewell to my family and dashed off down the road towards the Ridgeway.

First impressions were not good. The bike felt slower than its aluminium predecessor. I was convinced that I should be going faster than this and a nagging feeling of regret started to seep forward in my mind. I came to the first road hill, changed down and gave it some thigh muscle. Then the bike started to respond and I began to understand it. It wanted "welly", it needed a good kick. The titanium frame was not going to coast me down the road, it was going to make me work for my speed, but if I put in the effort it would respond.

The bike and I were starting to understand each other. After a few miles I crested the hills, and the bike and I stared down the first bridleway of the ride. It felt like the bike was daring me to attack the track faster and harder than I'd ever tried before, and so I did.

The two of us flew over a mile and a half of dry, straight, bumpy singletrack. I provided the forward force and balance and the bike responded with speed, traction and compensation for all of the poor lines I decided to follow. It didn't take me long to appreciate the suppleness of the frame, which forgives a cyclist straying onto poor ground and flows with bumps rather than bucking like an agitated pony.

I'd ridden that bridleway wordlessly hundreds of times; today I stopped and addressed my bike ... "You little minx." Roads and tracks were quickly eaten by the ride as I steered us towards our first off-road ascent. The bike gobbled up the chalky gully and spat me out at the top of it; breathlessly I threw the bike round the corner and powered on towards the Ridgeway.

This bike didn't want to stop and nor did I. A section of "multiple choice" singletrack found us negotiating deep ruts. The bike held the line I told it to, it took its orders and obeyed them to the letter. We gained more speed and I'm sure that the bike sensed the long technical downhill was ahead; it was trying to get there as quickly as it could. And so on to the rocky, rooty descent. A tight singletrack drop losing a large amount of height in a small amount of distance. Normally I approach it with trepidation and respect; however the bike stuck two fingers in the air and threw us down the track as if Ti Nirvana existed at the bottom.

I'd found my perfect trail companion. We held hands all of the way back and hugged tightly as we descended for the final time, the sunset chasing us home. I gently parked her in the garage and returned to my armchair, quietly contemplating my new purchase. This bike comes with a subliminal cycling cox, who shouts at me to go faster, harder tighter. A cox who demands excitement and won't settle for getting from A to B without a grimace, smile, whoop, shout or expletive. I gambled on my Russian bride and I won. I'm convinced that we'll be happy together for many years and she's an attractive young filly, so I doubt I'll find my eyes straying. Like all marriages, I'm sure we'll have our ups and downs; in fact being a mountain biker I sincerely hope we have many of them.

Chapter 4

Sanctimony

The world's full of sanctimonious people and us cyclists are many of them. You know the sort I mean, people who bang on about doing what they do and how great it is and how everybody else should be doing it as well. Some of the religious types have honed this to a fine art and will even wage war on your country if you don't quite agree. Us cyclists tend to be a bit more moderate. We won't invade your semi-detached and occupy it killing Grandma in the process but we will chunter away about the benefits of two wheeled malarky as opposed to other pursuits.

I'm as guilty as the rest. I'm constantly extolling the virtues of cycling to anyone who will listen, usually only my therapist. But sometimes even my cycling friends fail to see the logic in my arguments, particularly when the weather is bad and they really cannot be arsed.

If a cycling map of the world were drawn and labelled with weather, California would get "hot and dry", Spain something similar, France probably "mostly good sometimes amazing" and the UK would have a great big arrow labelled "character building". I'm amazed any of us bother riding at all when the forecast is usually "rain" or the classic "sunny intervals" which means long periods of rain interspersed with a few rays of light whilst the rainclouds recoup.

Many cyclists hibernate through the British winter, but I was in the Scouts and Baden Powell told me that "A Scout smiles and whistles under all circumstances" including when it's pissing it down and he wants to ride his bike. So I did. I rode my bike through bad winters and all sorts of inclement weather. This in turn developed a weird sort of sanctimony in my actions. There had to be a reason why I was doing this? Surely I was better than those cooped up inside?

All I could come up with was "The Knowledge", a phrase previously attached to London cab drivers. You'll find out what "The Knowledge" is by reading the rest of the piece. Hopefully it will become clear and hopefully you'll be sensible and ignore it. Wet days are for sitting inside and watching the telly. Only an idiot would ride their bike as these writings attest. The article actually made it into print in Singletrackworld Magazine in 2004, the one and only mountain bike magazine ever to publish my work. They should be proud!

The Knowledge

This week I fought one of the hardest cycling battles of the year. It wasn't a frantic sprint to the line, it wasn't the cleaning of a highly technical descent and it certainly wasn't a personal best. It was against my central heating, and I won. The preceding days bought me a cold, an unnecessary car crash, a kitchen stuffed with Christmas food and the filthy cold weather that so characterises the British winter. Nature's winter eraser has eradicated all trace of dry trails and morphed my locality into a semi fluid landscape of mud, clay, flattened crops and fallen leaves.

The climate and the home comforts of middle England had coerced in a bold attempt to steal my riding motivation. I found myself deliberately wasting time, posting inanities to internet forums, peering in virtual shop windows and poring over the small print TV listings. Technology and low pressure isobars started to hoist the flag of victory until I was suddenly reminded of "The Knowledge".

I can't remember which chain of thought led to my revelation, maybe a gradual piecing together of past memories, maybe a brief snippet of conversation or maybe I caught sight of the flagpole and used "The Knowledge" as a final line of defence. "The Knowledge" polarised me, it gathered my mountain biking paraphernalia and coarsely assembled me into semi-prepared cyclist. It dulled the pain of squeezing overdressed feet into rock hard winter boots and it allowed me to flatly ignore the sub-zero wind that pointed out all of the neglected repair jobs on my rickety garage. Buoyed by "The Knowledge" I struggled with a poorly installed up and over garage door and threw my singlespeed onto the front drive. A garbled "farewell" was thrown over my shoulder to my wife and engaged in singlespeed I sped towards the nearest road/countryside interface.

It quickly became clear that I had made the right decision. This day was perfect for rediscovering "The Knowledge" and a skywards glance confirmed this, clouds parted to reveal deep blue sky serrated by the trails of aircraft stuffed full with those oblivious to my impending meeting. The dark forces rallied and threw their final obstacle in my path as I drew closer to my first bridleway. I briefly regained my sense of smell that had deserted me mid-cold and identified the defining odour of a rustic country pub. Matured ale, wood smoke and fried steak pulled at my legs through my nose. These three sirens sang hard to tempt me away from the trail, but today I was strong, the scent of "The Knowledge" filled my nostrils and spurred me on past the pub and into my first puddle.

The cold kiss of muddy water shocked my embarrassed calves into action and like the most determined posse of religious zealots the bike and I attacked the marshy track spraying clods and grass in our wake. As the mud deepened we passed a field of rain ravaged sheep whose jaded glance barely registered our heroic victory over the Wiltshire clay. Thirty minutes into the ride, things were starting to warm up and as I was getting closer to "The Knowledge".

Pent up aggression surfaced as I attacked inclines, fought ruts and ploughed through that which "dare" resist me. Competitive urges were fed with glances at my stop watch and the setting and gaining of minor trail target times. My eyes gulped in the surrounding winter vista and my ears registered the silence shattered by my machine and its machinations. A long inclined track tested my recently gained singlespeed resolve as I fought gravity and pain in order to gain my first scenic outlook of the ride. At the top I paused, breathed and drank. My privileged eyes scanned the collage of countryside laid out below me and I pondered upon that which had brought me here. My bike and its assembly. Mines had liberated metals, which in turn had been mixed into alloys that were forged or milled into constituent components. Chemical synthesis had led to the plastics and a designer's board or computer had dictated every shape. Each component had taken a different journey from source via distributor to shop to my garage.

Thousands of miles had been travelled, thousands of hours worked and thousands of measurements had been taken and documented in order to ensure that everything fell into place. Energy had been liberated from coal, oil, wind, wave and the sun to make this bike. I myself had digested numerous magazines, internet forums, the advice of friends and years of accumulated knowledge in order to build this bike. My bike sat upon the Ridgeway, an ancient track carved over centuries by little else but the fur wrapped feet of ancient man. Somehow, I felt humbled, and this harried on my journey towards "The Knowledge".

I sucked hard on my Camelback, breathed deep on the cold winter air and continued onwards. "The Knowledge" was beckoning and it wasn't far away. I passed a horse and rider, we shared greetings our circumstances similar yet so far apart. She was sat aloft, well dressed, rested and issuing commands to her stead by a loose pair of reins. I was slumped over my transport, hot, sweaty and filthy, exuding steam and snot as I fought its controls attempting to maintain velocity and a straight line. I was close to "The Knowledge", she had taken a step towards it, but more effort was needed as I will explain.

Trail gave way to road and a brief respite as I gathered myself in preparation for the final descent of the ride. I hopped a kerb and twisted through hedge to gain the bridleway and winked a sly "Hello" to Ladder Lane. Ladder Lane is the perfect summer descent, steep, rooty, rutted, technical and committing. The gradient lulls the rider into high speed and then challenges them with route choice once terminal velocity is achieved.

In winter Ladder Lane is best described as a natural colon, veined with slippery roots, filled with partly digested winter foliage and ready to spit the rider out into a lavatorial field at the bottom.

This is the point at which you're expecting me to reveal the true meaning of "The Knowledge". You're waiting for an epic tale of bravado and daring as the intrepid rider fought the greasy technical descent at speed and with courage, emerging at the other end bloodied but proud, ready for a celebratory beer in the pub afterwards. You're also waiting for me to describe "The Knowledge" as a feeling of exuberance gained from conquering a technical challenge or overcoming a particular fear. But, I'm afraid it didn't happen like that and I'm also afraid that "The Knowledge" is something entirely different altogether.

The truth is I dribbled down the descent in a frenzy of clasped brakes and dabbed feet. My bike skipped from left to right as its tyre lost purchase on roots and my knobbly tyres gathered leaves and mud. I survived the descent, just. I rode on into a muddy field where all traces of the right of way had been ruthlessly eradicated by the farmer's plough, and my bike stopped. The winter mud and scattered foliage had combined to build a wattle and daub wall firmly adhered to my front forks.

My wheels would turn no more and I fell sideways off the bike into a drainage ditch my arms lacerated with brambles that had kindly attempted to break my fall. I lay there wet, muddy, cold, hurting and completely and utterly alone. I picked myself up and started to laugh, my face split with a grin as wide as Renton's * I was in "The Knowledge". You see "The Knowledge" has nothing to do with achievement, conquest or valour.

It's not about rider skill, ability or speed and it's got nothing to do with distance, difficulty or terrain. "The Knowledge" is the feeling of being in an uncomfortable situation, yet enjoying it. It's about taking pleasure from the participation in a sport that by design induces discomfort, yet learning to love it. It's the ability to lie there dirty, cold, wet and hurting and still feel privileged to be in that position. The ability to feel a sense of sorrow for those in their comfortable heated and air-conditioned environments and the fact that many of them will never have "The Knowledge".

They will never take that step into a slightly hostile environment and feel the masochistic pleasure that arises from the odd little "nip" the climate or countryside may deliver. Maybe I'm the only person who has "The Knowledge", but I doubt it. Every mountain biker I talk to has had their own particular brush with the countryside and I find it rare to hear them discuss it with anything but a tinge of fondness, and often anticipation for the next tussle that they will experience. "The Knowledge" comes to the fore when you discuss your escapades with one that has not been there.

They cannot and will not understand the pleasure you derive, they will shake their head and question your sanity, no amount of explanation

36

will convince them that you are having fun. This is when you have "The Knowledge". Don't get me wrong, sometimes our terrain bites harder than we can handle. "The Knowledge" has risk and we as dabblers have to accept that our calling can be dangerous and may even take friends from us or us from them. But as a biker with "The Knowledge" you have achieved a huge summit. Professional cyclists have their names upon trophies and within publications and we should respect their achievements.

However, you have broken away from "The norm", your name is inscribed within the tyre marks you leave on the winter landscape, your trophy is the feeling of sanctimony that arises from having taken a step that the vast majority of the human race will never take. You have ejected comfort and convenience in favour of another mad winter dash towards "The Knowledge". You're special, and I salute you.

At the beginning of the film Trainspotting the character Renton is stopped by a car as he flees a shoplifting incident. He finds his own personal "Knowledge" as his face cracks into a wide grin and he laughs manically at the driver.

Chapter 5

Unfinished Business

Shortly after you're inducted into road cycling you start to hear some of the myths. You're told of men who raced holding their handlebars with their teeth after breaking arms (true), you hear about the rider who rode Land's End John O'Groats in under two days (true) and then somebody informs you in hushed tones about the hardest route in the UK, The Fred Whitton Challenge. This ride is a particularly brutal hundred miles over the highest and hardest British Lake District passes. It's run annually as a tribute to Fred Whitton, the club secretary of the Lakes Road Club who organise the event in his name.

As soon as you hear about this so called "hardest ride" a slight hint of vexation shrouds your previous outings. Surely they were harder? Surely our hills are higher? It's in the Lake District, aren't lakes flat? My friend Andy and I were certainly piqued. With a slight sense of outrage we set out to conquer this Lakeland loop and it very nearly won. I'll never forget the hot summer's day where we collapsed under a signpost at the bottom of the Kirkstone Pass and desperately emptied our pockets in search of sustenance.

We had a gel and a mars bar between the two and shared these out like plane crash survivors rationing their last morsels of food. We'd ridden way beyond our personal comfort zones and everything was beginning to hurt. Then we headed off up the pass and it broke us in half. My vision actually went red for a period. This was that moment when two "dabblers" realised just how hard road cycling can be. I'm sure many more have had this epiphany and many more have it to come.

Cycling sometimes holds open the door, but asks whether you are really tough enough to enter and join the party. That day Andy and I were almost ejected by the bouncers. But we felt we were made of sterner stuff vowing to return and do the route in proper style. A year later we returned with two others. For some strange reason Andy thought it would be easier on a mountain bike. Cycling opened the door, looked at his gear and almost shut it again, but he was motioned in for the entertainment of others.

To make things worse he'd cajoled our friend Ryan to ride "small wheeled" as well. I was sticking to the road bike. This is the story of that subsequent ride. I managed to convince Cycling Plus to feature it in their magazine and Trev "The Sparky" was recruited once more to take the pictures. We can own up now that one of them was faked. A perfect scene of three riders crossing a picturesque bridge was constructed in Photoshop after the event. Perfect revenge for them printing the shot of me collapsed over my bars at the top of the Honister Pass.

Mismatch in the Lakes

A defining trait of any great cycle ride, is that which drags the rider back again and again to repeat its majesty, savouring a rediscovered view or delivering an improved statistic. The passes of the English Lakes command many repeat performances and have an uncanny ability to fade that "never again" feeling almost as fast as the lactic acid has drained from weary calves. Any rider that has experienced the call of the Lakes will understand why four of us were assembled in Ambleside ready to take on the hardest British bike ride. However, the keen observer would have realised something was up.

The peleton that left the car park consisted of two very shiny road bikes and a couple of mountain bikes with slick tyres. Andy and I had ridden the route a year before. Inadequate gear ratios, fitness and nutrition had forced us to curtail our planned route and miss out the Newlands and Whinlatter passes. We had received our annual call from the Lakes and it was time to go back. I had upgraded my fitness and road bike,

Andy had trained hard and decided that a mountain bike and wider gear ratios were for him. Ryan and Mark were dragged into our conspiracy and each decided to take a different side. Ryan proudly assembled his mountain bike whilst Mark held on tightly to his super light Litespeed racer. Who would be quickest? Who would survive? Would the riders stay together? Who would walk the climbs?

Thus began our great Lakeland experiment. Our route had been meticulously planned using the latest digital mapping technology and downloaded to a GPS receiver. Paper maps were consigned to pockets as we left Ambleside following the electronic paper trail displayed upon our navigator's handlebars. Our first objective on this crisp April morning, the Kirkstone Pass. Amiable banter ceased as the road coiled upwards. After no more than 100 metres it became apparent that the road bike riders were to own this climb. The Kirkstone Pass is a relatively steady gradient.

Mark and I eased up the block and climbed comfortably

opening a clear gap upon the mountain bikers. Andy and Ryan had shot through the ratios and were spinning furiously but making little ground. As we neared the top Mark looked over his shoulder and the lack of mountain bikers in his view prompted him to turn to me and quip, "One nil to the road bikes". We topped out and caught our breath. A whiff of temptation seeped from the Kirkstone Inn. Perched at 1500 feet, it proudly took its place as the third highest pub in England. A few minutes later the others arrived looking equally comfortable but a tad frustrated. Clearly the defining lesson of the day had been delivered early and we still had a further 90 miles and six passes to cover.

After four caught breaths Kirkstone threw us out at the bottom onto the gently undulating terrain that skirts Ullswater before climbing again through Dickray, Thornythwaite and Matterdale End. We worked well together as a group, swapping leads and pointing out the poor investments in the road surface.

The sun gave the odd glint around the high cloud and all indicators pointed towards a fulfilling ride. Our route skirted the Northern Lake district and delivered us into Keswick via a feast of country lanes slightly tainted by a small portion of A66. From Keswick we climbed easily above Derwent Water widely known as "Queen of Lakes". Our single track road clung resolutely to Cats Bells.

Attempts at climbing heroics were suppressed as each of us sucked in the surrounding views and shared the vista mixed with camaraderie. This was without doubt the defining moment within the ride at which we were four cyclists rather than two roadies and a pair of mountain bikers. The bikes had worked well together and we had progressed at a respectable speed, all riders appeared relatively fresh. We passed the 7th century hamlet of Grange which nestles below Castle Crag in the jaws of Borrowdale. Grange-in-Borrowdale refers to the "granary in the valley with a fort" and was one of the Northern granaries for Furness Abbey at Barrow-in-Furness. With a tinge of regret we lost our height and descended into Rosthwaite.

A flurry of bottle sucking and energy bar consumption signalled the impending gradients of the Honister Pass. "I think this one's a bit steep at the start" Mark euphemistically offered. We turned right and began to climb. Kirsktone had lulled me into a false sense of security which was cruelly exposed by the 25% gradient at the beginning of the Honister Pass. I rapidly used all options on my rear block and watched with envy as Mark climbed ahead of me with apparent ease. Determination mixed with grunting saw me over the initial steep sections and I stayed within sight of Mark.

Our mountain bike tail had been lost in a frenzy of upshifting and leg spinning. The final right hand bend saw the end of the climb. I stopped, recovered and assessed the experience. Honister had turned out to be a steep, sweaty, uncomfortable climb with little opportunity for rest. Yet somehow it lacks real teeth, it's on the verge of destroying the rider but suddenly gives up and lets them escape into the valley below with nothing more than a stern ticking off. Suitably chastised we re-grouped and plunged down the valley.

A few quick glances at Buttermere were grabbed before we were climbing again heading up over the Newlands Pass. A steady but exposed climb saw us sweaty at the top with the road bikers carrying out the ritual finger drumming whilst awaiting the offroaders. Our patience was extended by the spectacular view afforded by Moss Force waterfall. In my mind the descent from Newlands was the best of the day.

A fast, relatively straight road produced a very surprised motorcycle rider who shamefacedly acknowledged the waving road bikers who overtook him. Here, the cyclist has time to relish the speed whilst catching the scenery to the right, unlike many other mountain descents which tend to enclose the rider and suffocate their eyes. From Braithwaite we headed up the Whinlatter Pass taking a shady road hidden from the sun by its evergreen wrapper. The gradient offered little challenge to the lightweight road bikers, however, Ryan was starting to flag. We stopped to let him catch up. No real damage done but the effort of turning smaller wheels on bigger gears was beginning to show. Andy masked a jealous glint at the road bikes and I said a silent "Thank you" to my strange geometry that prevented a halfway swap of bikes.

For some reason we had imagined the next 35 miles as a gently undulating ride, briskly skirting the northern fells of Ennerdale and an opportunity for respite before the horrors of Hardknott and Wrynose. Next time we'll pay better attention to the height profile. We climbed and descended, ascended, went down, gained height, then lost it, defied gravity, complied with it. In fact we messed with gravity so much that I'm convinced we altered some poor soul's astrological chart. Catching sight of the climb beyond Ennerdale Bridge, we somehow convinced ourselves it was the Hardknott Pass and hung on to the vain hope that it's gradient had shallowed over the past year.

A further glance at the GPS soon shattered our illusions as the satellites confirmed it was a minor hill, well out of the Hardknott league. In short these were 35 hard miles and halfway in Ryan gave the cyclists equivalent of the Captain Oates speech."Just go on ahead lads, I'll see you at the car, I'll be happier at my own pace".

How often have we heard these words and how often have we complied unwittingly consigning the lone rider to the further torment of headwinds, poor motivation and an extended time out in the open. We were having none of it. He was sent to the back and ordered to draft ruthlessly. We kept him on our back wheels up the hills and shared the thrill of the descents. Thirty minutes later motivation had returned and he was back with us.

We made good time to Gosforth. We covered the counter of the local newsagents in loose change in exchange for sugary drinks to prepare ourselves for the final two passes. Secretly I was considering defeat. Up to this point we had ridden over 80 miles and climbed over 10,000 feet. My legs were tired and I felt for my mountain biking colleagues as my bike weighed some ten pounds less than theirs.

I knew that the final two climbs were the hardest and I also knew that Hardknott was steeper than Honister. I envied the 32 tooth sprockets at the rear of the mountain bikes and cursed their granny rings. Conquering Hardknott was going to take more than muscle, oxygen and bone. I wasn't sure I had it. Time was up and Mark led us to the ascent and calmly set about the mountain pass rapidly opening up a gap on the rest of us.

This proved to be my saving grace. On seeing a rider in front of me conquer the gradient, I knew it was achievable. I visualised myself guiding the bike up the path traced by Mark and found the climb was possible, even with tired legs, rasping lungs and a myriad of biological warning lights. Let's be clear. Hardknot was, and is, the hardest climb I have ever ridden on any bike. I'm a reasonably fit rider and it took every physical and mental reserve to pull my skinny frame over its 33% sections. I arrived at the top with nothing left at all. The ticking off given by Honister had been replaced by a full on thrashing by headmaster Hardknot. We all found it hard, even the mountain bikers with their advantageous ratios struggled to the top.

I collapsed over my bars. There's been a road through here for 2000 years, though it's had tarmac for less than fifty. The Romans were first, and they called this the Tenth Highway, linking forts at Waterhead and Ravenglass. I wonder if the Centurions complained as vociferously as my calves whilst climbing it. Wrynose loomed a few miles beyond. We cut short our celebrations and descended towards the final pass of the day. The 25% gradients near the top were no joke, but somehow seemed less painful when compared to the struggle up Hardknott.

The descent from Wrynose was punctuated with potholes and poor surfaces and my rear inner tube exploded in protest at the bottom. The puncture was hastily repaired and we ground out the remaining few miles back to the car park at Ambleside. And so it was done.

The Lakes had called and we had answered. We'd completed a classic loop with little incident. We'd clearly concluded that the road bike was by far the most sensible steed, yet we'd each revelled in that sense of achievement that comes from stretching the boundaries of a ride right up to personal limits. The Lakeland loop is a classic regardless of how it is ridden. It will call me again and I'll be back. I've got a feeling that it's one of those rides that can never be "done".

Chapter 6

Inspiration and the Wild

Anyone who has ever attempted any sort of creative writing will know that sometimes the inspiration for an article or idea comes from the strangest of places. This is obviously old news to physicists who simply sit under trees until fruit falls on them. Apparently Shakespeare sought inspiration from the bible, the miracle of creation and also nature.

There we go, great minds think alike! Because I too have been inspired to write by nature, or more specifically, Sir David Attenborough. You'll be tempted to think that Sir David's narration over the majestic migration of wildebeast crossing the Serengeti plain spurred me on to draw cycling peleton analogies. You'd be wrong. Neither was it his loquacious concern over the plight of polar bears fighting for survival as global warming melted their ice. Clearly they would have an affinity with time trialists who are desperately scared that their beloved dual carriageways will one day be replaced by trains.

In fact it was monkeys. A troupe of them had learnt to harvest nuts by picking up great big rocks and dropping them onto the hard shells until they broke. Sir David was rabbiting on about their ingenuity, one of the only mammals to have discovered tools, almost implying that they be able to fill out a tax return next whilst opening a milk carton with zero spillage.

That day I'd had to replace a Campagnolo integrated shifter on my road bike. This proved to be a near impossible task. I struggled for nearly an hour to get the cables threaded through only to realise that I had the brake and gears the wrong way round. It took another hour to seat the shifter properly on the bars and align it with the other side. Then I came to the bar tape and the incredibly dark art of winding it on properly, evenly and with no gaps below the lever.

Once this was all done I attempted to index the gears. Another few hours flitted merrily past as I danced frustratedly to the beautiful music of slipping gears and chains clashing with spokes. Halfway through the first ride the cable stretch undid all of that good work.

Sat watching those monkeys so coveted by Sir David I had a single thought. "Wildlife has it easy". I wish I was a monkey, I wish all I had to do was drop rocks on nuts subsequently gaining high praise from knighted naturalist luminaries whose brother can get them into movies for free.

Wildlife Has it Easy

Wildlife simply needs to be born and then survive. Most skills required are mandatory or wildlife fails. For us humans it is a bit more complicated. Many of us are born into a society when survival is such a high probability that it is a given and we are able to pick and choose from the available skill sets on offer. And in affluent western society, what a choice that is.

As we grow older many of us choose sport, there are a plethora of sports and an associated abundance of new skill sets to be acquired. Some simple, some complex. As an active and competitive cyclist I've discussed these with non-cycling friends. For them it is simple. All we do is turn the pedals round and point the bike in the right direction. In racing, whoever turns the pedals the quickest will win, it's as simple as that. For them cycling is a purely physical pastime and we all look so stupid dressing for it, hence cyclists must be at the lower end of the intelligence scale.

However, I've been thinking about this long and hard. I've catalogued the skills that I've acquired in my ten years as a fanatical pedal pusher and they need to think again as I present my argument for cycling as the all encompassing pastime.

Let's start with the physical aspects. We've got pretty good legs. The lungs aren't half bad either. As far as I am aware we have strong hearts and even the arms see some development from wrestling with bars. The modern roads and their caring occupants have ensured that our observation and hand/eye co-ordination are required to be spot on. If you ignore the biceps and the odd protruding tummy, us cyclists are pretty well physically developed all round. Well, most of the time.

All of us have suffered from some malady or other throughout our cycling careers and funnily enough, most of us know how to treat them. We've strapped up our knees, iced our ankles, taken painkillers, supplements and all sorts of remedies. We know how to treat coughs, colds, viruses, road rash, breaks, infections, cuts, bruises and I've even seen a major dislocation fixed on the road. Mention a medical problem on any Sunday club run and I can guarantee that there will be no shortage of advice or opinion proffered.

So not only are we perfect physical specimens, we're doctors as well. But it doesn't end there. We know how to stretch, we know when to rest, we know how to address aching legs. Physiotherapy has bled well into our sport and many of us may call ourselves amateur biomechanics as well.

Having a finely tuned engine is all very well, but it needs fuel. And so we move onto another aspect of the committed cyclists skill set, dietician. Everyone of us has their own formula for keeping the legs turning on the bike. Some of us swear by gruel made of oats, fruit or whatever we can find in the cupboard. Others prefer the more traditional approach fried and covered in sugary red/brown type sauces.

I've known riders who forgo pre-ride meals in order to promote weight loss, existing on expresso only for the first hour of a ride. Many of us religiously read the labels on food products on shop shelves, hunting down the tastiest combination of carbohydrate content versus flavour. The biscuit was taken however, by a close friend who constructs an intricate spreadsheet for each challenge ride he attempts. He carefully plans his carbohydrate intake against the course profile and his expected timings in order to ensure that he completes the course on target.

It doesn't just stop with food though, we fill our bottles with all sorts of concoctions, some natural but most purchased after intensive research. We have fuels to keep us going longer, drinks for hot days, powder for long days and I expect that out there is a product specially formulated for those with ginger hair.

All of these are carefully weighed and measured in order to make sure that we carry the maximum hit for minimum weight. Sometimes we get it right and end the last mile on the last bite. Other times we're found spent and foodless, miles from the finish contemplating eating grass/leaves/gravel anything to get us home. Cyclists aren't just dieticians, we're gamblers as well, or as we all like to call ourselves, "calculated risk takers".

Strength, speed, medicine, physiology, diet and risk calculation. That's not a bad list so far and I've only just begun. Look at the skills needed to plan a ride before the bike is even pushed out of the garage.

Firstly, the bike needs to work and that is a whole skillset in itself. Cyclists need to understand basic mechanics, if you can't wave a spanner about semi-effectively then you are going to be in trouble from the start. We need to understand gearing and how to move the bike forwards and most importantly upwards given the limitations of our legs and lungs. We also need to know how to stop the bike, this includes wheel braking sequences, pressures and which brakes and pad combinations to use. Maintenance is also important and cyclists require a working knowledge of lubrication, cable tension maintenance, tyre pressure settings, wheel alignment and bearings. Many modern handlebar accessories require the skills of a computer programmer as well in order to ensure their proper operation.

Next, the cyclist needs to know where they are going to go. This is often made easy by tagging along with a local club run or training ride. But for many of us solo types we stray into a whole new area of ability, planning and navigation. A large number of cyclists spend more time poring over maps than sweating upon their handlebars.

We are able to read the terrain from the myriad of different coloured lines and meticulously plan a route to take the optimal path required by our ride. This is often supplemented by a deep local knowledge of the road or track network, including traffic timings, road conditions, diversions and most importantly gradient. In fact were Ordnance survey to unexpectedly lose their mapping database the solution would be straightforward. All that they would need to do would be to approach the local cycling clubs for each region and demand that the ride leaders step forward with pencils. Within a week they would have their maps back, improved, with comments.

Many cyclists (including me) have taken this a step further and invested in satellite navigation devices and computer based mapping. This takes ride planning to a whole new level with routes built upon digital maps sometimes linked to aerial photography and even previewed in glorious 3D. Computer operations and GPS understanding and usage can also be added to the encyclopaedia of cyclist's abilities.

And then there's the quick glance out of the window to assess the current weather conditions. I can almost guarantee that this is not the first time our committed cyclist has given consideration to the weather. Most cyclists I know have a wide variety of channels they will use to gain the most "optimistic" forecast possible for their ride. Some tune into the regional news, others swear by the farming forecast or various websites that offer up to the minute updates concerning weather conditions. I bet there's someone out there who's taken the shipping forecast into account before chucking leg over bike.

Even out on the bike, cyclists are keeping track of menacing clouds and assessing the strength and direction of the wind. Listen to us talk, we're constantly rabbiting on about the impending weather change and the best days to get out and ride. Weather makes or breaks our rides and every single one of us can put a tick next to "forecasting" in our book of cycling skills.

Voyeur, navigator, planner, project manager, meteorologist, nutritionist, mechanic, doctor, physiotherapist the list goes on. Us cyclists are a complex lot and David Attenborough needs to swing his lamp around and take a long hard look at us for a while. Eat, sleep, reproduce, die. That's all his subjects ever seem to get up to, I'm surprised any cyclist manages to find the time and energy to actually ride their bike given all of the other supporting activity and knowledge required.

Chapter 7

Restlessness

I'm a restless soul and consequently do not cope well in the absence of change. The bike collection clearly attests to this view as new models come in and out of the door and existing models regularly sport new components..and dents. Unfortunately this applies to my working life as well. Many sit in their cubicles dreading the day that the manager announces that there are "changes" afoot. I'm the opposite, a streak of blinding optimism runs through me and every time I hear the word "change" I assume that the Managing Director position is finally mine.

Of course it never happens. I've been regraded into exactly the same job on a number of occasions. Once I was pulled into an office and heartily congratulated on gaining the position of "Job Value 2". Champagne flowed that evening, but not in my house we stuck to Vimto instead.

The restlessness doesn't last long though as I eventually pack it all in and go and do something else. It's almost become a regular occurrence for me to walk out of a perfectly good job in search of pastures new. Strangely this usually occurs after an epic cycling holiday which in turn provides huge opportunity for reflection. My wife has become accustomed to this with the first question on my return being "So, do I have to start selling stuff again?".

The first time saw me leave the Royal Mail and form my own business with a guy I'd met about three times. We built a shed in my back garden and ran it from there. Change happened daily as Grant would make a sale for something that we'd casually chatted about the week before. My job was to rapidly translate the "talk" into computer programs whilst Grant reassured the customer that it would be with them next week.

Life was never boring running our business from the shed. We followed all sorts of bizarre avenues to gain new custom becoming experts in Welsh language services and software for the blind. None of us could speak a word of Welsh or read braille.

It was also incredibly tiring. I've never worked so hard in my life and rarely left the keyboard as we fought, like all small businesses do, to stay afloat in a sea full of sharks. One September I came close to cracking with the weight of the work. I needed an outlet to refresh the thought process and offer the change that would prevent the inevitable resignation. What better way to achieve this then cycle through Ireland? A cheeky email to Dan Joyce at the CTC gained some funding for the trip in the form of a magazine commission. The article below is the result, slightly toned down for the tender ears of the CTC readership.

Read it, then get yourself over to Cork. This is one of the greatest rides I've ever done. I'm convinced that the "Alpine Style" is how cycle touring should be carried out. It liberates all the joys of riding without hinderance whilst delivering you into the care of a vast community of interesting, eccentric and often deeply caring hostelry owners.

As for the business, within five years we'd been bought by a larger company. They made me wear a suit, carry out appraisals and sit in meetings with people who said "out of the box". I only lasted a few years and after a cycling holiday in the Alps......

Ireland - Alpine Style

As a cyclist I dread the word "challenge",I know it is going to immediately lead me astray. Mere mention of a "challenging" climb will add it to my tick list. I've now completed at least four "challenging" Gran Fondos and seriously "challenged" myself when cycling from Land's End to John O'Groats with little preparation or training.

I should have closed my ears to the suggestion of "credit card touring" that I overheard in conversation, especially given that the dialogue was littered with the word "challenging". Instead I butted in and asked to know more. It turned out that the concept was simple, "credit card touring" describes the act of completing a cycle tour in absolute minimalist fashion, carrying the bare essentials for riding and a credit card to pay for accommodation. I was hooked immediately and all that I needed was a candidate cycle tour on which to live out the challenge.

To be truly challenging the route needed to be; long enough to stretch limited resources, scenic enough to maintain interest and challenging enough to push the rider. I initially considered the UK end to end but felt it had too much of the "known" about it and then my sights turned towards Ireland, Mizan Head to Malin Head, the Irish End to End. That would do nicely, Ireland a land famed for its rugged countryside, its hospitality and also its inclement weather.

Could it be ridden lightweight? I couldn't find anyone who'd tried...

All too quickly I found myself waving "goodbye" to the Swansea Cork ferry, armed with only the cycling clothes I stood in, a bicycle a pair of shorts, a t-shirt, a few maps, a vague route plan, some cash, a credit card and precious little else.

I was committed to the ride. The task seemed simple enough, ride from Cork to Mizen Head, Ireland's most southerly point. Next head north and take as scenic route as possible towards Malin Head. Have a brief celebration and then work out some way of getting back home to England.

I left the ferry port shrouded in early morning mist and escaped the clutches of Cork into traffic free undulating country lanes. Solitude heightened my early sense of commitment, heading steadily west I began to get a feel for the Irish touring experience.

The road meandered lazily between towns and villages grabbing views as it climbed hill and dropped down to investigate valley bottom. Surface quality varied from the occasional luxury of a rumble free pristine tarmac section to the more frequent rough pitted country lane. The countryside was dotted with history, my ride was being constantly interrupted by burial grounds, ruins, vistas, stone circles and follies each beckoning me away from the road for a brief investigation.

During one of these interruptions I wheeled my bike up to the Drombeg stone circle only to find a small child squatting over something shiny in the middle. Closer investigation revealed a scattering of small change left by superstitious tourists. Smiling to myself, I looked skywards, I'd found a pot of gold and a potential leprechaun but alas the rainbow was nowhere to be seen.

My route flirted with the west coast all the way to Skibbereen passing through a procession of pretty seaside villages. The sun widened a gap in the clouds and the smile on my face. So far I'd hardly seen another car. I felt relaxed and under no pressure to let drivers pass. It was as if the roads had been reserved for cyclists.

Draped in the afternoon sun I stood at Mizen Head staring out to sea taking a severe lashing from the sharp southerly wind. The ride "proper" was about to begin. I'd already covered ninety miles, I had a fair few more to go. Riding north with the wind up the west coast my legs were hurting, however, my Irish end to end had only just begun. Typical of Ireland, the scenery did not let up. After my first night's rest, I left Bantry and climbed steadily, gawping at the Caha mountains to my left. I gained an "alpine" feel as ahead of me I espied Molls Gap framed by the stone wall that lazily wound up the valley. The beautiful green/brown patchwork of rugged countryside compensated for my fatigue, what a way to begin a day's ride!

It got better, a drop down into the Black valley and switchback ride towards the gap of Dunloe. Cars are banned from this road and, apart from the horse drawn carriages stuffed full of camera touting tourists, the cyclist is king. My flow was frequently interrupted. These traps take up a large portion of the narrow road, and travel largely at the whim of the horses. All too frequently I found myself standing on the grass verge watching them go by.

Riding easily through the valley all was well until the road rudely turned back on itself and headed steeply upwards. I was wondering what I had done to deserve the sudden punishment when the road relented leaving me staring down the beautiful Gap of Dunloe. High valley walls framed a crystal clear stream and lake system, sheep lazily foraged in the sun, food choice being no problem with the abundant green surroundings. With mixed emotions I sped down the valley, buoyed by the thrill of the downhill speed, yet brushed with regret at letting the vista pass so quickly.

Tired legs forced me round the Stacks mountains and I dragged the bike on towards the Tarbet Ferry. Upon the ferry I sat surrounded by cars with a wry smile upon my face. I had earned my passage across the Shannon estuary what had they done to justify their ride? This was the most traffic I had seen all day. I leant back and mused upon a good night's sleep in Kilrush, today's destination.

So far, the lightweight touring method had served me well. I had found no problems in locating accommodation and without exception had been welcomed in along with my bike. The lack of luggage was speeding my progress and I was covering in excess of one hundred miles a day. I didn't need to carry food as every garage or shop seemed to have a sandwich counter that made my lunchtime baguette to order. I quickly developed an evening ritual of washing my clothes and squeezing them dry between two towels. Visiting the local corner shop and buying water and food for the next morning. Heading out in search of take-away food or a shop with yet another of the ubiquitous sandwich counters and eating it whilst scanning the TV for news and hoping for another good weather forecast.

My lightweight rituals seemed to soak up so much time that the evenings were gone in a flash. Before I knew it I was dragging myself out of bed, pealing on tepid cycling gear and shoving down yet another full Irish fried breakfast.

Up to this point the credit card tour had been going well. And then, it rained, properly. Ireland had clearly been playing with me, soaking me in nothing but countryside and treating me to tail winds and September sun. I left Kilrush in the pouring rain and headed out towards the west coast, dragged away from the direct route by the spectacular cliffs of Moher.

My lightweight breathable waterproof top resisted the rain for as long as it could before giving in and tormenting me with a mixture of warm sweat and cold rainwater. Yet somehow it was more bearable than a wet autumn ride back home, maybe due to the lack of traffic and the ever varying landscape that dragged my mind away from feelings of self pity.

In fact the rain seemed to complement the rock swept landscape cleaved by the Burren coast road. I caught a rare sighting of two other cyclists at Black Head point. While I took in the lighthouse, they argued over a map. I left them and the beautiful landscape to it as I rounded Galway bay and followed a nondescript road into Cong, wet, bedraggled and in need of an understanding landlady.

Clearly Ireland was not going to let me have it all my way on this trip. Water had found ingress into everything, including my evening clothes. I learnt that double wrapping in plastic bags was mandatory if items were to stay dry. I festooned my room in drying clothes and maps whilst flicking from channel to channel on the television desperately searching for the most optimistic weather forecast. I had the mountains and loughs of county Mayo on the next day's itinerary and was in serious need of a view without any obstructions.

The weather didn't disappoint and I had what felt like my most isolated day, starting with a brief tussle with the Partry mountains followed by a beautiful run along the coast of Lough Mask. Increasingly the roads were lined by peat bogs littered with discarded gathering bags. I was disappointed not to encounter any peat cutters but caught the acrid whiff of a peat fire snaking from a moor side Inn further up the road.

I began to celebrate my credit card tour. I was cycling in near wilderness with only the wind and random thought for company. I was riding my favourite lightweight titanium bike, my pride and joy, a racing bike without mudguards or racks or anything remotely useful for cycle touring. All of my possessions were stuffed within a tiny bar bag.

Somehow this felt right, the surroundings egged me on towards further discovery rather than dragging me back for another look. The light bike relieved the effort of a high daily mileage and was a major factor in my making the north east coast above Sligo that evening. With a fair wind I'd make Malin Head the next day and my challenge would be accomplished. Sadly, I awoke to a completely unfair headwind of nearly twenty miles an hour.

There was no escaping the main road heading north east through Donegal. I had limited time away from work and needed to get the ride done within the week. On a day like this the N15 had little to offer a tired yet committed cyclist. I grudgingly put my head down and ground against the wind. All surroundings were lost on me. Views and landscapes were discarded by my fractious mental state.

Towns passed me slowly by, rain showers paid me visits of ever increasing length. Cars and lorries showed me no sympathy, forcing me to hug the hard shoulder and look up malevolently from my relentless grind. I entered an almost trance like state of   suffering, punctuated with bursts of mental arithmetic as I converted kilometres to my more familiar miles and counted down the slow progress towards the northern tip of Ireland.

Turning due north, the feelings of hopelessness dissipated. I twigged that my objective was within reach. I was in Buncrana, once again away from the traffic and main roads, once again in the company of mountains and grand vistas. From nowhere I summoned speed and determination, I forgot all of the earlier toiling and kicked the bike northwards with an increasing realisation that I was going to make it. The rain started to come down, but I didn't care, the wind picked up, I still didn't care. Malin Head was close enough to ride to, and that was all that mattered.

At Malin a sign told me that I had a further ten miles cycling to reach Malin Head. I'd already cycled one hundred miles in appalling conditions, so I treated myself to a hotel room. I briskly dumped as much filthy wet kit as I could, glanced mournfully at the large bed and shower then sped off to complete the challenge.

Ireland had another treat in store for me. The narrow road leading up to Malin Head twists and turns and climbs and dives around the rocky coast. It is windswept and unkempt, dragging the eye from tussles of greenery, to rocks and then out to the rough waters of the North Atlantic. I passed beautiful beaches, derelict buildings, non-plussed grazing animals and the occasional local. All of this was shared with nobody else. A fitting finale to a tour that had felt so quiet.

Ireland does not give Malin Head up without a fight. The last hundred metres were by far the steepest of the tour and after a brief aerobic struggle I was looking out to sea from the most northerly point in Ireland. I'd completed the Irish end to end.

Malin Head does not have a visitor centre. There is no signpost for you to label with your home town and point south. In fact, all Malin Head has is a couple of ruined buildings and a spectacular view of the coast and the North Atlantic ocean and somehow, that seems just right.

I dismounted my bike and stared into the wind, contemplating the challenge. The Irish end to end is a committing ride and when completed outside of the tourist season the sense of isolation is real. The variable weather, rugged scenery and ever changing riding conditions never let up, constantly reminding the rider that they are in the "real" outdoors.

I'd risen well to the challenge of lightweight touring, and found that it suited me to leave behind the encumbrance of luggage. In fact I'd relished the daily challenge of finding some suitable accommodation and smiling sweetly at the proprietor whilst either dripping wet or sweating profusely. However, this was rarely a problem, the Irish people are consistently welcoming and budget accommodation abounds. The greatest challenge I had was that the smaller B&B's did not accept credit cards. The ride had become a "credit card and cash" tour instead.

Cycling Ireland end to end offers a steady string of highlights. The ever changing surroundings, lack of traffic and my minimal resources added a constant feel of adventure. Climbers talk of conquering mountains "Alpine style", travelling lightweight with no support. I felt that I've ridden Ireland Alpine style, it had been a worthy challenge and Ireland deserves something out of the ordinary.

Usually I complete a long ride with a sense of relief, glad that the mileage has been done and that I'll be hanging up the cycling shoes for a while. However, it was with a huge sense of regret that I mounted my bike and headed back to Malin. I'd found a major disadvantage of lightweight touring. The Irish end to end was over far too soon.

Chapter 8

Try Before You Die

There's probably some really famous quote out there about trying everything once before you die. In fact I seem to remember that it makes a couple of exceptions one of which may be anal sex. As a cyclist who regularly ventures off road, the anal sex one wouldn't bother me that much as I've spent well over ten years battering my arse with hard leather, plastic and occasionally the ground when it all goes wrong. I once came perilously close to anal sex with my bicycle as the seatpost snapped on the climb leaving a five inch carbon rod pointing invitingly up towards my nether regions.

However, I'm a great fan of the sentiment of try everything once. A series of ticks to be had that can be used in drunken oneupmanship cycling discussions. My list of ticks required is huge. These articles are symptomatic of that as I rush around trying things and equally quickly deciding that they are just not for me. Time trialing is one of them.

My first "25" will probably be my last. I left the start line with my heart rate set to maximum, powered bravely up the first climb with a beats-per-minute that I'd never recorded before and never will hence. A few miles later I was completely done, I looked at my cycle computer and had eighteen more to go. These miles were all passed regretting that I'd ever been born whilst listening to the ominous rumbling of the disk wheels belonging to the proper riders who regularly overtook.

These setbacks never diminish the curiosity though. As soon as any new genre makes itself known I feel I have to give it a go, mainly to see what it's like but often in the misguided belief that this is the one that will make me World Champ. Sometimes, some of them stick. Track cycling's a prime example of that. There's no greater thrill than hurtling round a wall of death, on a bike with no brakes, about two inches from the rider in front and a stupidly obtuse angle to the ground. I don't do it enough mainly due to the complete absence of a local velodrome.

Singlespeeding is another one that's stuck. But not as described below. I regularly ride a singlespeed cyclocross bike off road and it makes a guest appearance later in this book. This article documents the genesis of my singlespeeding, for those that don't know what it is, it's a bike with one gear like we all had when we were young.

The Tao of Singlespeeding

Like any good politician I regularly make a habit of reneging upon statements made in the past. In the early days of my mountain biking career I "pooh pooed" the idea of suspension forks, I can even remember the slightly tipsy argument in the Beehive. One month later, I slunk out of my garage and onto the Ridgeway with a suspicious Girvin shaped bounce at the front of my bike. My next target was rear suspension, "A total and utter waste of money", I loudly proclaimed whilst steadying myself at the bar. It must only have been a matter of days before Express Cycles took my order for a Marin East Peak full suspension bike, which bounced me round England and Wales for the next year or so. I've slagged off clipless pedals, carbon handlebars, disc brakes, expensive stems, energy powder, 2.1" tyres and more. Every single one of them has subsequently depleted my cash reserves and become a regular feature upon my bike. Last month it was singlespeeds.

"I can't see the point in putting yourself through the pain"

"People will do anything to appear slightly different, at the end it just make them the same"

"He's only doing it so he won't feel left out"

"Waste of a good frame"

"There's sycophants, fashion victims, attention seekers, and there's people with gears on their bikes"

All of these had made it into my recent vocabulary, so I suppose the outcome was inevitable.

Yesterday I rode my new singlespeed. I'd recently deconstructed my hardtail and full suspension bikes into a single, shiny all purpose titanium hardtail. The full suspension frame and nice shiny bits were dispersed to more loving garages around the county.

In a Dickensian twist I was left to look after all of the ugly, smelly bits, Deore hubs, worn Mavic rims, an old Specialized Rockhopper frame, dated Avid V brakes and some chipped and scratched old handlebars. I nearly sold the frame, but a closer inspection threw up an alarming dint in the chainstays. My conscience got the better of me and I emailed the bad news to a relieved punter. This pile of tat nagged at me daily, it had served me well and didn't deserve to be strewn around my garage like a student's soiled underwear. I gathered it up and formed my cunning plan.

I'd build a singlespeed, and then I'd sell it. I'd prey upon the fashion conscious mountain biking community and their lust for non-conformity. "Singlespeed for Sale" .. that'll get 'em, they'll be queuing up like old ladies outside of a broken lavvy, desperate to relieve themselves of their beer tokens. A probing (yet confidential) email to a friend heightened my enthusiasm. All I needed were some spacers, a new chain, a singulator and a cog at the back.

One phonecall later and a package was duly forced through the letter box by our ever caring postman. I set my 'productivity bot' to email an inane question to my business partner every hour and disappeared into the garage clutching bits, tools and a Toffee Crisp that had mysteriously found it's way in with the bicycle parts. I was momentarily distracted by the promise of a weekend living like a pop idol emblazoned across the Toffee Crisp, but couldn't be arsed to make the phone call. Tinkering commenced.

I can honestly say that I've never spent "quality time" in my garage fixing my bike. The truth is I fucking hate it. Sorry for swearing, but that's really how I feel. Adjusting things made of metal is my own personal hell. If Dante lived in modern times, his "Inferno" would contain the paragraph:-

"..and I descended lower into the seventh level where the inept mountain bike mechanics howled with rage and impatience as they attempted to re-assemble the freehub. Beelzebub himself sauntered into the room carrying a wheel to which was attached a Hope Mini, his smile widening as he span the wheel and pulled the lever. "Squeak, squeak, squeak, squeak". I turned to my guide, "And what crime hath these god forsaken creatures committed?", he stopped and shuddered, "Ah, these are they who posted 'What tyre?' threads"

Anyway, my point is that assembling the singlespeed was easy.

I took 2 rings off my XT chain set, stuck some shorter bolts on and affixed the 32 tooth ring. I put the 16 tooth cog and some spaces on my rear hub, lined it up with the front ring. I set the chain to the right length. I bolted the singulator on. I added the V brakes, stuck some tyres on the wheels, whacked on a few pedals, and it was all over. It only took me two hours. I lifted the bike off the floor, it was light. The angel on my left shoulder calmly asked me to walk back into the house and get it on eBay.

However, it was the devil on the right who I listened to. "Ride the fucker, ride it hard man, fucking get out there and fucking stitch the fucker through some mud, get this fucker dirty boy and then get it dirty some more, just fucking ride it NOW!" And that is really what it felt like. I went back into the house and cautiously announced to my family that I was going out for a little ride.

My wife surveyed my blackened hands, stained jeans, frayed fingernails, the rain sliding down the kitchen window, the clock, the darkness and then she peeked round the corner and saw the (sort of) new bike. I fought past the knowing look, sprayed myself in lycra and waterproofs, hastily adorned the bike with lights. I pushed the bike out into the street. I furtively looked left then right, like a dirty old man walking out of a sex shop and then dived on top of it and down the road we went.

To get from my house to the trails takes a mile. It starts on the road and gradually heads downhill to a sharp bend. The rider is then dragged up and over a couple of short steep hills before tarmac bleeds into bridleway. I set off at a moderate pace, but it didn't take long for me to end up spinning my legs like a cartoon character in mid-air. I couldn't keep it up and soon found myself coasting. Both hands were reaching for phantom shifters, I needed a bigger ring and wanted to go faster, but I couldn't, I was trapped at a moderate pace and no amount of leg windmilling could do anything to improve it. I nearly stopped and went home, and would have if it wasn't for the hill. The gradient ate into my cadence and as I mounted a motorway bridge, the bike was starting to make me work.

I got out of the saddle and fought back, my thumbs were still searching for shifters, but the legs and lungs ignored them as they began to concentrate upon the task in hand. I was enjoying it. The road swept me downwards as hill gave way to valley and again my legs ceased to have any useful function as the bike's speed exceeded any sensible pedalling velocity. I was ready for the next hill and attacked it, revelling in the lightness of the bike and the simplicity of the task. Just pedal, that's all you do, there's no fannying about with gears, no waiting with bated breath for an unreliable upshift of downshift, no noise, no clunks or grates, you just pedal.

The task became more familiar as I left the road and wrapped myself in bridleway. The bikes gearing was close to that which I would normally have selected, however, something was different. It was the silence. Bumps and ruts simply moved the bike upwards, gone was the usual cacophony of chain banging derailleur magnified by the winter grit. It's clichéd, but the bike really did purr along the trail.

I was starting to get what it was all about. Bridleway became rutted track and I was starting to get a feel for the Zen of singlespeeding. For me it's about pace. On my geared bike my pace will change with environment, hills slow me down, roads speed me up, but on the singlespeed I seemed to want to go everywhere at roughly the same speed. (How bloody obvious is that?) The off road hills were harder, I found myself out of the saddle much more and a few aches appeared in areas normally silent during a ride. I was waiting for the mythical exploding knee, but it failed to make an appearance.

For sure the quads and calves complained a bit more than usual, however it all felt manageable. I was writing this article in my head, about 10 miles from home. I was going to sing the praises of singlespeeding, salute it's simplicity and castigate myself for having been an unbeliever for so long, and then it happened. My singulator waved "goodbye" to the cog tensioning the chain. The cog took umbrage and flew off into the dark in a seething rage and the chain gave up its tension and fell off. Oh fuck.

I scoured the area for the cog and associated bolt. I looked enquiringly at passing rabbits, I renounced my atheism and pleaded with St Anthony. All to no avail.

The only option left to me was to ride the ten miles back using the cog shaft to tension the chain. It would wear the chain and the shaft, and would probably break. However, the casting vote was given to the cold and dark and I slunk my way home. That evening I brooded upon my mistake, I hadn't tightened the cog bolt hard enough and more frustrating than that, I hadn't tackled a long off road climb on the singlespeed. The next day I rushed the kids to the cinema and back and then recommenced battle in the garage. One Heath Robinson moment later and my bike was ready to go again sporting a newly bastdardised singulator along with an LX cog.

This time I completed the whole loop.

Twenty miles of spinning madly downhill, gurning uphill and hacking along at a constant pace on anything flat. It normally takes me an hour and forty five to do those twenty miles. Today took one hour fifty. Not bad for a bike with only one gear. However, if we introduce cleaning time into the mix then the singlespeed took on a whole new dimension. A quick dusting with the hose and the bike was gleaming like a crown jewel. My legs are feeling it as I type this text. My body is telling me that I did something different today that it's not used to, and the question it's also asking is "Am I going to do it again?".

Well, the answer is "Yes". I'm happy to say that I can understand why people do singlespeeding and I'm not going to sell the bike. It's hard to summarise my feelings about singlespeeding without descending into tired clichés or conclusions straight from the Ministry of the Bleeding Obvious. However, the impressions made upon me are as follows:-

- Making singlespeeds is enjoyable, quick and easy. If I were in my garage and heard the four minute warning, I'd probably make a quick singlespeed and then wait for the blast.

- Singlespeeding downhill is crap, you can never get the bike to the speed you're used to on your geared steed and you look like a ten year old kid frantically leaving the scene of a failed scrumping mission.

- Singlespeeding off road and uphill is great, routes need "energy planning" to make sure you have the muscles for the hills when you need them. A singlespeed will not let you off no matter how tired you are. It's committing riding and you won't catch me going out all day on the singlespeed.

- Singlespeeds, winter and night riding were made for each other. The simplicity of the drive train reduces noise and introduces the sounds of the darkness into your ride. My next ride with gears will be like having a stereo on. Also, the singlespeed will get cleaned at the end of a night ride, the geared bike will have to bloody well wait till tomorrow.

- Singlespeeding can be hard, I don't normally ache at the end of this ride, but tonight I do. However, for me this is a good thing. I can see singlespeeding entering my training program to help me develop power and cadence.

Would I recommend singlespeeding? Would I bollocks. For me singlespeeding is something you discover, something furtive and something that you could end up regretting. From my experience I can see all sides of the singlespeed argument and like the gutless non-commiter I am, I'm sticking my feet firmly in both camps. Singlespeeding definitely has a point and I'm going to keep on doing it until I discover exactly what it is.

Chapter 9

A Brief Attempt At Comedy

OK, let's stick with singlespeeding for a few more paragraphs. As you can see from the previous article there's something slightly irrational about those who decide to make life harder for themselves by deleting gears from their bike.

I began to wonder if singlespeeding was more than a shedding of cogs, was it a mental state as well? This led to the "Would anyone famous have singlesped?" thought, and the rest, as they say, is history.

This article appeared a copy of the Outcast magazine, a fanzine for those with a predilection for a single gear. I'm not sure if it's still going?

Singlespeeding Through History

Let's face it, Singlespeeding splits lugies in the face of common sense, it leaves a flaming parcel of dog shit on the doorstep of normality and vents falafel tinged colon gas in the general direction of logic. As a singlespeeder you may view it as your right to consider yourself the crazy paving, a pioneering idiot breaking a virgin trail, the singlemost foolhardy individual in time gone by. But you'd be wrong. History is littered with Singlespeeders if you look hard enough .

Take a glance down your street and hazard a guess as to who has a Betamax video recorder in their attic. Singlespeeder. The fact that there are fuck all tapes that will fit in it is immaterial. It's "better" and that's what counts. The Betamax owner will drone on like an air raid siren extolling the virtues of Betamax over VHS whilst glossing over the fact that the vast majority of the public have bought something else and think they are a knob for going on about Beta. Singlespeeders go back further than that though.

For instance Sir Walter Raleigh was sent off by Elizabeth the First to discover the world and claim it for England. The twat returned with a potato and then to make matters worse shagged one of the Queen's maids and got caught. Soon after, Elizabeth had his head. Definite singlespeed attitude.

Then there was Thomas Telford. The total moron built a network of canals throughout the UK without even considering that the car would be invented in the next century. I mean come on Tom, everybody knew that straight and simple was not the way forward. The great British public needed complexity, junctions, roundabouts and congestion. However, Telford's Singlespeed credentials are slightly slurred with the omission that he built a bridge with suspension over the Menai strait, and then it gets worse as he gives up his canals and starts making roads. Bloody traitor. Dabbles with singlespeeding ethics and then goes back to the mainstream. Telford's singlespeed legacy lives on though, kept alive by the sandal wearing, lentil snorting longboat dwellers busily going nowhere on their festering aqua bridleways.

Don't forget Benjamin Franklin, who fastened an iron spike to a silk kite and flew it in a thunderstorm just to prove that lightening was electricity. What a total and utter knobhead. Any normal cyclist would have handed the kite string to their wife, not Benjamin though, he's a singlespeeder, he hung on himself and survived long enough to write a shed load of waffle that keeps America free to this day, or something like that.

Other cases for consideration:-

- William Shakespeare - not singlespeeder, too complicated, text too small not enough pictures

- Winston Churchill - fat bastard, smoked cigars, half pissed most nights, shagged Germans. Definite singlespeeder.

- Henry the Eighth - nope, got far too much sex to be a singlespeeder

- Queen Boudica - she's in, but only 'cos she fitted gurt big knife blades to her chariot in an attempt to make it look less shonky

- Vincent Van Gogh - cut off body parts to save weight, a bit too jey for singlespeeding we think

- The Duke of York - pointlessly walked up and down hills. Appointed life member and presented with singlespeeder medal of honour.

- Napoleon - fuck off! he's French.

So, don't go thinking there's something unique or clever in your one speed dalliances, the fact is many others have been laughed at well before you. To paraphrase Oscar Wilde "Gears are the curse of the thinking classes".

Chapter 10

Friendship

If I had to pick one thing that cycling has given me over the years from a list my finger would have a lot of items to traverse. The change in body shape would be near to top but so would all of the scars that litter my limbs. Then I'd have to consider fiscal damage to my personal accounts balanced against the renewed love of our countryside. Cycling has provided me with many tales (you're probably fed up with them by now) and many pieces of metal, plastic and carbon. But my finger would stop and stay at the entry marked "Friends".

I value my cycling friendships above everything else that the sport has shoved my way. I've met legions of interesting, eccentric, determined, smelly, tall, thin, fat and even Polish people all of whom have shared their love of two wheels with me. If you've read this fat you might have skimmed through my story of L'Etape. There you'd have been introduced to Peter and his obsession with spreadsheets and calorie counting whilst cycling. L'Etape was the first time we'd met.

What the story doesn't tell is the friendship that emerged as a result, it crops up throughout these tales though as Peter features in at least three, maybe more (you don't expect me to go back and read all this waffle again do you?). Peter and his wife Annie became great friends and as a result and we've stayed in touch ever since I rode the event. I'm immensely proud of both of them for raising a gentle two fingers at highly paid jobs in favour of running a Bed and Breakfast for outdoor types on the east coast of Sardinia. Why not have a quick google for The Lemon House?

Their new business is thriving, completely underpinned by who they are. A couple that take great pleasure in helping others to have a bloody good time. Climbers, cyclists, walkers, kayakers and even the odd journalist all beat their way to the door of the Lemon House looking for a little bit of off the beaten track adventure. Peter shares a few of my own personal traits. Luckily they're not nose picking, arguing about religion or a taste for eighties punk rock.

Peter likes to continually push himself harder on the bike. He's always on the hunt for the next challenge and as a result has ridden most of the major European amateur events. Let's also introduce Cronan, a fine upstanding young Irish lad who had been resident in the same accommodation as us during L'Etape. He'd not ridden with us, but was clearly handy on the bike, lean but with that determined look on his face that tells you if he's starting something he's going to get it done. We'd all clicked glasses on our last night in France and drunkenly resolved to see each other again.

Peter didn't mess about. He was straight on the internet searching for "event much harder than the Etape that will probably kill an Irish bloke and some weird mountain-biker". He found it in the Fausto Coppi and convinced the two of us to bring our partners along for the ride. None of us had any real idea of the undertaking we had signed up to. You'll discover that in the writing below. For my part I became strangely hooked and returned a further three times to beast myself upon the Italian slopes. I've let my love affair with "The Coppi" lapse a little and writing this I feel it's time to go back and give it one more shot.

Coppi? or Cop Out?

The start-line ritual of racing cyclists defines and separates the species. Until I can change mine, I shall never know what it is to win a race, and this became apparent as I lined up at the start of the Fausto Coppi memorial Gran Fondo in Cuneo, Italy.

As always I sat astride my down tube and castigated myself for all my omissions in kit and preparation. Two huge alpine climbs awaited me and my legs had only done one this year. My rear sprocket was clearly missing a few teeth, highlighted by the dinner plates on the back of other bikes. My white legs sprouted hair while all others around me were shaved and tanned. I hadn't learned one single Italian phrase to be relayed as an excuse to the multitude of riders that would pass me. Why do I always start these rides regretting my inadequate preparation? And why do I always forget something?

I bet Fausto Coppi never felt like this. I bet he couldn't wait to get started, I bet he couldn't have cared less about his gear, I bet he always felt prepared, I bet he just wanted to win and that's how he felt at the beginning of every race.

And so, as the minutes counted down to the 7 am start, I reflected upon the ride ahead of me ... One hundred and twenty-five miles through the Italian Alps surrounding Cuneo. Fifteen thousand feet of climbing, mostly within the first sixty miles. One thousand riders, all of a high standard and many returning to the race from previous years. Two companion riders with me, Cronan and Peter, none of us having ridden together before and with no idea of our relative abilities. And finally, three spectating wives, all willing their husbands on towards a good performance. We were doing the Fausto Coppi.

The Fausto Coppi Gran Fondo is run annually, and attracts up to 1,000 riders, all of a relatively high standard. Every year the route changes subtly but always starts and finishes at the market square of the photogenic town of Cuneo. The race fee includes a rider shirt that MUST be worn throughout the ride. If this year's shirt is anything to go by, it is usually designed to illicit maximum comment from club members when worn again back home. My road club comrades currently refer to it as "That kit". I can only describe it as a symphony in orange finished off with the flags of all major European countries except Ireland (much to the disgust of the pure-blooded Irishman, Cronan).

Peter and I had migrated to the Coppi after completing last year's Etape du Tour as silver medallists. Cronan was back in action following an extended lay-off brought on by over-training.

And so we waited for the starter's orders. I scanned the façades that surround the market square of Cuneo, the early morning sunlight picking out its favourite buildings. My reflection was interrupted by the quick-fire Italian that shot from the starter's loudspeaker, and we were off.

The pack shuffled forward and it took no more than a few minutes for my transponder to register at the start line. A cobbled street restricted the initial pace before the race turned out of the town centre and headed out towards the mountains.

The previous evening our "team" had met over the dinner table and discussed race tactics: we were to ride fast up to the mountains in order to avoid any bottlenecks once the climbing started. On the day our tactics evaporated. I'm not sure whether it was nerves, pessimism or simply the fact that we were not aware of each individual's pace, but we were passing riders while remaining squarely in the middle of the pack.

The first twenty miles were uneventful. The alpine views were hindered by low cloud as riders were beginning to settle and find their pace.

At Valdieri the foothills of the Alps made their presence felt, as a sharp right took us into the village and we started our first major climb. Two poorly parked support vehicles hindered many riders and I only just made it through the gap between them. The congestion forced Peter and Cronan to dismount and walk past the vans. Meanwhile, I had begun the struggle up the Madonna Del Colletto.

Believing Peter and Cronan were with me, I set a good early pace and climbed comfortably past riders who had expended more effort in the early stages. I found my rhythm and arrived at the top slightly sweaty but elated that the Col had surrendered so easily. We regrouped, refuelled, re-clothed and clipped in. A glance over the left shoulder and the pack was rejoined for a cautious descent down a narrow, pock-marked road into the valley below.

As the downward incline gradually levelled out I caught sight of our next undertaking. The valley rose steadily for miles ahead of us; there was to be no rest, brake levers would be released as we began to climb, swapping effort from the front to the back of our legs. The sky brightened with early sun and jackets were relegated to back pockets. My chain skipped up the block as the valley forced us higher. Our first serious climb, the ascent of the Fauniera had begun.

I could spend paragraphs detailing the gradients, their length, and our performance over them, using the usual superlatives that pepper cycling articles. I could finish by describing our elation at reaching the summit and how privileged we felt to have been able to accomplish it. But that would skip over the secret truths shared by us semi-competitive types. And I am going to own up.

For me the climb was characterised by a single emotion. Within my group I did not want to fail and I didn't want to be the last. I was driven by visions of post-race conversation - I didn't want to be making excuses, I didn't want to be congratulating others for things that I hadn't achieved. In the bar I wanted to celebrate my performance in the same breath as that of others. And it is that which drove me up.

It was clear that Cronan's racing gearing was going to make the climbing hard for him. Peter and I made a few early attempts to keep us all together but the gap between us and Cronan steadily increased and he was left behind. Peter was probably concentrating on the scenery or his heart-rate monitor; me, I was concentrating on him. I was determined to finish at his heel and thus set my cadence and climb rate to his. As it happened, we switched the lead many times as the climb progressed and after two hours we gained the Col and a typical Gran Fondo chaotic feeding station. 5680 feet climbed, sixteen miles travelled a temperature drop of nearly eighteen degrees centigrade, I couldn't care less. I'd matched Peter and that's what mattered to me.

And it is here that we made our first mistake. We waited for Cronan. Alpine climbs are differentiated from their UK cousins by two things: their length and the change in climate and temperature from the bottom to the top. Ten minutes passed before Cronan rejoined us, during which I donned all of my spare clothing and gathered spare food and water. But ten minutes is too long. I became cold quickly, with little prospect of warming up, given the long winding descent ahead. I learned a valuable Alpine lesson: if you're going to wait, then wait at the bottom. At least there is the prospect of warming up quickly if you become cold, when you start the next climb.

The descent from the Fauniera split the race, with 50% of riders turning off to complete a short course of 60 miles. This gave us a clear road ahead on the way down and so we dared each other ever faster to the bottom, twisting between trees and criss-crossing the mountain stream that took the direct route down.

I'd been told that the Fausto Coppi is one of the hardest European Gran Fondos and the reason was about to become clear. Its two major climbs are separated by a descent, and nothing else. Only a few miles of respite before the effort had to begin again. A marshal waved us left up a steepening slope and the geography made it quite clear to me that we were to escape this valley the hard way, up its side. My private battle with Peter had recommenced.

I don't have many good memories of the ascent of the Col de Sampeyre. I already had two climbs in my legs and the gradients were harsher, with extended sections of 18%. My 25-tooth rear cog had become an optimistic overstatement and I glared jealously at Peter's larger cog. A flattish section of one kilometre gave some respite before the climbing became steeper and the terrain more exposed. The final four miles were climbed in the mind rather than by the legs. I refused to let Peter move ahead of me, I cursed the signs that counted down the remaining distance to the top, I silently mouthed catchy lines from dated pop tunes, I fixed my attention on riders in the distance and willed myself closer to them, I furiously calculated average speeds and distances to convince myself that the top was near; I even stopped and poured away most of the water from my bottles to reduce weight. I emptied my mental arsenal in order to will myself to the top and after one and a half hours of effort I did it.

The illusion I had created of myself as a good climber was shattered by the reality I encountered at the top. It was clear that many other riders had been through the feeding station, and that we were to the rear of the field. I realised that heroics on the English hills do not translate to the European cols, where a different breed of strength and endurance are needed to compete near the head of the pack.

Cronan had not climbed with us. Again, we waited, longer this time, until we finally twigged that we would do better to continue before becoming victims to the cold. A marshal handed me newspaper for the descent and I proudly stuffed it down my jersey to keep my chest warm. This was old-school cycling - disposable clothing to be discarded at the bottom. The descent was the worst part of the race. We shared the narrow winding road with cars ascending for an afternoon picnic at the top. Every corner delivered its open unique sense of fear, laced with the anticipation of another poorly concentrating driver. I didn't enjoy it at all, and it was with a huge sense of relief that I discarded my newspaper into a welcoming marshal's hands at the bottom.

The challenge was unrelenting. There were still fifty miles to go to the finish line. We had nearly 13,000 ft of climbing in our legs and we were on our own. No packs to shelter in, no drafting. The two of us upped our cadence and set off in search of others willing to bear the burden of the continuing fight against wind resistance.

A few miles down the road and we had picked up some fellow stragglers. In the next twenty miles our group sighted another and we then descended into a fit of "chain-ganging" in an attempt to catch it. We'd meet up and then continue at pace; some would keep up with us whilst others relaxed off at the back. It was hard work, with Peter and me the main protagonists, urging others on towards the next objective. Eventually we joined a group of ten and were able to relax into a steady pace of about eighteen miles per hour. Peter began to chat in Italian with our fellow riders whilst I marvelled at the cyclist next to me, a double amputee who had fitted carbon lower legs yet was able to comfortably match our pace.

Our peleton meandered on, until we reached a small town and met our mini-fan club, our dedicated wives, who had waited for us for hours with food, water and encouragement. Torn between an easy ride back with our loved ones or finishing the race, we made the right choice and, after a brief chat - during which we learned that Cronan had been contacted, was OK and making steady progress - a snack and a kiss goodbye, we sped off to finish the race.

Peter and I excelled on this final leg. We found the spirit to up our tempo and share the load of the race towards the line. In the relatively flat terrain we tore up the miles and soon we hit the outskirts of Cuneo, even picking up a straggler who fixed himself to our rear. Eventually stray wisps of loudspeaker noise announced the finish line, Peter and I turned left from a cobbled street and saw the beckoning arch of the finish line.

A quick glance, a smile and we sprinted for the line. Justice was done as we crossed it together in exactly the same time. A few minutes later we welcomed Cronan over the line, the first Irish rider home! He looked tired, but I saw a glint of satisfaction in his eyes. He'd known early that his high gearing would make it hard, but had persevered; a lesser rider would have packed it in and blamed the bike.

We'd finished, and there followed the post-race ceremony of the amateur cyclist. The "well done" from a partner, the gathering of trinkets, certificates and finish positions, the consumption of free food and drink and the reflection upon how we could have done so much better, if only …

And so, the reflection. There is no doubting the pedigree of the Fausto Coppi Gran Fondo. It is a serious undertaking when considered statistically: 15,000 feet of climbing, 125 miles long, average gradients in excess of 12%. Geographically, the back-to-back climbs add to the challenge, the vast majority of the 15,000 being covered within a distance of forty miles. The "weekend warriors" were absent, we were fit, trained competitive cyclists and yet found ourselves at the back of the pack. In summary, it is an event for the tough and committed rider. The Fausto Coppi Gran Fondo is the ideal tribute to its namesake; it shares his defining characteristics as a rider.

Our sense of achievement was dampened by our finish position. However, we've shelved our excuses and clearly defined the improvements necessary for next year. From the starting line we're going to race hard in order to get near the front before the mountains. We're going to believe in ourselves and ride harder on the climbs. We're not going to wait for anyone at the top; we'll take food and water and then be off. If we can, we'll ride with a pack and help drive it to the finish at speed.

The trials of this ride haven't dented me at all; in fact I feel they'll help form me as a cyclist. I'm going back to do it better next time. Because I'm convinced that is exactly what Fausto would have wanted me to do.

Chapter 11

Genres

————————

Cycling, like many other sports, has it genres. You'll know this by now as I've gone through a few of them in the articles so far. The problem with genres is that they are often deemed to be mutually exclusive even though they aren't. Yet us humans love labelling things and cycling's no exception. My Dad is also a "labeller", I believe this stems from his strict upbringing within the RAF. When I grew up everything in the house had to be marked with it's purpose (or "for the use of" to give it Dad's technical term).

We had brushes for cleaning our shoes. One was covered in polish, clearly for putting it on and the other wasn't, so you'd use that one for polishing it off. Dad clearly labelled each, "Putter-on" and "Taker-off". Mum bought him a DynoTape machine that allowed him to create his own labels in minutes, soon after it all got out of hand. Everything in the house had to be labelled. We had labels above the phone telling us the number of the speaking clock. His wooden pencil case had its own inscription advising the reader of the contents and pointing out that it was his. Our car had numerous instructions affixed to it, including the fact that the cigarette lighter did not work. I imagine my brother and sister were both labelled with their names but they probably fell off in a scrap with their elder sibling.

Cycling's the same. It's obsessed with labelling. Bikes are labelled as racing machines, sportive suitable, all mountain, cross country, cyclocross, hybrid, shopper and there's even the new genre of "fat bikes" designed for riding in the snow! It gets worse when you turn to the riders as they end up labeled as well. You're marked as a roadie or mountain biker or tourer or trials rider or any other number of labels that attempt to pigeonhole you as the rider you are. What's worse is that often the association is deemed to be for life and woe betide any cyclist who strays from the chosen pack into that of another.

I began cycling life labelled a mountain biker. This meant compulsory beer, absolutely no leg shaving whatsoever, loose clothing and frequent moisturising to fight off any evidence of the encroachment of age. Then I dabbled about with the road bike. My mountain biking brethren were appalled. "Dave, you know where this will lead don't you? Tea, smooth legs, tight clothes and conversations and Saga holidays". But I ignored them and all of their predictions came true (apart from the smooth legs as I'm not very good with the razor).

However, my love of mountain biking remained. In fact it got stronger as an alternative approach allowed me to "Vive le difference". I wanted to explain this to my friends but they were too busy hucking off drops. So I wrote this little analogy instead. The editor Mike Davies kindly published it for me on the mountain biking site Bikemagic and much online discussion was had as a result.

The Bigamist

About eight years ago I found myself dressed in the best gear Burtons could supply, travelling back from London after the usual series on unproductive business meetings. Bored and fed up, I entertained myself by eavesdropping upon the surrounding conversations. Mobile phones had yet to intrude the commuter's routine. Most failed to catch my ear, until I overheard a frustrated couple discussing the crossword. "A member of two unions simultaneously", the husband repeated whilst impatiently drumming his fingers against the window. His wife rapidly emptied her cranial thesaurus and began to freeform around the names of British trade unions. I knew the answer instantly, it was "bigamist".

I'm hopeless at crosswords, I doubt I've ever completed one in my life, but for once I'd unravelled a slightly cryptic clue. Imagine my torment, torn between proudly announcing the answer or keeping it to myself in a self satisfied smug smile folded arms sort of way. A few minutes later I blurted it out. The wife politely thanked me whilst her husband tinged red and furiously attempted to disprove my theory. He couldn't and the word "bigamist" has stuck in my mind ever since. Eight years later and I've finally put the word into practise. Not in my love life I hasten to add, bigamy would be very difficult for one with my appearance and table manners. However, were marriage law to be applied to cycling then I would quickly find myself answering charges of first degree bigamy.

I've got a road bike and a mountain bike and I love them both the same. In order to explain my crime, I need to give you some background. So let's start with mountain biking and how it led me down the aisle. I bought my first mountain bike in 1998, my friends were buying them and my knees were insisting that cross country running had played its role more than adequately in removing my 30 year old puppy fat. Being a slightly obsessive character I set out to ride it as often and as fast as I could. The bike led to 4 others, a myriad of accessories, a darker section of my front drive, an increased mileage on both my car and camper van and a number of pocket draining holidays in the USA. Mountain biking was certainly my first cycling love, kindled over the ruts and chalk of the Wiltshire Ridgeway but set alight in the English forests and Welsh mountain passes. Whilst mountain biking I have collected a whole new group of friends and plenty of material to bore my grandchildren senseless with as I descend into senility.

I've raced, I've explored I've been lost and found as well. I've had nasty injuries and seen friends put out of action completely. I've joined a club and stayed up till early hours drinking and giggling incoherently. I've bought a rainforest's worth of magazines and wasted hours on internet forums. I've taken photographs and written reports. I've nodded knowingly and laughed at the reports of others. I've ridden alone and in groups, night and day in every season. I've tested myself, won and lost. I've felt frustration, elation, apathy, empathy, and on certain occasions a belief that nobody in the world is having a better time than I.

I've catalogued volumes of new knowledge, learned new skills and techniques and maybe even matured a bit along the way. Mountain biking has taken me to some of the most scenic corners of Britain, it has given me views that only the minority will glimpse. If I think about it hard enough the essence of my mountain biking is that which surrounds me whilst I'm doing it. Be that companionship, scenery, weather conditions or the lack of a certain problem that's been weighing me down.

So, that seems like a perfectly reasonable seduction. Who wouldn't be happy in a marriage that delivers those characteristics and why on earth would anybody hanker for more? Well, as stated earlier I'm a slightly obsessive character. I find it hard to sit still and equally hard to sit back without any attempt to improve. Mountain biking has delivered a new degree of fitness for me, however, in true 21st century male fashion, I'm not satisfied and I want some more.

That's why I've recently had an affair with road biking, which has now escalated out of control to the point that we nipped down the registry office a few months back and signed on the line. Or put another way, I've joined a road club. "Why?", I hear the committed mud warrior cry, "Surely you could get fitter and ride your mountain bike at the same time". Well I've been thinking about that. Every mountain bike ride offers me the opportunity to stop, take a breath, look around, read a plaque on a memorial, admire a sunset or wonder "What the fuck was that?" and wish I'd not come out alone in the dark.

Every ride has a hint of uncertainty about it and I'd hate to turn up the opportunity to view a naked couple romping as my training schedule forbade it. Put simply, I'm not about to ruin my mountain biking with rigour, schedule, targets or monitoring. So I joined a road club.

Now you understand my reasoning, I imagine that you are still confused. Bigamists have two marriages. It's clear where the love for mountain biking comes from, but surely road biking is purgatory punctuated with angry motorists, boring routes and miserable companions. Isn't it more akin to a mother-in-law rather than a second bride? Well, no. I really enjoy road biking and joining the club has only served to increase that pleasure. I'll try and explain why.

The essence of a road club is the club run, a regular ride often run at weekends and usually covering a fair distance. Our club run sets off on Sunday mornings and covers between 60 and 70 miles around the back-roads of rural Wiltshire. The Sunday club run is billed as the "fast" one and usually averages a pace of somewhere between 17-19mph over the distance. Between seven and ten riders usually turn out all wearing the club colours. From the outset we ride in formation, a mini peleton designed to be as aerodynamic and energy efficient as possible.

The peleton has a life and dynamic of its own as we flatten out to let motorists pass or re-order to take tired riders off the front and replace them with a fresh set of legs. We ride close together and a blithe banter ripples up and down the group. Riders at the front unconsciously point out hazards in the road to those behind such as potholes or pedestrians.

The statement that road cyclists are unskilled is a myth. Precise bike handling skills are necessary in order to remain within inches of the wheel of another whilst ridiculing the shameful chat up lines they produced during the previous evening's drinking session. Occasionally a road sign or boundary marker causes conversation to cease, followed by a rattling of chains and a marked increase in the pace of the group. It's a club run sprint, the objective of every rider is to be first to the marker, and it's taken me a while to be able to play this game.

The first time it happened, I dashed enthusiastically off the front of the group only to descend into a ragged hell of lactic acid and cramp as the rest of the group cruised effortlessly past. This was followed by a quick and efficient burst of speed from the winner to claim the sprint. I hold back now, I can't win the sprints on the flat but the hill climbs are a different matter (mountain bike legs you see).

Some sprints are traditional, others are spontaneous. If we're honest we're imitating our heroes in the major races. But I find it certainly adds flavour and interest to the Sunday run. Every cyclist we pass is waved at and any overtaken are invited to climb on for a tow. I've read so many things about bad tempered roadies, but can't find them in my club. After a few hours we stop to refuel. The conversations round the table echo those I encounter whilst mountain biking, invariably descending to base male subjects centred around alcohol, women or sporting prowess but sprinkled with sarcasm and self depreciation. Admittedly the scenery is not as good as that found off-road.

However, I've had sunny winter panoramics of the Cotswolds, frost nipped rolling Wiltshire downs and guest appearances from the Mendips on one particularly long ride. Our club runs are deliberately run at a pace and they're demanding. We all turn up to get fitter or maintain whatever fitness we have. We share that objective and we work hard yet collectively to ensure that we all end the ride together having maximised our workout. I recently descended further into the freemasonary of road riding by completing my first time trial. But that is another story altogether. I hope you can now appreciate that whilst my bigamy has no excuse, the reasons are clearly understandable.

Both of my marriages are strong because they have been entered into for entirely different reasons. Mountain biking feeds my soul and delivers the antidote necessary to survive some of the darker side effects of modern existence. Road riding feeds my ambition to be a better and faster rider and participation within a road club pushes me harder towards that ambition. I wouldn't for a second advise that every cyclist become a bigamist. My route has been formed by a connection of synapses within my head that are peculiar to me. What lights my candle may well extinguish your forest fire.

Chapter 12

Victimised By Genetics

Genetics is a wonderful thing. Well it is for those who have benefited from the right strains of DNA passed down the line. Unfortunately for a lot of us some errant chromosomes have made their way into our DNA and caused a little bit of bodily havoc. Prince Charles may own most of Devon, but he can't go outside in a strong wind due to the massive lugholes he inherited from a German Tzar. Jeremy Clarkson unfortunately inherited far too much skin for his face causing it to flap around like a black bag in the wind as he sets out on yet another pointless derision of those on two wheels.

And then there's me and the saddle bags I inherited from my Dad. Combine these with my Mum's svelte figure and you end up with a very strange shape indeed. My problem is that I only accumulate weight around the waist area. Fat resolutely refuses to attach itself to my arms or legs, areas where it is desperately needed in order to create a proper sense of bodily proportion. You'll have read in the introduction that I ballooned a number of years back. I absolutely cannot let this occur again as I start to resemble a human toffee apple made from a pear as a result.

So with my genetics it is possible to exist as one of two shapes. Famine victim or man with a 360 degree fleshy bum bag. Famine victim is preferable as depending upon the current vogue I can point to size zero models and claim that I am fashionably thin. This has certain advantages when cycling, clearly it gives me an advantage going up hills. The mass of the earth is pulling on me a little less hard than some of my more rotund cycling companions who occasionally resort to devious means to redress this balance.

In 2002 I cycled France end to end with colleagues from the Swindon Road Club. A few were clearly getting annoyed at the stick-on-a-bike who kept nipping away when we came to the hills. One long drag proved particularly hard for me though and I couldn't understand why? It wasn't particularly steep and there wasn't much wind. It took a few minutes to register that it was actually Smithy cunningly attached to my seatpost by his hand and enjoying the free ride.

The end of season came and I appeared to have a little bit of surplus fitness. I found out that my club ran a hill climb competition every

October, what better place to get my revenge on Mr Smith as he usually entered. The article below gives a brief insight into what went down at that event. What it fails to tell is that I did this competition and then went on to complete the Sunday ride. A number of others did this as well which made for an unusual thirty miles to the tea stop. Usually we'd chatter away about this and that, but that Sunday we simply coughed, hacked and spat the hill climb out of our lungs.

The Hill Climb

Looking from the outside in, many sporting pastimes make little sense to the casual observer. I for one have never been able to see the point of the athletic discipline that is walking. Why on earth do individuals deliberately suppress the urge to run, in order to travel between two points in the shortest time possible? The steeplechase baffles me, scatter obstacles over a perfectly good running track and humiliate yourself stumbling over them in the later reaches of fatigue. The butterfly stroke, bowls that don't roll in a straight line and of course oval shaped footballs. All of these leave me scratching my head.

And so I sympathise with the non-cyclist trying to fathom the hill climb. Why on earth would a pack of perfectly sane cyclists wave "goodbye" to their competitive season with a race up a steep hill? In the age of the internal combustion engine where is the pleasure in racing against Newton's great discovery with legs? This season I made a pact with myself to find out.

I've always been a good climber on the bike. Personally, I'm convinced that it is down to training, mental attitude and natural talent and that is why I wilfully ignore the shouts of "There goes that skinny bugger again" on the club runs. I suppose my lack of weight must contribute a bit, but I'm going to stand firm and talk about "power to weight ratios". Being a good climber doesn't help much in the British chain gang.

It only gets you the road signs that nobody else wants to go for and often a win up a steep incline is swiftly followed by being shot off the back as soon as it gets flat (and they've all recovered). So, you can understand why I have been looking forward to our club's annual hill climb championship. It's the only road race I've really got a chance at.

My preparation had been pretty good. Base fitness was fine, I was near the front of the chain gang and doing a high weekly mileage. I'd included a large amount of climbing in my weekly miles and had even attempted a few sessions of hill reps. I'd ridden the course on several occasions and beaten the times of last year's winner. I'd even been visualising, I pictured myself on Salthrop Hill, staring mockingly back into the eyes of a beaten Armstrong as I glided away upwards from his contorted sweating exertions. As an added bonus my main rival had a walking weekend that clashed with the competition. I had convinced myself that he was afraid.

The night before the race I prepared in my usual fashion by sleeping poorly, drinking too much alcohol and eating mounds of food devoid of carbohydrates. I awoke feeling awful and dehydrated. Breakfast did nothing to perk me up and the 3 mile ride out to the course was characterised by a high heart rate and low average speed. It was all going wrong, and it got worse.

On arrival I was greeted by a number of unfamiliar faces that were attached to skinny powerful looking riders on lightweight bikes. One had even brought his fiancé, he must be serious (as must she). Not only was I in a poor physical state, but I had competition. How dare they, didn't they understand that this ride was to be mine?

Against better judgment I put my name against number one on the start sheet and intelligently used the twenty minutes before start by not warming up at all. Instead I attempted to psych out my opponents with a nonchalant "devil may care" attitude whilst removing from my bike and person as many weight bearing objects as possible. All too quickly I found myself clipped in and supported by the "pusher offer". The thirty second call released far too much adrenaline into my blood stream and on the call of "go" my legs spun like a Dutch windmill in a hurricane.

In preparation I'd told others that I would ease into the climb and leave my acceleration for the steeper sections where I would gain maximum benefit. In the heat of the race I expended all of my available energy on the lower sections of the hill in a fit of high ratio ultra cadence. This destroyed any hope of my gaining a rhythm on the steeper sections and as the gradient increased I found myself out of the seat jerking my bike from left to right desperately scratching for height.

I'd like to be able to clearly narrate the next 250 metres, but the truth is I can't remember them. They were lost in a haze of gasping, wrenching, rasping, face pulling and spitting. My brain was so occupied with pacifying screaming muscles and complaining tendons that it failed to switch on any memory capability. Somehow, I emerged at the lip of the hill and through streaming eyes caught a blurry vision of the finish line two hundred metres ahead. I found the resolve to change down a gear and even managed to attempt a feeble sprint for the line. The sympathetic sound of encouragement drifted towards me and gave me the resolve to maintain the hurt and pass the finish marker.

As I coasted to a halt I felt no sense of relief. In fact the pain in my legs became more profound, I coughed and wretched, my eyes continued to stream and I barely had the strength to maintain my grip on the bars. At that moment I was the worst possible advert for the healthy benefits of cycling. I had momentarily destroyed myself for the sake of a position in a results table. There weren't even that many competitors.

I gingerly turned the bike back towards the finish line and watched the other riders who followed. They all looked remarkably smooth and composed. They all looked faster than me. I was convinced that I'd be beaten and so I began to catalogue my list of excuses. I'd be a graceful loser, but of course there would be mitigating circumstances.

I checked my time with the finish line marshal and free-wheeled down the hill. The pain was taking a long time to dissipate, however the endorphins were beginning to help. I had a little giggle to myself, suddenly I'd spotted the point of fast walking, the steeplechase made sense and it was entirely reasonable to play rugby.

The hill climb is a perfectly logical end to the road cycling season. It demands an intense degree of suffering for the lowest possible speed. It celebrates the cyclist's ability to cope with pain in order to make progress. It's almost akin to a pagan rite of passage into the winter, a short self sacrifice to ensure a better performance in the coming year. I still haven't got a clue why swimmers bother with the butterfly stroke, but I think I get the point of the hill climb.

I ambled up the hill after the final rider and dejectedly approached the group huddled around the finish sheet. The race organiser looked up and gave me a smile, "Well done Dave". I'd won my first hill climb, by two seconds.

Chapter 13

Relationships

An interesting facet of cycling is the impact it can have upon relationships. Some are formed on two wheels as partners are introduced in forests, at cafes, on mountaintops, in valleys and I even know of a couple who met after crashing into each other at a road junction. Other relationships are strained by cycling. For example, an errant wheeler inconsiderately spending far too much time on their bike and not enough on their partner. Then there are the relationships that are augmented by cycling. A couple I know spend a week of each year following Le Tour. They've done it for years and I get the sense they always will. I guess it's become part of who they are and why they're together.

I'm too scared to ask my wife which category ours falls into. She might tell me that we're squarely in the "strained" category. I actually believe it crosses into all three. We didn't meet on the bike, it was at a karaoke evening, but it wasn't long until we were riding together. That didn't last. I convinced Helen that the Isle of Wight was flat and we should ride round it one weekend. It took her twenty miles of hills to hand me her panniers along with the phrase "never again".

We have both shared a love of Le Tour, excitedly hanging around roadsides for hours waiting to cheer the British riders on. We enjoy watching it together on TV and I'm sure that Helen is particularly enthralled by my long monologues that accompany mountain stages where I have ridden up one or two of the inclines myself. I might not have turned her into a tourer but I will claim to have pushed a little bit of my cycle racing passion her way.

The "errant" bit is a little harder to defend. To be frank, I'm guilty as charged. We used to do deals whereby I'd nip off somewhere nice for some mountain biking and Helen would go skiing instead. Then I started to gatecrash the skiing whilst carrying on with the cycling breaks. For Helen it's got steadily worse. Cycling now encroaches almost every holiday we have. My pouty bottom lip makes itself known unless I'm allowed to travel with a bike and sneak off for some epic during the break.

This would be manageable were I to confine my misdemeanours to my own relationship. Sadly I'm known to lead others astray. We've shared a number of holidays with friends and their kids. If Dad's into cycling, then

Dave inevitably pops up with a two wheeled distraction to take the fathers away. What's worse is that it's wrapped up as a benefit to the ladies concerned. Allowing them to have a "relaxed day doing just whatever they want to do" whilst negating to mention that they'll be looking after the kids and dealing with two broken men who will inevitably return later than planned covered in mud.

I won't hide the fact that collusion can occur. My friend Malcolm is in a similar domestic situation and we are slowly mastering the art of sugar coating the discussions with our wives concerning cycling breaks. Hopefully neither of the wives will read this far and understand that men discussing things in hushed tones in the garage is never a good sign.

Big Hills Fat Bikes

That first day at school feeling, do you remember it? Entering a strange room and glancing round at unfamiliar classmates, wondering whether or not you will fit in. I had a touch of this as Malcolm and I entered the Chalet TinTin in Sainte Foy. We had three days to sate our mountain biking appetites whilst our partners battled with weather and children 300 miles further north. Neither of us had any alpine off-road experience. We had no idea what the riding would be like or whether we would be up to it. What better way to find out than a long weekend pitting ourselves against southern France's pointy high bits.

Chalet TinTin is run by "The White Room" or Stevo and Iona if you are on first name terms. They're a young Scottish couple who tired of the UK rat race and relocated to the Alps for a stress free life of winter ski chalet hosting and summer mountain bike guiding. I'm not sure that they've achieved the stress free objective given some of their previous clients. In particular the Barter family who had invaded their chalet several years previously for a Xmas skiing holiday. It had been one of our best ever trips and I'd been looking for an excuse to partake of their summer hospitality when opportunity presented itself.

My wife colluded with Malcolm's and suggested a two week camping holiday in France. We raised eyebrows and mentioned that the Alps happened to sit in the same country. Negotiations commenced and in a break from stereotype, Malcolm and I emerged with three days child free mountain biking for very little penalty. Clearly we are model husbands to deserve such a bounty, or could it be that the wives would pay any price for a spouse free long weekend?

Regardless, the two of us hired a small car, filled it full of bikes and cycling tat, abandoned the family at a rain sodden campsite and drove south to Sainte Foy. Iona welcomed us into the chalet late afternoon and we tentatively crept into the communal area wondering who our riding compadres would be. This is where it all got a little bit like school, but in reverse. Malcolm and I were the oldest by decades. Oh shit. Three days of limping after whippersnappers who lacked the fear, family responsibilities and ageing bodies of us over-forties. We were introduced to Richard, Ellie, Richard II, Alison, Callum and Alex. Fresh faced, exuberant, clearly experienced mountain bikers.

Things took a turn for the worse when we glimpsed their bikes..... Firstly, I was unable to spot any gaffer tape, cable ties or oil leaks. Next I noticed that they were properly clean and exhibited signs of maintenance. Finally, they appeared to have rather a large amount of travel attached to them, making mine and Malcolm's bikes appear comparatively "jey" with our measly dose of 140mm.

We left the chalet and took a brief walk to mull over our predicament. The hills bore the scars of the ski station. I looked up at my winter ski runs with mixed emotion. A thrilling tree lined white avenue had morphed into a grey twisted fire road, made worse by the spittle that began to fall from the clouds. And then the phone rang.

Iona was conscious that we'd only booked for three days. The following day's forecast was for torrential rain with brief periods of heavy rain as respite. Iona urged us to get a quick ride in before dark. This is the sort of service you just won't see elsewhere. Iona was more bothered about our riding than her evening chores. Malcolm and I sprung into action and ambled back to the chalet at a furious pace (it must have been the altitude). Thirty minutes later we were crudely recognisable as mountain bikers and pedalled left out of the chalet up a hill. Iona had texted us instructions, they were perfect..but due to the limitations of txt speak a little understated. I reproduce them below with some commentary:-

"Directions! L out of chalet, R at dble track t-junction, R at dble track y-junction (signed 'le monal') continue up this till you see large elec pylon and car park"

Perfectly clear and correct, however, if Iona had more time and text space she might have replaced:-

"continue up this"

with

"gentlemen, this ride begins with a f**k off great climb up to the car park that is steep in places and goes on for a tad".

Somehow, Malcolm and I had assumed that our quick evening ride would be an easy, flat dally through some scenic singletrack. Iona was clearly made of tougher stuff though and the two of us sweated our way up to the car park constantly checking with each other that we had "got this right".

"Take sngle track at R, far end of car park signed 'la raie' and 'vtt1' follow down lots of switchbacks to tarmac road."

I did have a quick giggle at Iona's sentence précis on that one. With the only edit being a single "i" removed from "single". But this was probably the most understated direction of the lot. The "sngle track at R", dived steeply into the forest and fired unrelentingly down the mountain. Malcolm dropped his saddle as my intestines prepared to drop something else. We quickly carved final will and testament into a trailside tree and then headed down. Bloody hell it was steep.

Within a minute I'd lost sight of Malcolm who'd got to grips with the trail a lot quicker than I had. It was dark, steep, rooty with occasional consequence and I hung to my brakes quietly mumbling "Mummy" to myself most of the way down. One steep corner consisted entirely of tree root and I was relieved to see Malcolm stopped and wheeling his way round. Thank f**k for that, I now felt no pressure to ride it myself and joined the mini-mincing parade. More steepness, more rocks and more speed as I acclimatised to the roots and turned up the "boldness" dial a little more. I began to get glimpses of Malc as the enjoyment synapses in my brain started to make themselves heard.

The feeling of "I can do this" coincided with the end of the trail. A tarmac road cut through the dark forest forcing me to reach for my phone.

"R at the road (remember to ride on the right h side!) after 1km take R on road signed 'ste foy ski station' follow road back up to chalet"

You've just gotta love Iona's text directions.

"remember to ride on the right h side!"

This statement actually saved our lives. Caught up in the mayhem of the roots and switchbacks, both of us had forgotten. If it wasn't for Iona we'd still be traveling south now glued to a Frenchman's bonnet. Then we have:-

"after 1km take R on road signed 'ste foy ski station' follow road back up to chalet"

I might rephrase that slightly as:-

"Lads, I hope you enjoyed the downhill bit, it was a blast wasn't it, not quite the rolling clay hills you are used to in Wiltshire. Now, a little bit of bad news, you have a blinking long road climb ahead of you. Almost 5km of it at a gradient of about 6%. If you were on roadie bikes then all would be fine and you'd probably enjoy the scenery as you spun your way up. But sadly, you are replete with big wide knobbly tyres and suspension so it's going to be a bit of a grind".

And grind is exactly what the two of us did. I felt really slow initially and couldn't work out why? until I glanced down and noticed that my rear shock had suffered an absence of air. This seemed strange as the bike shop had serviced the bike 5 days previously. We struggled on up the hill and were passed by Iona in her car. She drove alongside and chatted briefly. This would have appeared a tad incongruous to a bystander who would have wondered why the Director Sportive insisted her team train on mountain bikes? The hill soon relented. Dressed and showered we discovered that Iona was set to give us a lift, but we'd looked comfortable pedalling up the hill so she'd left us to it. Next time I'll gurn and cry like a baby.

Over dinner we learnt more about the other guests. Ellie and Richard were on honeymoon and possessed the cleanest bikes of the lot. Ellie remarked that Richard enjoyed a quick fettle, relieved that she was referring to the bike I pushed a little more.

"Did Richard know anything about shocks?",
"Yes",
"Fox shocks",
"Yes",
"Would sir kindly accompany me to the workshop?"

Thirty minutes later Richard was staring at the inside of my shock and shaking his head a lot. A gelatinous blue goo oozed out of the air can and was not looking good to Richard's mechanic's eye. He meticulously cleaned it all out and reassembled the shock filling it with the proper weight oil. We shoved it full of air and the seal held. In fact the seal held for the remaining three days.

My bike shop 0 : Richard 1

The rest of the evening was spent worrying about the weather. Stevo and Iona were certain of rain. My Android phone had a weather app which assured me that the rain would cease at 11:26am. I reassured the others with this information. Their youthful cynicism shone through though, or should I say they completely took the piss out of me for the rest of the night.

"It's OK, Dave's app says it will be sunny at 11:26" became the standard answer to any question concerning the next day's weather. I made a mental note to book Saga holidays in the future. (For the record, the sun did in fact shine at 11:26am. However, it pissed it down for the remainder of the afternoon).

Our first proper day's riding began with an uplift. Ironically the van climbed the tracks that Malcolm and I had thrutched our way up the day before. We disembarked high above the Sainte Foy ski station close to the Fogglietta lift. Malcolm and I were to spend the day with Stevo including ups as well as downs, so we sped off down singletrack following Stevo's rapidly disappearing arse. Thankfully the previous day's misgivings were gone and I found myself in the unusual position of being able to keep up. The rain was holding off as Stevo led the two us us up and down the local trails. The old gits were coping well and looked in reasonable condition as we stopped for cake next to a remote gite. I had no idea where we were but couldn't care less as eyes feasted on the high mountain landscape.

A few minutes later Stevo came up with a choice. Press on as planned, or take a "wee diversion" up a climb for an "interesting" rocky descent. Soon we were to learn that if Iona is understatement's "Queen" then Stevo must be appointed its king. A sodding great steep lung busting climb led us to the top of the trail. Malcolm and I almost got out ropes to finish the last section of pedalling. Stevo had sensibly decided to walk. We came back together at the top of the "interesting" rocky descent.

For "interesting", read "rocky and technical as hell for you chalk riding Wiltshire based Sassenach types". Stevo showed the way down, Malcolm and I bumped, bashed, bounced and many other "b"s from rock to rock, furiously competing to be the most inelegant descender. I think it is fair to say that Malcolm won, purely by forgetting to lower his seat and consequently falling off a lot. I made it down with dabs and smiles, for once unscathed. We then headed off cross country, traversing the local Alps on our way to a long singletrack descent. The route climbed through meadows hanging precariously to the valley side. Eventually pitching up at our lunch spot and high point for the day which I have subsequently christened Twattinggreatrock.

I sat and enjoyed the view, eyes drawn to the cloud in the valley below, which seemed to be moving towards us at quite some rate. Within minutes we were shrouded in moisture or to use its technical term, rain. The cloud density made it clear that the precipitation was setting in for the rest of the day. With jackets on and sunglasses pocketed we rode through bushes and onto tight steep wooded singletrack taking us back down into the valley. For me the riding was a bundle of descriptors; fast, sketchy, challenging, thrutchy, precipitous, exposed with a smattering of wet. I fought hard to hang onto Stevo and Malcolm, willing myself onto their wheels whilst fighting the urge to brake and get off. I'd struggle to describe the trail in detail, my memories are formed of snapshots that include steep switchbacks, narrow contouring paths, rocks, a sketchy bridge and the ever present trees.

A coffee stop intervened after a road and Gite appeared from nowhere. The pouring rain turned it into a double coffee stop with extended chat. Finally we found the will to carry on down. More singletrack, more concentration, more rain but it didn't matter. Stevo led us confidently, countering moisture with speed and creating that perfect balance of fear verses elation.

A final few kilometres of road and we were reunited with the rest of the group in the uplift van. I expected to see rain damped frowns and requests to go back. Not so. The seats were filled with smiles, air soaked with laughter as Malcolm and I were urged into the van for "one last uplift". And up we went, high above the town of Sainte Foy and back down through woods and trees.

The larger group egged itself on. A clear hierarchy of speed had formed and it was no surprise to find myself near the back. At the first switchback I slowed, weighted the outside of the bike, shifted weight back, fixed eyes on the exit and stuffed my bike into a tree." Are you alright Dave?" Ellie enquired. A phrase that follows me wherever I ride my mountain bike. I was. A quick brush off, a little laugh and back on the bike.

Dinner that evening was animated as we shared exploits, mishaps and mountain bike mimes. The conversation meandered as the wine disappeared. Is skin waterproof? lectures on sanitation, the chemistry of halogen lighting IT systems in car manufacturing, credit card hacking and the inevitable piss taking of my phone's weather app.

The following day showed promise. Rain had cleared and the cloud systems appeared to be dissipating. We were scheduled to ride together and there were no signs of lethargy as bikes were wiped, adjusted and wheelied in anticipation. I gave my Zesty the once over. Richard's shock maintenance had held with no perceptible loss of air, but things had gone badly wrong at the front.

The disk calliper mount was missing a bolt. How on earth had this happened? I had my suspicions given the recent bike shop service. Iona passed me a box of bolts sadly lacking in M6 disk adaptor mounts. We delved deeper and found a candidate bolt, right thread, wrong length. A brief hacksaw session saw to that and the Zesty was back in business.

This debacle had not gone unnoticed with piss taking being deflected away from my weather app and on to my bike. This fuelled conversation during the uplift and ensured that large gaps were left to my back wheel as we descended down through the woods. I was starting to get it now. This didn't make me any faster, I just found myself enjoying it more. If I had to use two words to describe the difference between the Alps and Wiltshire they would be "bloody steep". The steepness causes switchbacks, some wide, some rocky, some tight, some downright impossible. Ellie gave me one bit of advice "Outside foot forwards". Once this had sunk in I found myself able to ride them, not fast, but I was getting myself round.

We paused in a clearing and stood admiring the view. I walked down the hill a little and looked back at the others. A tableau had formed. More riding, some meadows and then a talking to. Stevo advised that the next trail was graded "black". There were sections where we'd stop and have a look, it was up to us whether we'd ride them or not. Proceed at your own discretion. In the future when this conversation comes up I'm going to hand the guide a note from my Mum.

"Dear Guide,

Thank you for informing Dave that the next section is hard. He suffers from a strange mental condition that disconnects his aspiration from his ability. You will ride down something and make it look easy. Despite large amounts of evidence to the contrary Dave will believe he can do the same.

He can't.

Please remind him of this fact and hand him the camera instead.

Regards

Dave's Mum"

The first problem was a rocky chute leading to steep, tight switchbacks. To be fair I made it down this intact as did Malcolm who showed real skill by appearing to endo his way down. The next section was much harder. A near vertical rock drop-off leading into a rock garden. Most of the group applied discretion. Stevo and Richard rode it with finesse. I couldn't help myself, I had to have a go.

I knew that stopping at the drop would magnify doubt. I had to keep the bike rolling, arse back, off the brakes. There was no problem with that bit, I rolled in and in Stevo's words "panicked" turning the wheel inexplicably to the left. Lots of bangs, bumps, bashes and a great big hiss ensued. The bangs, bumps and bashes were me bouncing off rocks and then Iona who'd had the foresight to get between me and the really sharp rocks, skilfully fending me away. The hiss was my front tubeless tyre leaving the rim and taking in a decent sized portion of dirt and rock. I was as deflated as my tyre. For me the hard bit was attempting the drop

90

off and that had gone to plan. I wanted another go, but it was clear that the wheel would need a long period of love and attention. We tried to reseal it to no avail and so in went a tube.

Fifty metres later I pinch flatted it. The group waited for me at the bottom, revelling in the new piss taking material that my bike had to offer. Post lunch we piled in the van and were driven up to the Col de Petit Saint Bernard. "Downhill all the way" Stevo told us. We mulled over his understatement on the fire road climb that shortly ensued. A short technical ridge led us to switchbacks or "one million" switchbacks as Stevo advised. Given his talent for understatement I became a little concerned, needlessly. The ground had dried out and the trail wound tightly through woods. I bloody loved it, for once I could ride these things reasonably quickly.

Ellie's advice became a mantra. Outside foot forward, outside foot forward. This made a real difference and combined with looking onwards round the corner I was getting round at something approximating speed. I didn't want this to end as we swooped our way down, but it did. We lay in the sunshine watching the walkers alight the summer lifts. If the day had ended then I'd have been content. But the Alps seem to have a habit of getting just a little bit better to catch you off guard.

The next trail was fast, actually, scratch "fast" and replace it with "hoon". I have no idea of its length, descent or any sort of statistics. I think it ended in Seez. Suffice to say we piled down it, tyres on edge, elbows out, pleading with gravity for a little more pull to drag us to the rider in front. The singletrack spat us into a car park where we regrouped, laughed and began the chant.

"Again, again, again".

Stevo's the right kind of guide. He didn't even glance at his watch, simply stuffed us all back in the van and drove back up to the top. More speed, more hooning, more smiles and guess who punctured in the last hundred metres? Piss taking took a subtle turn towards my tubeless tyres as the rest of the group noted that their inner tubes were remarkably intact. Monday night was the last chalet evening for Malcolm and I. Ellie marked this fact by transferring a significant volume of red wine from it's bottle into our glasses. With no thought to the remaining day's riding, we drank it.

Tuesday morning started in slow motion with heads, eyes and legs rubbed in that order. But Tuesday was "Backcountry" day and determined to make the most of it we quickly perked up, our recovery aided by the best banana pancakes I have ever eaten courtesy of Mansel and Amy our chalet hosts. Tuesday's bike inspection delivered a startling lack of missing components, broken shocks, punctures and mud. The Zesty appeared as keen as I was to get out into the mountains and ride. The plan was as follows:-

- uplift to Aime La Plagne ski stationclimb
- up to col (hmmm, more Stevo understatement?)
- descend down to mountain refuge
- lunch
- descend,descend,descend,descend
- bit more descent with some descending
- train from Moutiers back to Bourg Saint Maurice
- uplift back to chalet

The uplift to Aime La Plagne went without incident. I probably can't say the same about the climb. It was a bit of a stinker, and that's coming from a man who's not strayed far from his birthweight. I'm not really sure of the stats, but I am sure that it was high enough for the altitude to take effect and steep enough to make me wonder whether a 40 tooth rear cog was feasible.

Some of us ground our way up it and others sensibly pushed. On one particularly steep switchback I glanced left at Alex. He was riding a 40lb downhill bike with a single large chain ring at the front and small road block at the rear. He didn't seem that troubled by it at all. But, he's fresh out of university and his brain hasn't developed the proper pain synapses yet. Many minutes later we arrived at a ramp. I'd been dragged up this a few winters previously by a ski lift. It was long, loosely surfaced and steep, somewhere near 30%. Again the dreaded words:-

"Only Stevo and our guide Yvan have ridden up this".

I wish I'd had that note from my Mum. Whilst others pushed, I pedalled onto the start of the ramp with the bike in the lowest gear. The first few metres seemed ok, I was still going upwards and could breathe. A few pedal strokes more and it got a bit harder. The loose surface needed momentum to keep traction and I knew that slowing down would mark the end of my attempt. More height, more pedalling and then that familiar burning sensation that begins at the base of your lungs and works up to your throat. I was now in oxygen debt. I was about to get off and give up when someone called "Go on Dave!".

The shout spurred me on. But halfway up the climb steepened and I spied a single line of hardpack that led to the top. Carefully I inched the steeply inclined bike over loose stones towards the hardpack. The front of the saddle dug hard into my arse as the cold air scraped away at my lungs. More shouts, more pain, when the f**k was this ramp going to end? I gingerly eased the bike round the last steep corner and collapsed victoriously at the top.

At over 2000 metres altitude this climb had taken its toll. I coughed like a smoker for the next hour as my lungs rejected all excess baggage in order to repay a significant oxygen debt. I should have realised that more climbing was yet to come. A brief singletrack descent was followed by a long push through flowing green alpine meadows to a striking col view. This was it now. All climbing done, 2000 metres of descent! We traversed down the valley singletrack avoiding the electric fences that criss-crossed the grass.

The mountain refuge was soon gained, bikes discarded on the grass. Richard confidently strode into the restaurant and requested chips. The proprietor confidently took the piss out of him for the requesting of chips, sentences peppered with "non". I played safe with coffee and milk and suffered a mild jibe about the proffered 50 euro note. If you're ever stuck for entertainment then visit the refuge at La Plagne and laugh yourself to death at the red faced owner and his witty retorts.

After a group effort to consume Alison's tartiflette we departed on singletrack down the mountain. Well, the others departed down the mountain. I sat and fettled with the mysterious puncture that had appeared in my one remaining tubeless tyre. The hole entered and exited high up the tyre sidewall. It could not have happened on the trail, I had suspicions of foul play. Iona waited patiently as I swore my way through a tubeless repair inflating the tyre on the second attempt.

She then set off gracefully weaving down tight singletrack that contoured a ridge system down to forest. I pedalled hard to keep up and leant deeper into corners than I normally would. This is how I like to ride, following others who know what to do and guide me beyond my limits. It didn't take long to reunite with the rest of the group. It didn't take long for the grins to appear and the fingers to point at my tubeless repair. I hinted at sabotage but was met with denial, the mystery unsolved. Could it have been a particularly aggressive bee? Or maybe Mr Red Face in retribution for the requesting of chips?

We were in forest now. The trails steepened, switchbacked and increased in difficulty. The enjoyment was there, but it wasn't my day. I waved Ellie past as her brakes began to squeal in my ear and took my rightful position firmly at the back. The riding was hard, then easy, then up a little bit, then impossible, then a little wet, then scarily rooty, then rocky, then grassy, then road, then steep again. The full menagerie of mountain bike challenges were thrown at us.

We fell off bits, walked bits, rode impossibly fast down sections, laughed at each other, pulled wheelies, trackstood, apologised to walkers and stacked a little bit more. Ellie's victory salute at her penultimate crash said it all. Every single rider was trying hard, sometimes a little bit too hard but loving the day. It all came to an end at the side of a road. We'd run out of mountain. Yvan advised us to de-pad and set suspension to hard as we had a kilometre of road to ride to the train. This was it, my three days in the Alps were done. I sat back in the sun and wound back to the start.

All "first-day-at-school" feelings were gone. We'd eased into the group and had bonded through a common love of the bike and the outdoors. Some rode better than others, but it didn't matter as trail performance had been graded in smiles rather than technique. Our guides had completed the perfect balancing act pitting us against challenging terrain whilst ensuring that we went home in one piece. Stevo and Iona are mountain bikers who happen to run a guiding company, rather than guides who happen to mountain bike. It feels like you're riding with friends, willing you down the trails at speeds dictated by fun rather than paper disclaimers. As for the Alps. Well, they're not Wiltshire are they? Driving back to our wives later that evening, Malcolm and I had little to say. I sensed we were both lost in thought, processing three days saturated with experience. As we headed north Richard's parting words rang in my ear. "Dave, I'm going to miss your punctures you know"

Chapter 14

Bloggers

Blogging, it's rubbish really isn't it? Thousands upon thousands of misguided souls seeking attention from the rest of the internet. What did all of the bloggers do before the internet was invented? I have this feeling that parish newsletters must have been really rich and fulfilling in those days, filled with the observations of thousands who were slightly annoyed with a car that passed too close to them. Bloggers without a parish mag. probably just kept a diary and simply marked each day with the food they ate, their current spot count and the fact that they've been dumped by Karen Davison .

These days you can't move for blogs. In fact it has got so bad that certain individuals are cutting and pasting their diatribe into word processors and passing them off as books. If you look hard enough there is a blog about everything. I met a young lady who works in the area of sanitation, her expertise is basically ... faeces, she even lectures on it. Over dinner she told me that she had a blog. I resisted for days but eventually couldn't help myself and navigated over for a quick peep. It was about mountain bikes.

But I'm proud of the bloggers. I have to be as I'm one myself. One man's "self promoting spurious words that have all been done before" is another man's "free entertainment for fifteen minutes instead of working on that report". I've read lots and lots of blogs and been inspired by many of them, particularly my friend Alex who wrote an amazing piece about killing his washing machine with cycling filth. I'm waiting for him to forget about it so I can rob it and use it in mine. Reading some American blogs led me to the "Fat Cyclist".

He appears to be a minor celebrity in the USA, mainly because he was fat, cycled a lot and now isn't. If you've read the introduction to this book you'll understand that I felt quite aggrieved. He's not the only one who's shed a few pounds and then gone on to write a few words. It just so happened that the day I rocked up, he'd written a request for others to contribute to his blog. The challenge was to write about "My Proudest Moment on my Bike". I surfed around his site some more and discovered that he had all sorts of sponsorship, merchandise and much worse fawning blog fans. Every post he ever made was "Awesome", and so was he. He was mates with Lance Armstrong and Levi Leipheimer and regularly name checked the two. Where the fuck were my fans? How come David Millar has never heard of me? Surely my fifty hits a day deserved at least one internet stalker?

I then began to imagine the contributions that would come in. Sorry to offend any Americans, but you lot let George W Bush run your country for a bit. A little bit of sick came up in my throat at the thought of the tales of endeavour from lard ass doughnut eaters who'd cycled ten miles to raise money for their aunt who was tragically afflicted with gout. I couldn't imagine any of his fawners approaching the task with humour or irony. And so the challenge was set. I penned the article below designed as a little bit of citrus within his sugary mire. I hoped he'd enjoy something a little more refreshing. But clearly it was shit as I never even got a reply. Me? I'm not bitter.

My Proudest Moment On My Bike

I was flitting around the internet yesterday in a fit of work avoidance when I came across a posting from the Fat Cyclist. The rotund fellow appears to have a decent sized following and he was sticking to type via a request for others to do his work for him. This is clearly how he ended up a size twenty and I was severely tempted to send him an email berating his work ethic and carry on with my time wasting. But then I thought about his request, he was looking for riders to write about their proudest moment upon their bike. I pondered this for a while and suddenly realised the enormity of the task.

I'm sure I could waffle on for several thousand words about a few decent moments that I've had...but think of the competition. There are people out there who have ridden through all sorts of adversity, from overcoming illness to the loss of several limbs. I've been overtaken by a lad with two carbon legs in a race before. This was after one hundred miles of climbing in the Alps and he looked like he was ready for one hundred more. If he sent in a blog contribution it would kick my arse.

The cancer survivors, extreme weight losers, deaf, diabetic or anaemic would all have better stories to tell than me. Unfortunately (well actually fortunately probably) the greatest adversity I have ever had to overcome whilst cycling is whisky created hangover coupled with a cold. There's no way that fatty is going to pay lip service to that story.

Then there's those who have achieved fantastic things upon their bike. I've never ridden round the world, I've not won a major stage race, I've certainly never ridden for more than 24 hours. So my meagre palmares are not going to cut it either. I can just imagine the Fat Cyclist in-box filter receiving a contribution from Eddy Merckx closely followed by mine. You wouldn't need human intervention to filter that one. Even a lowly computer would recognise the disparity in achievement and would probably silently move my message over into "spam". Things were not looking good and so I resisted the urge to put finger to keyboard, but then a little voice in my mind piped up "Think left field Dave, think left field". At first I wondered what the hell a mainstream drum and bass band had to do with cycling, but then it hit me.

The voice was hinting that being on the bike wasn't just adversity and achievement, there's other stuff as well. Mental cogs ground harder and I slowly relived a lifetime's worth of cycling to seek out even the most tenuous proudest moment. I tried hard to remember whether I had invented anything completely awesome whilst turning the pedals. Sadly that angle failed as the handlebar mounted airbag I'd conceived several years earlier had only managed to generate laughter from venture capitalists. I turned my mind to other feats and remembered the first time I'd ridden "no handed" in a group. I must admit I was pleased with the smoothness of the sit up followed by the deft reach for the Power Bar in my jersey pocket.

The transition to mouth for unwrapping had gone without a hitch but after that it all started to fall apart as I chewed desperately at the wrapper to try and get it undone. Minutes of this ended in abject failure and with amazing stealth I returned the soggy, yet unopened bar back to the pocket and cycled on. I was pretty damned proud that I pulled this off without comment, given that I ride with a group whose sole purpose is to somehow humiliate one of their members as soon as a display of ineptitude becomes visible. I doubted that fatty would be interested in that story either.

Could a proudest moment be something I'd seen or a weird happening? Anyone riding a bike for any period of time will at some point encounter the surreal. Last year I was tapping along minding my own business when a van pulled up next to me. The passenger window was wound down and a Jack Russell dog was held out of the window directly into my face. The dog gave me a look of resignation and managed a timid yap. My pride was in my composure, I simply "woofed" back at the dog and carried on with my ride. Truth is I couldn't believe that it was actually happening and thought it was some fatigue based hallucination. Clutching at straws, I turned my mind to mountain biking, was there anything I was proud of that had happened off road?

Well, I've fixed my broken bike with all sorts of vegetation and managed to get home. From grass stuffed tyres that saved me from a forgotten inner tube to the huge great log I once used to whack my bent wheel back into almost true. I wasn't sure that these met the criteria. So I looked into whether I'd ever been awesome down a descent. The plain truth was "no", all I've ever done is survive, I guess I should be proud that I've made it this far still relatively intact but I doubt readers would be inspired by that. Thus I realised that I didn't really have any proudest moments on my bike that were going to stand up against those submitted by others.

My cycling mediocrity would prevent me from sending in an entry and I was about to consign my efforts to the trash icon until I had this revelation. I haven't got a single proudest moment on the bike, I'm just proud that I carry on riding it. Cycling is one of those weird pastimes where the participant is continually faced with adversity, mediocrity and many other reasons to stop and go and do something more rewarding instead. Yet I and others carry on doing it, because we can and we love it. And so I realised that I'm proud of all of my moments on the bike and none of them shall take precedence. I'll send this piece to fatty anyway. Like the rest of my cycling I doubt it will bubble to the top but I've strangely enjoyed the therapy of bashing it out.

Chapter 15

Sometimes It All Goes Wrong

Lots can go wrong when you're out cycling, especially given that you share the roads with any number of lunatics who have been handed a piece of paper entitling them to drive a car. I never cease to be amazed by the antics that they get up to when encountering a cyclist. I've had my arse slapped, half finished McDonald's meals thrown at me, been spat at, shouted at and had a Jack Russell held in my face by the passenger of a passing white van. I've been hit by cars and once by a lorry.

Luckily I've survived each encounter and shared merry banter with the assailant usually comprising of vigorous waving of single fingers accompanied by imaginative swearing. But it's not just motorists that make cycling things go wrong. Mechanicals play their part as well. I've abandoned countless rides due to component failure the worst being a freehub that decided to freewheel in both directions. There's nothing more frustrating than pushing a bike for ten miles when at first glance it looks perfectly functional. All of the passing motorists think you're a little too tired hence pushing on the flat. I've also had the occasional failure down to nutrition.

We've all heard of "the bonk" and many of us have suffered it. Including me. It's much worse when you're in a relationship as you inevitably phone home and feign some mechanical issue whilst begging for a lift. I'll hold up my hand, I've done this in the past returning from a 60 mile ride to Bristol. I've also seen tough love in action on a club ride, when a junior stopped and phoned Dad to ask for a lift, his legs had clearly had enough.

Dad was a seasoned rider though and told him to "sod off", it would be "character building" to ride the rest of the way home. Pete "the snotter" stepped in calling his wife instead and we waved goodbye to the two of them as they were driven home. Good strategy by Pete who could use the junior as an excuse for baling out early. But we knew the truth as Pete had been blowing out of his arse.

Crashes are the worst instance of when it goes wrong. Fortunately most of mine are relatively benign with the greatest injury being a dented pride as friends point and laugh at me face down in a ditch. I've only been hospitalised twice. The first time stacking the mountain bike in the middle of nowhere and smashing my shoulder into the ground. Helen was called to come and find me for a ride to A&E. X-rays showed no lasting damage and I was sent on my way with an Aspirin. The second occasion was worse.

My helmet peak came off and jammed the front wheel. I now know why you never wear peaks on a road bike. I had no time to react and hit the ground with my head, bending my neck very hard in the process. I'd read that in this instance you should lie still and do nothing. If it was broken, the slightest movement could cause lasting damage. This time it was far too serious for Helen and an ambulance ferried me away. Fortunately the X-rays were kind to me again. I apologised profusely to the A&E staff, but they would not accept it. "You did the right thing" were the doctor's passing words. This next article concerns another serious crash. This one happened in a foreign country.

Crash

Four and a half hours into the race, my year's training efforts came to an abrupt end. My prone, cut and bruised body was halted by a traffic barrier. Six months of hard work slid down the road undone by a single mistake. My season's objective out of reach. Or was it? I'm a voracious reader. I have the ability to read and digest at speed, much to the annoyance of my wife, who often teeters on the brink of sleep only to be disturbed by my rapid and regular page turning in bed. I've made it my mission to plough through a library's worth of cycling biographies and training manuals and never cease to be inspired by those who have taken on the mountains and won.

In my cycling lifetime I've set out to understand and empathise with my heroes by taking on the role of a climber and setting about the gradients encountered on the club run. Every year I make my annual pilgrimage to the mountains of Europe to test myself further in a long Gran Fondo that climbs a mountain or two. Usually I do "OK", but my late night reading was giving me the impression that "OK" is just not good enough. So this year, I trained to go hard. And I really did train. I rode hundreds of miles every week. I rode an additional two hours after every club Sunday ride. I time trialled, I raced, I recovery rode and performed interval training.

I rode nearly one hundred hill repetitions and really showed my mettle by removing every strand of hair from my legs in an extended two hour shaving session. Four thousand seven hundred training miles couldn't be wrong, especially given that they had got progressively faster. My objective was the one hundred and twenty mile long "Fausto Coppi" Gran

Fondo. I'd ridden it before in nearly ten hours, suffering badly on its two major climbs. This year, my master plan said "eight hours".

Recent performances showed that I could achieve this and I also believed that I could. Self belief is usually worth an additional ten percent. And so I crossed the start line and began to live the truth of my training manuals. To give them credit they were mostly right. I comfortably rode through the pack to join the lead group and stayed with them till the slopes of the first col beckoned with crooked finger. My bike raised an eyebrow in surprise as I piloted it to the top minutes faster than the previous year. So far, the eight hours were in reach. The next thirty kilometres must have been hidden in the training manual small print as I don't remember the bit about the pain remaining even when the fitness has increased. After a brief descent the race went skywards again.

An eighteen kilometre climb, in hot sun and without respite. Initially, I maintained a high pace and high gear, however, each new kilometre saw my legs fade a little further until I had run out of gears and had ceased passing others. I was beginning to understand that faster legs simply hasten the body to the point at which the pain begins. There does not appear to be a training program for self synthesis of morphine, I'm certainly going to be working on it. However, the news was not all bad. I found that my training allowed me to ride through the pain and accept it.

Others were in a similar position. The field had thinned out by the time we reached the top of the first mountain. Manners were left waiting as we collectively scrambled for food and water from the feeding station and then pushed off to address the steep, narrow descent that snaked down the other side. I've always been a nervous descender on the bike. I've yet to find the courage to trust   my mental geometric calculations to guide me at high speed through any corner.

So, with no riders visible in front of me, my brakes remained firmly affixed to the wheel rims as I squeaked down the mountain. As I got lower, the road surface degenerated into "almost track" at one point requiring a dismount and short walk thanks to the Italian road builders who had removed the tarmac layer and then gone to lunch. As I lost height, the surface began to improve, riders began to catch and pass me at speed.

The road morphed into a series of fast swooping bends and I relinquished my iron grip on the brake levers and gathered more speed. The next rider that came past took longer to overtake. I realised my own speed and increasing bravado was a part of this and silently affirmed to follow his line to the bottom of the mountain. Inadvertently he led me directly into the crash barrier. Descending upon a bike gives a unique insight into the nature of courage.

Some riders will risk all to enter and leave each corner at the fastest speed possible, often taking a gamble that no vehicles are approaching from the other direction. Others promote self preservation and descend tentatively in the knowledge that maybe the time lost going down can be safely regained on the flat or a climb later in the ride. Finally, there's the hybrid descender.

Tentative in their own company, but willing to subscribe to the risks of a faster rider who may go pass. They abdicate their own judgement to the rider in front and assume that if they follow their line, then they too will arrive safely at the bottom. To me, it is unclear who has the greater courage. The faster rider undoubtedly has the guts to survive by their own judgement. They take on the road alone, secure in the knowledge that their decisions are right and their luck will hold. The self-preservist has the conviction to ignore the actions of their peers and descend at a rate that suits them.

This may well mean a faster climb is required later in the ride or a more sustained effort upon the flat. The self-preservist is prepared to magnify their future suffering in the name of safety. Finally, we have the follower. A rider who makes a split second decision to trust the judgement of a complete stranger. A rider who immediately assesses the ability of the cyclist in front matched with their own and decides in an instant to follow. A rider who is prepared to take someone else's chances. I'm a follower and thus found myself leaning into a corner at close to 40 miles per hour at the beck of another rider's line.

It was too fast.

I realised that I wasn't prepared to lean my bike over at that speed and instinctively pulled the brakes. Mistake. I can still vividly recall the moment at which I lost control. I'd locked the rear wheel up and the bike was trying to turn through 180 degrees. I felt myself lifted over the handlebars and clearly heard myself shout "Oh no!"."Oh No!", what kind of an epitaph is that? Would Nelson have been so fondly remembered for looking up at Hardy and groaning "Oh no"? Would King Charles have made such an impression had he mounted the stand, caught sight of the block, turned to the crowd and mumbled "Oh no!"? These were potentially my last words and the sentence didn't even contain a single profanity.

Next time I have resolved to do much better. I hit the ground hard on my left side. From that point onward all I can recall is motion. Fast, confused, blurred, disorienting motion. And then it stopped, hard, as I met the roadside crash barrier with my neck. A brief moment later my bike joined me and we lay there, a sorry pile of metal and flesh, alone at the bottom of a mountain pass. I lay there for nearly a minute before I gained the courage to attempt to move my legs. Relief mixed with pain flooded through me as I was able to rise to my knees.

My legs and arms were covered in blood with most of the skin removed from my elbows, shoulders and knees. I had a great deal of pain in my neck and my left hand, I hurt a lot, which meant I was alive. Other riders started to come past, but nobody stopped due to the gradient and the speed of their travel. I was on my own, I hadn't prepared for this and all that I could think to do was to get back on the bike and carry on. As soon as I was in the saddle I felt a weird kind of nausea.

I really didn't want to be doing this at all. Something bad had happened and I just wanted to get away from the bike and the scene as quickly as possible. But the bike was the only option. I coasted down the road until I found the next marshalling point. In a near daze I tried to continue along the race route and climbed onwards for nearly a hundred yards until my legs refused to turn the pedals anymore. I lacked the energy or mental capacity to unclip and simply fell sideways.

Two concerned marshals ran up the road and disentangled me from the bike. They caught sight of the blood and pointed back down the hill whilst jabbering in Italian. I haven't a clue what they said, I didn't need to know. They were telling me my race was over. And they were right. An hour later I found myself back at the finish, covered in Iodine, resplendent in ripped lycra and full of regret. Since the crash I had carried out a lot of mental arithmetic. I realised that I was on for a very quick race time, nowhere near the winner, but possibly within the target eight hours I had set myself.

That opportunity was now gone. I'd have to spend another year training, I'd have to lift my confidence in bike handling and kill the doubt that would whisper every time I started to lean the bike over. I'd have to clap my friends over the line and congratulate them on a ride completed whilst wishing I could share in their elation. I began to wonder whether I could have carried on after the crash. I'd managed to cycle back to the start, surely I could have recomposed myself, rested a while and then carried on. It took me a few weeks to carefully squeeze the positives from my unfortunate accident.

I have managed to rationalise it all. I was in the race to challenge myself to go faster but I had a crash. The crash was my fault. I was lucky enough to walk away. As for my wasted preparation? Ultimately training has to be largely formed of mental attitude. For my training to have succeeded, I needed to find the strength to leave the crash barrier behind. To get back on the bike and return a safer, yet more determined rider. And that's exactly what I plan to do. I'll do the race again next year. I'll gain the courage to descend pensively away from the wheels of others and I'll cross the line a far more satisfied rider. This year's training has by no means been in vain.

Chapter 16

Empathy With The Giants

Writing as an amateur can be a very lonely task. You hammer away at pieces that you're convinced are the best that any will ever read, submit them to editors and wait, and wait, and wait. Finally in desperation you stick them up on your own personal website and wait for the floodgates to open and the praise come washing in. Repeat the waiting thing again.

It's easy to get down hearted but I would hope that most writers don't. There's something desperately therapeutic about banging away at a keyboard trying to bring others into your world. In fact I've written a whole piece about that alone, but don't worry it hasn't made it into this book. Occasionally something comes out of the blue that makes it all worthwhile. An email from a reader that you've never met thanking you for the piece and pointing out passages that they identified with. Or a cheque from a magazine for an article you wrote (you'll write more words chasing payment than writing the article).

But sometimes, maybe once in a blue moon, something very special happens:-

"Dave, we want to commission an article about the Tour de France route that goes through London this summer (2007). Would you be prepared to ride it and come up with something for us. We'll get you on a Team Issue bike so that you can have the full Tour rider experience. Don't worry if you aren't interested" - Dan

I had to re-read that email over five times and then drink coffee to ensure that I wasn't dreaming. I was going to get paid to ride a super lightweight carbon bike along the Tour de France route. "Don't worry if you're not interested" Dan, I would have paid you! I tried to temper my excitement in the reply"

"Dan, YES YES YES YES..PICK ME ..PICK ME..."

I think that showed remarkable restraint. A week later the bike arrived, the latest model from Scott, their flagship Adict. I undid the cardboard box and the bike floated out and stuck to the ceiling. It was so incredibly light, and shiny and every single component on it was top shelf. The next few days were full of stress as I fretted over the bike. At night I hardly slept for fear that it would be wrestled from my garage regardless of the six locks that secured it to the walls, ceiling joists and workbench. This stress was tempered with excitement though, given the route I was going to ride, surely it would be a classic.

The day of the ride came and went. I was filled with quandary as it wasn't what I expected. This was going to cause me a problem as I wasn't sure what Dan wanted his readers to see. I dropped him a tentative email, but true to form he told me to write it how it was. No dressing up, no fabrication, your story. So I did just that and he told me it was a bit shit, too flat, not enough "Dave". Dan said it needed some "riffs". That advice has stayed with me over the years.

Taking on Le Tour

"And in a glorious triumph for British cycling, Dave Barter has taken the first stage of the Tour de France 2007 with a solo breakaway effort that destroyed the peleton on the outskirts of London". I could clearly hear David Duffield celebrating my victory as I freewheeled up The Mall ready to ride the route of the first stage. Swathed in dreams I clipped into the pedals, the only part of this thoroughbred race bike that belonged to me. Admiralty Arch beckoned me through and a fictitious crowd roared as I accelerated into Trafalgar Square.

A Taxi driver leant on his horn, a traffic light spat red and a thousand tourists ignored the lone rider staring at his GPS his moment shattered by the chaos of a Saturday's London traffic. I was seeking empathy with the Tour riders by taking on the first stage myself. The route dashes out of London and heads southeast to finish in Canterbury, calling at Maidstone, Tonbridge Wells and Ashford on the way. A loaned ultra light-weight Scott Adict carbon fibre race bike as ridden by the Saunier Duval Tour team completed the experiment. It was about as close to the Tour as I was ever going to get. The only closed roads were those undergoing maintenance. There were no route markers. Navigation consisted of a GPS containing a route hastily planned the night before.

The team car was a battered camper van staffed by director sportive Helen and two soigneurs Jake and Holly. Additionally, London was in the midst of preparations for the marathon. I'm sure that the Tour teams are better prepared than that. Clip, unclip, clip, Embankment, Parliament Square, Westminster Bridge, the sights were getting ticked off but progress was fitful, a recurring theme as the route wound its way through the City.

The Tour riders will be jostling with each other for position, my battle was with London itself. The Adict needed winding up, but London had other ideas, gruffly vocalised by a disgruntled lorry driver and his one fingered greeting. The tour riders will speed through London to salutations and applause.

For me it was hand gestures and expletives simply for taking my rightful place upon the road. A bus lane granted privileged access with a little welcome speed. My spirits were lifted a little by the welcoming spans of Tower Bridge. Ahead I espied a fellow cyclist and was back in the race as I fought to pull him in. A wasted effort, traffic lights called time and we paused to chat. By chance Marcus was due to do the route in July.

The "Tour 2007 cyclosportive" takes in the majority of the route. 5000 entries have been sold already and Marcus welcomed the challenge. We separated at a large roundabout, I peeled off onto a long straight and the Adict immediately took control. This bike clearly hates hanging about. So far it had sulked its way through the centre of London, moaning at every stop. For a few fleeting moments it was free and I held on for dear life as it raced the following traffic. A red light intervened.

The breakaway was short lived. I stuttered through Erith, Dartford and on towards Gravesend. Where was the team car? I needed a bottle, reassurance, encouragement, sympathy and a friendly face. Illusions of a glorious ride through historic surroundings had been elbowed aside, I needed to get out of London and into the countryside. Unlike the tour riders we had no race radio. Traffic noise obscured the enquiring texts and phone calls sent by Helen.

Eventually we met in a disused roadside garage. Five minutes separated our arrival time. London had done it's best to thwart me, but two wheels had just about kept up with four. Battered but unbroken, I vowed revenge and pushed on towards Gravesend. Progress was faster, streets gave way to roads, the Adict cheered up a bit but I was in need of some views. The Thames teased to the left but failed to make a grand appearance. Signposts promised history but then cruelly pointed away from my route. Starved of distractions I contrasted my ride with the race. As the roads became wider the traffic speed and volume forced me ever closer to the kerb.

These few feet carry the debris swept aside by speeding traffic, the holes and lumps at the bottom of maintenance priority lists and the caps and openings leading to drains. With closed roads, the racers see nothing of these as they gravitate to the middle of the road. The Adict had no sympathy, and signalled its displeasure with a constant battering of my nether regions.

The stiff carbon bike was not happy at all. Gravesend served only to heighten these differences further. I had mistakenly plotted my GPS route to exactly match that of the tour, unaware that the tour will go the WRONG way round the one way system. No problem when the roads are closed, but I discarded tens of minutes guessing my way across the town.

The breadcrumb trail plotted upon my GPS was regained and the A220 towards Rochester suffered my gripes and curses. The tour route dives under the River Medway through the Medway tunnel which is closed to cyclists. A welcome shortcut lifted me over the Medway via an impressive road bridge. I was halted by the view. The keep of Rochester Castle towers over the river. At 34.5 metres high it is the tallest Norman keep in the country.

Nipping up the side of the castle, I encountered my first closed road, sadly an inhibitor as today was market day. After a short walk followed by a nicely cobbled climb the strong scent of rape seed signalled the start of the English countryside. Absent cars and undulations forced up my speed, I was back with the Tour riders, the yellow rape seed fields replacing the sunflowers of France.

I rose from the saddle and attacked. The Adict responded instantly, recognising the moment, a willing companion towards speed. The fantasy held with the empty road traversing the hills above Wouldham. In response, the outskirts of Maidstone lurched forward and put paid to our plans with a wide dual carriageway jammed with Saturday shoppers. The team car sat lost amongst them. We entertained the shoppers with a shouted discussion peppered with bizarre sign language and the odd shaken bottle. They must have wondered what the camper van driver had done to deserve the attentions of such a clearly insane cyclist. Climbing through the backstreets of Maidstone I met Barrie who had agreed to keep me company for a few miles along the route.

He provided some welcome relief as we chatted towards Tonbridge and fought traffic through Royal Tunbridge Wells. Barrie stoically put up with my rantings on traffic, major roads and roundabouts. He smiled patiently as I made my excuses for being so late and probably wondered quietly to himself whether he had made a big mistake in agreeing to accompany such a whinger.

At last a lunch stop and my opportunity to pull one over the Tour. Team riders snack on energy bars and gels from a musette hastily grabbed in a feeding zone. We parked bikes in the beer garden of a roadside pub and sat back enjoying the sun. All was well until my team mate produced a surprise attack by placing a cool pint of beer and an overflowing bacon baguette on the table in front of him. A sly wink goaded me to follow suit, but the long silent stare of my director sportive convinced me to stay with the orange juice and tuna. Thirty minutes later we realised complacency had set it.

We had only covered 60 miles of the route and had at least another seventy to go. It was nearly 3pm and I didn't have a set of lights for the bike (I think the Adict would have thrown them off in disgust anyway). A quick glance at a map showed one more major town centre to navigate before Canterbury, so progress had to be quicker. Barrie and I parted just before Goudhurst as roads became more minor and the gradients undulating. I rushed up the climb into the village and claimed all of the "king of the Mountains" points. Haste paid dividends as Kent "proper" began to make itself known. I nipped from shade to sun below roadside trees that increased in frequency.

Buildings changed in shape and style, eccentric locals lining the route to wave me on. Crops varied from immature cereals to strange vines winding their way to the sky. It proved a welcome antidote to the previous 60 urban miles.

Consequently the speed reading on the GPS edged higher and higher. The Adict complied, a greyhound let off the leash, and together we barked through the Kent countryside romping in the sunshine but conscious that the race was now against dusk. The Adict was unable to suffer the ignominy of a finish in the dark so the pace strayed higher. The lightweight bike ate the inclines, at times it felt as if it was waiting for me at the top. At the rendezvous in Tenterton I informed the team that the race to Canterbury was on.

The little soigners offered a bottle from the window, it was accepted, thrust into its cage and whisked speedily up the road. Wedding bells provided the soundtrack for the climb into St. Michaels. What was the bride letting herself in for? Would she find herself with two kids in a clapped out camper van chasing her mad husband through the Kent countryside in ten years time? Ashford noisily interrupted. I had failed to account for the one way system. The consequences were dire as this was the main ring road and I had little option but to scurry across busy roads and seek out friendly cycle paths. I started to argue with my imaginary tour competitors.

They had it easy, they had closed roads and signs to point the way, they had cars to continuously hand them bottles and radios to tell them what was going on. They had briefings to talk them through the route and marshals to make sure that nothing impeded their progress. Me, I had a line on a GPS that was a long way from my current position and no idea whatsoever how to get to it. For sure I understood the training and commitment they have put in. But I wondered just how far behind they had left the struggles of an ordinary club cyclist like me.

Shear luck overcame frustration; I popped off another cycle path and caught the route to Canterbury. Valuable minutes had been lost but this was no time for excuses. Resentment started to drive my pedals faster. Resentment began to mask the lactic acid of the previous hundred miles and the Adict jumped forward in surprise. For once it was me telling the bike to "get on with it".

The legs were tired now though as I'd covered over one hundred miles. They fought hard with my mind as I dragged the bike up the long climb to Farthing common. I still don't know which won as we reached the summit and signed a collective truce for one final push into Canterbury. And here I gained my second wind.

At this point the tour riders will be either fighting to catch a breakaway or raising the pace ready for a sprint. For me, the end was less than ten miles away and somehow I found the pep to make the most of the long flat road that leads into Canterbury. I haven't a clue what I was racing against, but racing I was, buoyed with thoughts that the ride would be over soon. On cue the GPS gave me a "low battery" warning and I realised that if it switched off I would have to get the map out. I was too tired for rational thought, I needed guidance to get me to the end, I'd just have to go faster.

Bystanders must have wondered what had got into the sweaty looking bloke on the classy bike. Why was he gnashing and spitting so late in the afternoon, and where had he got that bike from anyway? But I didn't care. I raced cars through the centre of Canterbury and finally caught sight of the team van parked right on the finish line of the tour route. Suddenly I was out of the saddle and sprinting with all of my force. I had nobody to race but myself. As my legs finally gave out I sat up in the saddle and took the line with arms outstretched.

I'd finished the first stage of the 2007 Tour de France. Helen and the kids helped me off the bike and back into the van. I sat tired, contemplating the route. For me, it had not been a classic day out on the bike. I hadn't enjoyed the disconnected urban riding or the traffic filled major roads. The Scott Adict needs to be raced and it hadn't felt at home in slow moving traffic or bumpy roads. It was only in the latter half of the ride that the bike had really come alive. I'd faced the challenges of the everyday cyclist and was pleased to have come through. I was glad to have ridden the route, but next time I'll pick smaller roads and avoid the town centres.

Had I found the empathy I'd sought from the start? Frankly, "No". For the tour, things will be different. The riders will barely dip below 25 mph and the only cars they will sight will be their own. The urban sections will be lined with bunting and a curious public egging the riders on. They will have few distractions from the task of pedalling their bikes as fast as they can. For them this will be a memorable stage and I will be jealously watching their every move.

Chaper 17

To Grow A Mountain Biker

Any parent will tell you that it is a joy to watch a child develop from birth and go through a similar experience path to themselves. Well, I say "any" but I am sure there are a large number of exceptions to that rule, especially if the experience path is one of drugs, injury, depression or following Swindon Town football club. But that aside there is a hearty pleasure in leaning back with pipe in hand and reminiscing about when you were at that particular stage in life, what it felt like and the silly things you did.

It's the same with cycling and I'm sure that many of my club brethren and sisthren have smiled knowingly as I wrestled with my first club run puncture whilst others hurled abuse. I now know that the proper practice is to hold up the deflated tyre so that the club captain can see it whilst maintaining a look of extreme incompetence. He will then step in and sort it in order to get the ride underway in a timely fashion.

I've mentioned my friend Peter earlier in this book. We met as road cyclists and Peter was a fully inducted member of the two wheels and tarmac club. After a few years of running a Bed and Breakfast in Sardinia, he began to see the potential for developing mountain biking in the region. There were no off-road access problems as we have in the UK and plenty of dusty, dry unridden track to explore. Peter decided to become a mountain biker.

Similar to me he started on the wrong bike wearing the wrong gear and riding the wrong way. On our first off-road ride together he had no suspension and strapped his sandwiches to a pannier rack on the rear of the bike. He wore full roadie lycra cycling gear and looked a tad nervous on even the slightest off-road incline. I cruelly filmed him mincing down a wide trail and added the Steptoe and Son soundtrack to the clip. Peter, however, remained un-phased.

He'd caught the off-road bug and like the rest of us lived the evolutionary lifecycle of a mountain biker which begins with bike based upgrades and ends with "sessioning" difficult off-road problems in order to get them solved. These days Peter dresses like Steve Peat, rides a monster full suspension bike with a full faced helmet and full compliment of pads. He pushes himself to ride faster and harder down increasingly difficult technical terrain and in 2012 authored a Sardinian mountain bike guide.

The last time we rode together, the tables were turned as Peter took me down a series of steep angled switchbacks in the heart of Sardinia. This time it was me with the feet down and Peter who whooped round the corners and offered advice upon how they should be ridden properly. We had a great time though, just as we did the first ride out. Cycling's like that. People change, get better, faster, fitter and more confident but the basic pleasure of riding in the wild together is never diminished no matter who's ahead in the riding scales.

This article documents a Sardinian ride that the two of us did with a guide. I wrote it to promote mountain biking in the area and in particular the Lemon House run by my friends. Peter had ridden off road less than five times before, little did we know what lay ahead.

Rocks, Tracks, Wine and Italians

As a mountain biker it is all too tempting to seek out clichés when planning the annual holiday. UK trail centres, Utah, the Alps and the Canadian bike parks all spring to mind immediately. It is tempting to seek out miles of flowing way-marked singletrack, the pistes of the mountain biking world. This year I decided it was time for a change, time to venture off-piste a little and seek out routes with a few less tyre tracks marking their way. Given the lack of UK summer I needed some sun as well, along with the odd sandy beach and spectacular surroundings thrown in for good measure.

I "eeny meany miney mo'ed" around Europe until my finger alighted upon the East coast of Sardinia, specifically the Ogliastra region. Some deft internet searching produced a complete lack of documented mountain bike routes, yet Google Earth showed plenty of hills, valleys and gnarly bits. Sardinia has a fantastic weather record and some of the most beautiful beaches in Europe. A light bulb appeared above my head. I knew of a bed and breakfast run by friends and situated in an uncluttered seaside village.

My mind was made up and soon after Easyjet were a little bit richer. My hosts were Peter and Annie who run the Lemon House situated in Lotzorai. Lotzorai sits neatly sandwiched between sea and spectacular mountains, a perfect base for those wanting to indulge in a day's outdoor pursuits followed by an early evening dip in the sea to cool off. Peter knew Mauro Atzori, a local MTB guide, who organises trips during the summer, mainly for Italian bikers on holiday in the area. Mauro was leading a ride the next day, a quick phone call from Peter and we were in.

We awoke early, ate, stuffed our bikes into Peter's van and drove up to the town of Baunei, spectacularly perched at 1000 feet overlooking a wild plain semi-tamed by the local farmers. There we met Mauro and four others who had ridden with him before, repeat customers, always a good sign. The ride began typically, seven of us ambled out of Baunei in the morning sun, pointing at each others bikes, and sizing up the legs and ability that surrounded us. The fact that all conversation was in Italian was irrelevant. I hardly understood a word, but the meanings were definitely the same.

Somewhere in there I was ribbed for being too skinny, my scuffed frame was frowned upon and (worryingly) my baggy shorts were investigated, the Italians had all turned out in tight fitting lycra road kit. The first few miles saw us climb on empty roads that traversed the valley below. The group broadly stayed together as we made good time to our first venture off road. Dusty doubletrack dragged us away from the tarmac and occasionally pointed us towards the sun, impatient in its need to gain more altitude. I found myself tested on the steeper climbs as "competitiveness" definitely does not recognise the language barrier, graciously I allowed my hosts to crest first, or so I told myself.

The terrain became harsher the further we ventured away from the road. Sardinia certainly has its share of loose rock which adds challenge to switchbacked ascents and descents. The ride was becoming increasingly more technical and physically demanding and I held no envy for Peter who felt every bump as he banged about on his fully rigid hybrid folder! However, I was starting to gain that splendid sense of isolation that underpins my reason for riding off-road. In the last hour we had not seen or heard a single soul.

The only litter in evidence had been made and left by goats and we were now completely reliant upon Mauro to guide us through the maze of shepherd tracks and back to civilisation. I was beginning to panic about water, two hours of riding in the sun had emptied my Camelback and the frequent lizards were testament to the arid conditions.

A sheepfold proved my saviour and we crowded around a water trough fed from a natural spring below. Cooled and hydrated, we pedalled on for a few more miles until Mauro stopped and announced the end of the doubletrack. My Italian is poor but I definitely heard the phrase "singletrack" and "eight kilometres". Mauro pointed out a path twisting into the bushes and gleefully we sprinted off, ready to reap the reward promised by the previous climbs. As it turned out, my Italian wasn't as bad as I had thought. A narrow shepherd's track ran us through mountainous terrain and then twisted down to a hair-raising descent onto the Cala

Luna beach.

I don't think I've ever ridden a track with so many and varied challenges littered along it. We swooped through trees on flat packed twisting singletrack, barely maintained control on steep loose rocky descents scattered with babies heads, gurned up rocky granny ring climbs and fought bushes, scree, large rocks and stream beds in our quest to make it down. This trail was truly wild. The winter rains and lack of trail traffic hide any obvious lines. The rider is left on their own to negotiate any obstacles and make their own choices. Somehow I found that gratifying, this trail was not patronising my skills in any way as man made lines often can.

It was up to me to find my own way down it or just get off and walk. The trail was offering no help whatsoever delivering a reluctant nod as a rider conquers a challenging section. Several departed from their steeds on the way down, however the Italians are a tough race and they quickly remounted with a smile, waving off any concern. I was glad to survive. We regrouped at a natural arch, S'Arcada S'Architieddu Lupiri.

Well, I say regrouped, the first arrivals were hustled into hiding behind a gorse bush in an apparent attempt to humiliate those lagging behind into a belief that the gap was even further. The Italians are definitely tough, but I had concerns over their sense of humour. Jokes over, Mauro gave another pep talk.

I didn't understand it at all, but the faces around me increased in their gravity. In hindsight, I think he was warning us that the trail became steeper, rockier and much more challenging than anything we had ridden so far. I had the camera and was picked out for special attention, a few minutes and many hand gestures later I realised that I was being sent down first to take photos on a strategically placed corner. The others preened whilst I did my best to represent Great Britain, pulling of a passable impression of one who knew his way round a mountain bike.

As soon as they were out of sight, I just held on, as the rocks unceremoniously shoved me around the trail in some weird form of bike based rodeo. I reached the corner, threw the bike down in relief and snapped the others on their way down. Beach views proved a distraction, I realised that Mauro had steered us down towards a bay fringed with golden sands, crystal clear water and many a scantily clad distraction. Peter and I clapped each other on the back. We'd hung out with native bikers and survived, they'd tried to unsettle us with their dry, dusty, rocky deserted trails and we'd come through.

All we had to do now was to get through a short boat trip without turning green and our reputation would be sealed. Sadly this was not the case for one of our companions. He'd had a nasty fall on the rocky descent and opened up a large fissure just below the knee. The beach first aider took one look and called in a medi-boat, we later learnt that he'd been helicoptered off to hospital for stitches. Just as he was leaving we were asked by a council representative to pay a single euro as a "beach tax". I coughed up willingly having seen the service provided. We loaded bikes onto the boat and kicked back drinking coke and watching the sunbathers busily doing nothing in the afternoon heat.

How many of us have had those rides where we think we're at the end only to be told that we're merely half way round? Well, that's exactly how Peter and I felt as the boat pulled into a small beach and our companions began to unload bikes. The panic set in as they furiously gesticulated at us to get a move on and before we knew it we were back on terra-firma waving goodbye to our boat. I looked accusingly at Peter. Mauro had told Peter on the phone that we'd be getting the boat from Cala Luna, Peter had wrongly assumed we'd be coming back to Santa Maria Navarrese, the seaside town below the village of Baunei at 500m where our ride started.

It turns out that this beach really was half-way. We were to eat a long lunch in a seaside restaurant and then ride a long climb through a wild valley to a point a few miles above our start point. Peter and I exchanged glances and remembered half made promises to wives about meeting them shortly after lunch. We concocted our excuses and sat down at a table with our comrades ready to dash down some pasta and quickly retreat from the beach. They clearly had no such plans illustrated by a large carafe of wine, an order for starters and a long debate about which main course would be the largest. I must say that I enjoyed the relaxed attitude of the Italian riders.

They knew they had all day to get round, they knew the weather wouldn't break and they knew that they'd worked hard to get down to this beach. In fact I felt a tinge of envy as I wondered why all of my UK based rides seemed to be a mission to get the loop over as quickly as possible. Sadly, the clock dragged Peter and I away. We paid our share, shook hands, swore a lifetime of friendship, gathered up our bikes and struggled up the boulder littered path that led from the beach.

Peter knew the way back, a ten kilometre climb up a rough dirt track nestled in the depths of a spectacular rift valley. I can't remember if the climb was hard or not as my senses were continuously diverted from left to right as spectacular rock formations dragged my eyes towards them. Eventually we reached a plateau a few kilometres from our parked van and descended down switchbacks swathed in the glow of early evening light. As I coasted towards the van I began to reflect upon the day's ride. It's a cliché, but mountain bike rides share a common language regardless of location.

Smooth tracks provide the vowels, lumpy bits the consonants. Sentences are punctuated with incidents ranging from crashes to mechanicals and each chapter often starts and finishes at an eating place. The Italians certainly spoke a dialect of mountain bike that we could understand, it was definitely hotter and richer in scenery than many of the UK rides I have undertaken but the trail diction was considerably more primitive. My decision to venture off piste had been entirely vindicated, Sardinia provided a ride that felt wild and undiscovered, littered with variety, challenge and contrast. It's definitely a place that will drag me back, and next time, maybe I'll stay for the wine.

Chapter 18

The Wandering Mind

I've found that over the years my mind has wandered off to some fascinating places whilst out cycling. In fact I believe there are not many other sports where this luxury occurs. I can't believe for one minute that those who fence have time to cogitate on which was the best of the Star Wars films. I'm absolutely certain that the motorbike riders in the Isle of Man TT only have one thought in their minds as they reduce the island to a blur, my guess is that it is "Oh shit!!!!!!". However, cycling is different.

The vast majority of cyclists end up doing long rides at some point in their two wheeled career, often these rides will revisit lanes that they have travelled before. There is only so much nature that you can be in awe of and I'd challenge any of them to state that their mind hadn't meandered away from the bike and onto some other subject. I know for a fact that mine has and also that it happens on quite a regular basis.

Whilst riding I've invented all sorts of weird and wonderful things including; the mobile phone doorbell, a charging system for laptops using manure, wifi enabled radiators and a bicycle that becomes its own lock. Each will have its own day I'm sure and there have been others that I've forgotten, memory erased by a particularly nasty hill. It's not just inventions that occur in the wandering cyclist's mind. I've solved problems as well. Most of my career has been spent in IT and all us IT types ever do is solve problems. Most of them are of our own making. A computer system that won't work because we've tinkered with it, or a system that hasn't been delivered on time because we said it'd be easy, and it wasn't.

What better place than the bike to mull over these issues and contemplate a variety of solutions? Mainly due to the fact that the rider will be a long way from those who are directly suffering the consequences and looking to quietly wring their neck. I've composed tunes on the bike inspired by the whirring of gears, click of chains and snapping of components as they've fallen to the road. Bad poetry has also been the product of an elongated bike ride, fortunately I've never penned any of it to paper.

But I have dictated letters to editors, utility companies, members of parliament and a couple of resignations. The open air office is far more conducive than a stuffy cubicle shared with a flatulent colleague. Then there's the articles. I can guarantee that the vast majority of those penned within this book were conceived on the bike. It would be odd if they weren't as they are without exception cycling related.

However, some of them are the result of more than one ride. I come up with an idea add it to the "to do" list and then completely forget. Another ride later and the stimulus returns so I begin the mental dictation again. The "Back to School" piece is one of those, I'd spent many rides furiously calculating average speeds and wondered if others did as well? I imagined the frustration of those who hated maths but enjoyed cycling and were forced to reuse the skills they thought they'd left behind.

Back to School

For me cycling is supposed to be mostly about recreation, I don't live far enough from work to commute and I'll be buried before you find me on a bike with a basket on the front of it. Therefore, every time I mount the bike, I should be setting off on a journey that will be liberally sprinkled with enjoyment. So please explain to me how most of my rides recently have transported me right back to my first year in school, specifically mathematics. I've become obsessed by it, before during and after each ride I carry out. I find my mind racing with numbers, constantly recalculating averages, percentages, inclines and durations. It starts with route planning, I sketch out a loop in my head and estimate the number of miles.

I then have a quick guess at the height gain and some nether region of my brain subconsciously uses a Naismith type algorithm to work out how long it will take and what sort of average speed I can expect to attain. A deep analysis of the BBC weather chart allows me to deduce wind direction and I use sophisticated geospatial modelling to decide which way to ride the loop in order to return with the wind behind me. This in turn leads to nutritional calculus where a complicated set of internal equations leads me to decide how many bottles to place on the bike, the number of stale energy bars to stuff in my jersey and how much cheese and bread to stuff in my gob before setting off. Once on the bike, the mathematics increases in tempo.

One mile into the ride I have worked out my average speed from the time taken and am carrying out a whole series of forward calculations to ascertain whether or not I shall complete the ride in target time. This in turn triggers a decision as to whether or not I should speed up. The answer is usually "whether". It gets more complicated at around about 10 miles because the situation has usually been tainted by a touch of fatigue. The equations can often look a bit dodgy at this point, due to the high average speed required to complete the ride on time.

And so I branch into a whole new genus of arithmetic, "excusamatics". I invented "excusamatics" by the way, its a set of calculations designed to show with honour why you have not been able to complete a ride within your chosen target time. It fully takes into account time spent at traffic lights, adverse wind conditions and GPS speed miscalculations whilst subtly ignoring your fitness and ability to MTFU. But very occasionally, I get half way round a ride and notice that I am almost on track.

My average speed will usually be a little under that planned and so begins the complex art of working out what new average speed I need to achieve in order to ensure that I meet the average speed I had planned to achieve before I achieved the lower average speed. And sometimes having conquered this Vordermanesque little conundrum, I'll be going a little faster than I planned. Thus requiring some further numerical dabbling to work out whether I can afford a little rest and allow the oxygen debt to recede for a serene minute or two.

Then there's the distance/fatigue ratio that requires balancing. This is where I work out how far I have travelled and how knackered I am and then forward project this into the distance I have yet to travel. It's a rare form of masochism as the answer is always untenable and requires a furious recalculation to try and come up with another answer.

You'd think that arriving home it would all be over and I could give the maths a rest along with my poor little legs. But sadly, there's a whole raft of computations required as I coast down the road to my house. The ride has to be compared with previous performances, all of which are pulled from the memory bank and compared. Average speeds, incline ratios, distance travelled and all sorts of other little statistics are compared and contrasted to decide whether or not the ride has been any good. And so I start to understand why I'm sort of looking forward to winter. As the barometer falls so does my will to train on the bike, it's this will that clearly leads to an obsession with numbers and hence the non-stop mental fag packet scribbling. In winter I just ride the bike to not get fat, all echoes of first year mathematics a distant memory.

Chapter 19

Pilgrimage

Pilgrimages. One of those things that make humans stand out from the rest of the crowd. And don't go mentioning migrations as they are completely different. Migrations are designed to escape bad weather, find new food sources or make new and smaller versions of an existing animal. Pilgrimages achieve none of these, they are inherently pointless and the dictionary definition should say something along the lines of:-

"Pilgrimage - going somewhere that you don't live which is quite a long way away because other people have told you that you should"

Muslims are told to head off to Mecca at least once in their life and then to throw shoes at a wall and avoid being crushed by millions of others with a similar mission. Christians hot foot it to all sorts of different places where the mother of Christ has supposedly popped up and healed a few people or appeared in a slice of toast. There are Tibetans who crawl round large mountains in bare feet and British tramps who regularly stagger to off licences with the promise of enlightenment in cans of cheap cider.

Us cyclists prove to be no exception. We have our pilgrimages as well. As a hairy legged mountain biker I made an annual trip to Moab, or Mountain-bike-Mecca as it is often named. Moab offers a crucible of slickrock, a unique surface that grips and allows inept riders like me to do things on hills they wouldn't be able to do elsewhere. I made this trip four times, drawn back by the sunshine, terrain and $3 fried breakfast in the Moab Diner that came with maple syrup. The transition to road cycle comes with a pilgrimage that is properly serious. Not only does it include an iconic climb that is shrouded in fear, it involves the doffing of cap to a fallen rider who died on the hill.

A few mountain bikers have come to grief in Moab, but nobody rides out to the scene of their demise. Yet thousands of cyclists stop every year at the shrine to Tom Simpson, many leave a cycling artefact behind. Mont Ventoux is the ultimate cycling pilgrimage. Every roadie has an aspiration to ride this extraordinary hill and more importantly, make it safely back home. Tom Simpson didn't. Racing in the Tour de France he succumbed to the temptation of drugs and used amphetamines to bolster his stride.

121

It didn't work out on Ventoux, the heat and the effort of the climb did for poor Tom.

A shrine marks his deathbed less than a kilometre from the top of the mountain. Stopping at Tom's shrine is now part of the Ventoux ritual, this is what we roadies do. A moment to reflect upon a wasted life, a rider that could have been truly great if only he'd trusted his lungs and his legs. I made my own personal pilgrimage in 2010, it was part of the most amazing week where we rode many of the classic tour climbs with Ventoux saved till the very last. It's a pilgrimage that every road cyclist should make, not because of Tom, but because of the mountain itself.

Tom's story is tragic, but it wasn't the mountain that killed him. It has a majesty that goes way beyond the story of a single rider. Much of which is derived from the fact that it clearly doesn't belong in the terrain that it sits. It's almost as if it snuck in to the region one night waiting for unwary cyclists to happen upon its slopes.

Ventoux

Mention "Ventoux" to anyone and you'll get some sort of emotive response. Non-cyclists will scratch their head for a few seconds and then mention that they think they've seen that one on the Tour de France ... and didn't some bloke die up there? Cyclists will nod sagely and either tell you of the time that they grappled hard with the mountain, or the fact that it's definitely on their "tick list" sometime in the future. It's an emotive mountain, shrouded in endeavour, mystique, passion and tainted by drug taking and death.

Anyone who has heard of Mont Ventoux will make some comment or relive a memory intrinsically linked to cycling. The bicycle has given the mountain a reputation tinged with savagery and suffering. Without the bike Ventoux would be a strange, high lump emerging from the trees, slightly out of odds with the surrounding countryside. Mont Ventoux has sat on my tick list ever since I watched Pantani and Armstrong fight it out up the mountain in the harsh sunlight of the 2000 Tour de France.

It just doesn't get more stereotypical than that, middle aged bloke gets inspired to ride up a hard mountain having watched two sporting greats do it at near motorbike speed. And let me tell you it was some inspiration, as it took me more than 10 years to finally get round to having a bash at it.

Friday 1st October 2010 saw myself and Andy kitted up and spinning out of Bedoin, accompanied by perfect autumnal sunshine and a complete lack of any wind. We'd spent a week in the Alps, beasting ourselves up and down a series of Tour climbs, finely honing the art of riding together in silent unspoken competition. Truth is, Andy had taken most of the honours during the week, fuelled by extra fitness and a complete lack of about 20 pounds of body weight that he had been carrying last time I'd ridden with him. We chatted amicably as the gradient dithered upwards and a mile out of town had "that" conversation about how we were both quite tired and should "take it easy" and "just enjoy" the climb up to the summit. Utter bollocks.

As soon as the road began to reach for the sky proper, I gave my legs a few extra turns to see how they were feeling, and the feedback was positive. So I set into a rhythm and began to spin away at the hill. Andy spotted this, pulled up alongside and even offered up a brief session of half wheeling. I spun a little bit faster and he half wheeled a little bit more, until we reached an unspoken truce and agreed to have a damn good go at the hill together.

This all occurred less than 7 kilometres into the ride, we had a further 21k to climb to the summit and were neither "taking it easy" nor "just enjoying" the climb. The previous evening we'd sat and looked up at the mountain in the fading light. It was hard to see what all the fuss was about, for sure it looked reasonably high, but it didn't look that steep. In fact Ventoux from a distance reminded me of a gigantic dormant slug that had come to rest after a particularly fine feast of surrounding countryside.

But the road told a different story. Out of nowhere the gradient leapt up towards an average of about 10%..and it stayed there. Strangely, this coincided with the cessation of conversation and significant perspiration. I'd read about this section before and had been clearly warned that the forest stage of Ventoux was particularly steep and unrelenting. But the figure of 10% didn't worry me, as I live in Wiltshire and regularly huff my bike up climbs of 20% and steeper. However, I always forget to factor in the distance. A 20% hill back home is a mere finish line sprint when compared to alpine climbs.

The forest section of Ventoux equates to 10 kilometres of riding at a 9-10% gradient, none of the steep hills round my way are 6 miles long! So, as my legs were telling me, I'd ridden up to this hill with a degree of nonchalance only to find reality nibbling away at my arse in a determined fashion. The gradient really was unrelenting. Unlike other alpine climbs, there are no switchbacks or flattish sections to aid recovery. The road simply points up and rudely demands that the rider either ascend it, or go home.

There are no views to admire, only trees, steep tarmac and the occasional weaving cyclist. Nothing to divert attention away from the fact that your legs really hurt and there are double digit kilometres still to climb. Andy and I managed to negotiate a cadence and rhythm that sat somewhere between our competitive will and our physical limitations. And to be fair, it was reasonably brisk as we were passing cyclists but had yet to be overtaken ourselves. In fact, it all felt a bit Pantani/Armstrong, apart from the fact that I'm not bald and Andy has two testicles.

Anyhow, let's just say that the forest section was hard, which it was, and things were apparently going to get much worse as we rounded a corner and cafe, Chalet Reynard, came into view, as this is where the myths begin. I'd read that on passing the cafe we would be buffeted by extreme mistral winds, cooked to a crisp by unrelenting sunshine, freaked out mentally by lunar landscapes and probably accosted by a Death Eater from the Harry Potter novels. We must have caught the mountain on an off day, as the gradient eased off a bit and both of us really started to enjoy the experience.

Our tempo increased a little and we mercilessly chased down cyclists ahead of us in our quest for the summit. We must have been in another zone, as we cruised straight past the Tommy Simpson memorial without noticing it, focused upon the top. The last kilometre does have a sting though, I'm sure it got steeper. And as if to remind you that the mountain is still in control, a marker post has also been placed at the half kilometre point to niggle at you that "you may have done well, but you ain't finished yet". I should have become suspicious when Andy zipped up his jersey.

I should have known that something was up when he put his helmet on shortly before the final corner. And I damned well knew there was something fishy going on when he got out of his saddle and sprinted the final 200 metres. I could have maturely waved him off and let out a loud "tsk" at his youthful exuberance. But no, I decided to sprint after him shouting loudly something about f***king cheating b**st**d. The tourists at the top loved this little spectacle and we even attracted a smattering of applause and a few "chapeaus" for daring to give it some at the finish.

I found out why later as I had the opportunity to view some of the ashen faced corpses that dragged themselves to the top after us. And so, after a brief argument concerning the ethics of unannounced sprinting, we retired to the coffee shop at the top and reflected upon the climb. Andy and I were relatively fit, we'd climbed it in around about 1 hour 30 minutes and felt pretty good at the top. However, this was all hindsight, we had not forgotten the never ending forest section and were also agreed that it would be a completely different experience with 100 miles in the legs at the end of a long Tour stage.

We weren't sure that we had conquered Ventoux, more that we had ridden up its back without it turning round and biting us. Ventoux reminds me of a hippopotamus, which looks odd, seems clumsy yet is renowned as the most dangerous animal in Africa. The mountain shares similar characteristics, from first glance you wouldn't have thought it was going to do you that much damage. Yet tangle with it and you'll understand where it gets its reputation from.

Chapter 20

Caused By Casual Conversation

If you're anything like me then your cycling life will be heavily dictated by your friends. I would say that the vast majority of events that I've taken part in have been the result of a friend casually mentioning that they might like to have a go at it. Sometimes this reaps reward and other times it ends in a long drawn out chorus of "Why me?" as you wish that you'd never listened to a word that they'd said.

A prime example of this was the first ever Sleepless in the Saddle 24 hour mountain bike race. My friend Russ suggested that this might be an interesting event to enter as they had created a category for pairs. Russ and I regularly raced bike orienteering events as a pair so surely this was tailor made for the two of us? We trained for precisely zero hours and simply turned up with my camper van and some energy drink and bars for support.

The organisers lined us all up and read us the rules over the tannoy. The most important of which was "the baton". Each team or pair would be issued with a small baton on some string. This had to be carried by the racing member at all times, if it wasn't, instant disqualification. Russ and I nodded sagely, determined for our efforts not to go to waste by a forgotten baton. We retired to the van and plotted our tactics. I idly attached the camper van keys to a bit of string, I only had one set and the rider resting would need them to get back into the van (you know what's coming now don't you?).

Things seemed to go OK for the first six hours as we took it in turns to ride two laps each whilst the other rested and ate. I attacked the climbs with a little too much vigour determined to own the fastest lap of our pair. Seven laps down I felt a tinge of heaviness in the legs and understood why Russ had walked the big climb on most of his laps. Then came nightfall and a switch in tactics. Russ would set off and ride four laps on the trot, I'd get four hours sleep. We'd switch and then I'd ride four while he snoozed away.

I gave Russ the baton on the string (in the dark) and wandered back to the van. I reached round my neck for the key on the string and retrieved... the baton. Oh fuckityfuckityfuck. I ran as fast as I could back to the start but Russ was gone. Oh well, three hours sleep instead of four, I'd catch him as him came round for lap two. But I didn't. Fatigue had dulled my senses and somehow I missed him go past. I was locked out of the van, and becoming increasingly cold and very hungry indeed. Things got worse as I waited for the end of Russ's next lap.

Fortunately, a determined squint at each rider passing allowed me to find him at the end of lap three. We exchanged bits of string and I sullenly retired to the van for less than an hours kip most of which was lost to eating. I met Russ at the end of lap four and sulked my way out into the night. It was a disaster as the cold and lack of sleep took its toll. I think Russ may have sympathised and swapped after I'd ridden two. All I know is that I wanted it to end there and then, yet I had at least ten more hours of riding to do.

It all ended well, we came sixth and stood on a podium in front of hundreds of other bikers to be presented with our winner's prizes, mountain bike jerseys. They were too small for Russ, so he gave me his. I still wear them to remind me never to secure car keys on string.

This next article is inspired by a friend, but this time the driver is envy.

Destroyed by Average Speed and a Tandem

I had a email from my friend Andy who told me that he was knackered due to having just finished a hilly ride at an average of 20.3 mph. This got me a bit knarked to be honest as I was pretty pleased with a recent set of rides that had finished with an average of 18mph on the clock. I'm a bit weird with average speed, for some reason I have an aversion to looking at it during a ride and so I keep it as a big secret only to be revealed within the confines of my garage. Usually, it's a massive disappointment.

But tonight was different. I lobbed a bit of caution in the direction of moving air and set off with average speed clearly visible on the GPS. My target was Andy's 20.3 mph and within 3 miles I was on track...I live at the top of a hill. However, I have to say that focusing on average speed did make a real difference, instead of coasting downhill, I pedalled, on the flat I tried harder, going up hill, I made a real effort to keep power and speed constant, rather than sprinting then blowing.

After 10 miles I was ahead of target, riding at an average of approximately 20.5 mph, things were looking promising, until Ashbury hill. This is a ten percenter that goes on for nearly a mile and I could see the numbers slowly bleed away. At the top I was looking at an average of 18.9mph, it needed a big effort over the next few miles to get back on a par with Andy.

The downhill coincided with a tandem pulling out from a junction 50yds ahead of me. I caught it easily, said a breathless "hello" to the old(ish) couple pedalling it and passed them easily. Then I really put the hammer down, cranking up to 27mph on the gradual descent as I fought my average speed back up into the 20's.

"That's a nice titanium bike you have there", came the casual comment from the pilot of the tandem as it pulled up alongside me with ease. The wizened tandem riders merrily chatted away to me oblivious to the fact that I'd gone anaerobic. I puffed back curt responses but eventually gave in and explained my quest to the couple. They nodded sagely and carried on with their casual pedalling alongside me, I descended further into lactic hell.

How the fuck did they do that? Was it weight, was it two sets of legs? Or had I accidentally stubbled across two ex-pros sharing their retirement as they had earned their living. We carried on like this for a few miles, eventually they took pity and ACCELERATED off up the road. I was doing 26mph on the flat!!

20 miles in, I was on track, average speed 20.4 miles per hour. But a shed load of long hills remained. I really buried myself over them, forcing myself into the drops and switching gears to keep cadence as constant as possible. But it was largely in vain. As I summited the last big hill, the clock said 19 mph and I had 7 lumpy miles to go. My brain was only capable of approximations but these told me that I needed a pretty special average speed to meet Andy's target.

For brevity, I didn't make it. I got home in 1 hr 46 minutes at an average speed of 19.3 mph having climbed 2300 ft. At first I was gutted, then I remembered the last time I did that route, 17.8mph average. Andy's email had motivated me to push hard continuously and I'd done the ride nearly 10 minutes quicker!

So I wasn't too unhappy. Especially when Andy revealed that his ride was 16 miles long....technically, I'd had him. As for the tandem riders, can someone please tell me it was down to some basic physics.

Chapter 21

Straying Online

I come from a generation whose cycling has been heavily influenced by the internet. In fact just about everything that my generation does these days requires the internet, including talking to our children even when they are sat upstairs. I'm as bad as them though. When I'm not out exploring on the bike, I'm surfing around cycling sites looking for new adventures in the writing or photographs of others. I also use it to plan my trips, find accommodation, download routes, check weather and pay for the myriad of accessories that I probably don't really need.

I'd still cycle without the internet to help, but it would be a little bit harder to find things to do and the information required. I'd have to actually talk to people, or read books or, God forbid, visit a library. In fact I went to the library last week to look for a guide to building sheds. The rows of books sat unloved and unbrowsed, the computers with free internet access all had queues. Most of the computers were furiously loading Facebook pages or playing browser based arcade games.

It's hard to sit back and judge the internet based upon its impact upon cycling. On one hand it is there to inform, guide, facilitate, share experience and sell all sorts of shiny gear. On the other it has taken away the apprenticeship that pre-internet cyclists used to serve by learning just about everything from their Dad or members of their club.

However, cycling information on the internet has steered me well away from the darker recesses, like porn or Paul Daniel's blog site and so on balance I consider the internet to be a good thing for those partaking in two wheeled activities. By the way, I know I have said "two wheels" a few times in these pages but would like to make it clear that this is simply writing laziness. I do appreciate that there are tricyclists and unicyclists out there who are fed up of being excluded from phrases such as "two wheeled" brethren. And rightly so as they're flaming weirdos.

Anyway, back to the internet. Whilst there is no doubt that it has enriched the lives of many and expanded the wallets of a privileged few, it comes with its own set of dangers. Opening up a web browser is similar to walking into a financial advisor's convention. Some of the information and advice will be heartfelt and correct, but if you're not careful you'll end up listening to the thief in the room and before you know it the damage has been done. Cycling advise on the internet is similar, one man's "It's a straightforward descent anyone can ride it" is another man's weekend in Accident and Emergency.

Cyclists have to build all sorts of additional senses. We have to read the minds of motorists or errant/elderly pedestrians. We have to grow a very thick skin that is able to deflect the looks we're given when fully attired. And we have to filter through internet advise in order to work out what is applicable to us as individuals and the level we are at.

It does take some time to acclimatise yourself to the cycling-internet and work out just where you fit and when "It'll be fine" really does apply to you.

Three Peaks Cyclocross - Singlespeed

Twitter is a very dangerous piece of technology. It can get you into all sorts of trouble as many a tweeting politician will attest. However, it's not only those who tweet that are at risk, followers put themselves in the line of fire as well. I obsessively follow cyclists. I shouldn't, because the vast majority of them simply tweet their middle class credentials all day long. Inanely informing me of the latte they crave or the Ella Fitzgerald track that's just been played on Radio Two. But once in every while there's a danger-tweet;

"Entries now open for the 2011 Three Peaks Cyclocross ->[link to online entry]"

Why did I even bother to read it? I've never ridden a cyclocross event in my life. I don't possess a cyclocross bike and all I knew about this event was that it is supposed to be quite hard. I'm still unsure as to why I opened the online entry webpage and am completely and utterly stumped as to why I filled it all in. I was vaguely aware that it is oversubscribed every year so what chance did I have of getting in?

To make matters worse, I was presented with a box along the lines of "Why should we let you race if you've never done it before?". I haven't raced anything for years, so I scratched out a few palmares from the past that I hoped would cover my entry. Some of these may have been "bigged up" a little.

Podium finish in SITS 24 hour race (sixth mens pairs actually, but Pat Adams did get us on the podium and give us racing jerseys as a prize)

Hill climb championship winner (local road club, no more than 15 entries)

High placed in international alpine gran fondo (ninety forth .... but 1000 entries)

I didn't hold up much hope to be honest and forgot all about it. Until a month or so later I received an email telling me that I was in. Cough up the race fee now or lose the place. The email was opportune. I'd spent months riding hard road routes in a vague attempt to turn them into a book. Cycling had morphed into work and the only variety lay in the scenery and route. I needed a little bit of light relief, so what better than the hardest cyclocross race in the UK to break it all up a little. Twenty three credit card digits later and I was committed. Time to go looking for a bike.

The rules for 2011 were quite clear:-

"This race is for CYCLO-CROSS BIKES WITH DROP HANDLEBARS ONLY". Optimistically I opened the garage door and checked each of the fleet in turn for suitability. Three flat barred mountain bikes failed scrutineering immediately. Two road bikes looked keen but were clearly too light and too expensive to venture off road. The kid's bikes all hid, leaving only one suitable candidate, a dropped barred singlespeed hack bike with cantis, my On-One Pompino. Singlespeed would be nuts though.

Looking at the race route there was 5000 feet of climbing and surely some of this must be in the saddle? Furthermore the bike was running a 48:16 ratio, I can hardly get up my drive on that let alone Yorkshire hills. The bike had no gear hangers so adding derailleurs would be a pain. I googled hub gears, subtracted prices from my bank balance and was forced back to the garage by a set of negative numbers. Singlespeed, could I do it? More googling. A guy I knew had ridden fixed a few years back! I dropped him a line to ask for advice and it came in spades.

"You'll be alright Dave, it's doable if you make the cut-offs. But for f**ks sake don't try and ride on 48:16"

Cut-offs! Great. I projected forward to the humiliation I would feel as an unbending grim northern marshall held up a flat hand to an exhausted naive singlespeeder then pointed to the showers. The pressure was beginning to mount. Not only did I have to ride on one gear, I had to maintain a reasonable speed if I was to tick the finish.

The next few weeks followed an interesting cycle. I'd take the Pompino out for a off-road blast and buoy myself up. Returning home I'd be full of a future where crowds parted to cheer the macho singlespeeder home revelling in the awe of his thighs. Then I'd speak to someone who knew a mate who'd done it. Phrases like "It's nails" were uttered and heads would be shaken when I mentioned one gear. I'd pick up snippets on the internet that would reinforce this view. Self doubt would magnify and turn inward. Why was I doing this? I don't even like cyclocross. What's the point in going off-road without gears? I'll hurt myself and never finish writing this book.

It came to a head a week before the race. All my training said I'd be "OK". I'd managed near 100k rides off-road with hardly a walk. I was pretty fit and coping with riding reasonably technical stuff downhill. But the devil on my shoulder told me I'd fail. Late one evening I sent this email to the organiser:-

"Dear John,

I may not be able to make the race due to a commitment in Northumberland. Do you have a reserve list of riders and could somebody take my place?"

Cowardly shite. The commitment was of my own making and could be put off. I was looking for a way out before I'd even tried and hoping I'd get a "don't worry sonny someone else can ride" reply. John wrote back:-

"There are no reserve riders. Your name's in the programme"

Terse but exactly the swift hobnailed boot up the arse that I deserved. It took me back to a round of the national XC that I'd spectated at. An elite rider realised he was being caught by lesser mortals and so he packed. At interview he gave this excuse;

"The fans don't want to see me ride like that so I stopped"

"You arsehole" I fumed. You should have finished, lesser riders were going to beat you today and that's what they deserved. You've subverted their right to battle past and properly gain another place. Now I'm no elite rider, but I owed it to those who were going to beat me and those who'd missed out on a place. My name was in the programme. I'd not get to see it unless I took part. One line of text and memories of a distant XC race proved more powerful than any training ride. Fuck it, I'm going. If I fail I can at least point to the gears as an excuse, but I'd struggle to cope with the failure to even have a go.

Saturday 24th September 2011. I drove my motorhome into the campsite at Knight Stainforth and parked up. The Pompino was dragged from the van and briefly inspected:-

- seattube foam present - check

- 39:16 gearing set-up and working -check (slight grindy noise from freewheel but we'll live with that)

- front tyre inflated to 100psi - check

- rear tyre inflated to 100psi - shit, there appears to be about 20? Great! the valve on the new slime tube is knackered

- rear tube replaced with standard road tube - check
- rear wheel looking bloody stupid as only available road tube had deep section valve on it -check
- adjustable seat collar present - check (I'd out fox those cyclocross types on the descents by lowering my saddle, an old mountain bike trick)
- left hand crank still tightly on the spline - check (it had developed the worrying habit of undoing itself on training rides. Typically, I actually did something about this the night before the race by applying threadlock)

I put the bike back in the van. Ate some tea then promptly felt ill. From nowhere a mixture of nausea and head cold appeared, frustrating as hell as I'd only just ditched a cold. I attempted to mitigate by drinking lots and going to bed early. This resulted in a sleepless sweaty night and seven toilet visits. I should have remembered. There's never been a pre-race night when I've slept like a log. I toss, turn, worry, sweat and conjure up all sorts of strange thoughts that are about as motivational as a Gordon Brown speech.

But oddly the four hours sleep I did get seemed to work. I awoke on race day feeling refreshed. The phantom illness had morphed into a sweaty duvet allowing me to attack breakfast with zeal. The attack and strong coffee prompted a further three more extended toilet visits, but by 7.45am I was packed and ready to ride to the race. Skies were grey as I pedalled towards Helwith Bridge, however, I dismissed them in favour of the national weather forecast that suggested clement weather and a lack of serious rain.

Registration was smooth. I'd read the rules and presented my orange plastic survival bag, whistle and waterproof. Others tried to negotiate with space blankets and ignorance. The organisers were unbending and replaced protests with a bag sold for a bargain four pounds. In fact registration was far too smooth and I was done by 8:01am with the race scheduled to begin at 9:30. I scouted around for a few friends and shared some merry banter mostly at the expense of my gears.

Then it began to rain. We trouped to the start where a set of yellow placards awaited us. Each had a time range inscribed upon it and we were asked to stand near the card that represented our estimated finish time. Half the field had piled to the front and were looking to finish in under four hours. I crapped myself a little bit. FOUR HOURS! I was aiming for six. I'd be chuffed with 5.30 and anything higher was inconceivable for a singlespeed newbie like me. I mentioned this to fellow rider Clare. "Don't get left at the back, Dave", she advised, "You'll be queuing at the first ascent".

I shuffled forward to four hours fifteen. It felt fake, I highly doubted my ability to finish so fast. I was there to survive, no pretensions to race. Many more minutes of hanging about in the rain passed by. Jacket went on then off then on then off and back in the pack. The drizzle was falling but it felt warm and I hate stopping to faff. I gambled that the weather would clear but the time for fretting was gone as the race set off and the riders in front of me clipped in.

The race instructions say the following:-

"The first 5.5 kms will be escorted. Competitors will ride behind the lead car. Any rider passing or attempting to pass the lead car will be disqualified"

I'd expected a 5k warm up at a nice steady pace. The opposite happened and I would suggest the race organisers rephrase the above mentioned paragraph:-

"The first 5.5 kms will be escorted. Competitors will ride behind the lead car. Any rider passing or attempting to pass the lead car will qualify for the British Olympic track pursuit team"

I reckon I had 30 seconds of easy pedalling to the bridge then it all kicked off. Suddenly my cadence was in the 200rpm area as I fought tooth and nail to stick to the wheel in front. "Fuck me we're doing 27mph!" I heard. Didn't I know it. Within one mile I was at lactate threshold just trying to hold on. "A hill, a hill....my kingdom for a hill" I thought, anything to make the furious spinning stop. Less than five minutes into the race and I wanted to get off. Fortunately a gradient intervened and the big ring boys went backwards a bit. Shifters went off around me like a swarm of cicadas. I had no choice but to stand and gurn. They were clicking, I was stamping but the lack of gears forced me to climb hard and I gained places as we climbed all too briefly.

It was 6km before we headed off road for the first time. Marshals harried us into line and over a cattle grid, funnelling us out onto the moor. Two riders beside me discussed the best place for a beer. I envied their casual conversation, my mind was shouting, "Survive! survive! survive!". The course struck out onto increasingly inclined moorland. We rode a bit, carried a bit, rode, carried, rode, pushed, carried. Our objective was hidden in the mist, the steep climb of Simon Fell.

In my mind gears played no advantage over this section. Conditions were poor and traction only really available to water based lifeforms. I maintained my position within the group as we thrutched our way up to the wall that is Simon Fell. This climb is a Three Peaks legend. Countless pictures are captioned "The camera is not tilted" as riders are shown carrying their bikes up a 45 degree slope. I doubt they'll be many pictures this year. The mist shrouded us as we shouldered and made our way up. Banter stopped, replaced by breathing. I've never been surrounded by so much breathing.

It was everywhere. The ground was wet and horribly steep. I focused on each footstep. Find a foothold, press gently, then extend, look for the next. Riders were slipping and falling, clutching at clumps of grass to arrest their descent. Others dragged themselves up the wire fence to the left. Step, push, breath, step, push breath. Singlespeed, gears? it makes no odds here. all that matters is weight, muscles and lungs. I lost myself for a bit, focused on the task. It was over sooner than I'd thought it would be, the sense of relief was immense. One Three Peaks legend out of the way, three more to go. Next we fought our way to the top of Ingleborough.

Sometimes we rode, but conditions were wet, boggy and terrible. I'd describe it as more of a forwards slip than riding. Mostly we pushed and carried. I'd certainly have welcomed a lower gear but to this point 39:16 was survivable and not many were riding by me. A white line had been laid to guide us to the top. We needed it! The cloud was right down and visibility was close to nil. I found this helped as I concentrated on my local predicament rather than what faced me ahead.

Over one hour into my race I made my first dib (sportident transponder into timing system). At the top of Ingleborough I clocked 1:08:08, turned and faced the descent. I had no idea of my time, I'd left all timing devices in the van. But something odd had happened. "Survive" had been replaced by "Race". I felt in a pretty good state, things ached but there were no real complaints. The bike was riding without issue and I seemed to be maintaining my place in the bunch. Time to head down. Time to show these "cross boys" what descending is all about.

Actually, it wasn't. The descent from Ingleborough was a right mess. No obvious lines, deep peaty sections, messed up ruts and varying abilities of rider. Sometimes the hazard was on the ground in front of you, other times it was the rider who'd made a poor choice or decided to stop and carry. "Race" flipped back to "Survive" and I descended with care, saddle dropped, arse back, brakes covered.

"Thee's gam riding them gears laddo, or stupid"

I think that's what he said. "Both", I laughed back. The comments had come thick and fast from the start, everything from "Are you fixed?" to "I was planning on riding singlespeed this year". I tired a bit of "You've forgotten your gears mate" but had to laugh at "Your back wheel's going round..just". Riding singlespeed stimulated a certain amount of banter, but not much.

I was struck by how focused all of the riders were on their race. In other events I'd experienced more of a laid back attitude, but this seemed pretty serious. Riders only stopped when punctures or rocks forced them to. There wasn't much chat and if you eased up at any point a body on a bike would shoot by. As the descent eased I wound back into the race and could hear the encouraging crowds as I caught sight of the marshalling point at Cold Cotes.

A brief stop for a second dib, then a sketchy descent onto the road watched and cheered by many.

Someone shouted "Nicely done Swindon Road Club".

"Thank you". "Thank you" whoever you are and even if it was a lie. Another single line of shouted text that spurred me on. I stuck the head down, cadenced myself up and hammered out over 10km of road with a prevailing wind. This section felt good, there was enough climbing to keep the big ring boys at bay and I felt that I kept my position in the race. Occasionally I'd work with a rider and often lose them as the road went up. My road training and single gear paid dividends for this section.

I had time to eat and catch up on my drinking which had gone into arrears climbing up to Ingleborough. I made the first cut-off at Chapel-le-Dale with nearly an hour to spare, I had no idea of this at the time. Next, the climb up to Whernside. I've sat for ages stopped at this paragraph trying to remember it. All that comes back is steps. I think we started up a loosely surface lane that was hard going on the singlespeed and then I remember a brief descent followed by a carry up stone steps.

I could cheat and search the internet for another's account, but this is meant to be a dump from my mind. So steps it shall be. Loads of them and steep in places. Carrying was beginning to hurt now, I shut myself off for a while and listened to my breathing instead. Keep it rhythmical, don't draw too hard, align it to your footsteps. I think we rode briefly before the steep and loose finish to the top. Can't remember as a single statistic was going through my mind. 66% of peaks done at the top of this one. 66.666% of peaks done, 33.3333% to go.

Forgetting the ascent is possible but the descent from Whernside will always occupy a small corner of my memory, labelled frustration mixed with indecision. The descent started loose and rutty before morphing into more steps. At first the steps were easily rideable and the frustration came from those in front who'd get off and force me to brake just when I was getting into the swing. Then the steps got bigger. I could ride them, but I wasn't sure about the wheels. Thunk, thunk, thunk, thunk. Four steps, four big hits. Four moments of "Is the wheel really going to take this?". So I stopped and became the frustratee instead of the frustrated.

Fortunately the steps gave way to track and it was rideable. I sneaked up upon the wheel of another rider who appeared to know his way down. I agreed with all of his line choices and decided to follow. Suddenly a little bit of fun had crept in. He was blissfully unaware of the service he provided as I abdicated some line choice to him and his bike. We were off the fell in no time. Another dib and a view of Ribblehead Viaduct.

An overheard start line conversation had started something like this:-

"I love it when I see the viaduct at Ribblehead, it's then I know I am going to make it" I would have liked to gently shake the speaker by the throat as I faced 10 kilometres on the road into the wind on my own. The field was well split by now and no matter how fast I windmilled I couldn't catch the riders up the road. Others who caught me passed, I struggled to get the singlespeed into any kind of rhythm and strangely yearned for some off road to slow me down and give me some rest. If only I knew what was coming, I'd have sat up and enjoyed the tarmaced view. As it was I ate drank and moaned to myself until Horton and a drastic turn to the left.

The track to Pen-y-Ghent started shallow but kicked up after a few hundred metres. Not so bad with a 32 teeth cog at the back, but sheer terror on the singlespeed. Up until this point I'd only really wanted higher gears, but now I was begging my front ring to shrink and rear to expand. I had to dig really deep to drag the bike up this climb and caught two riders ahead. They were spinning away on lovely low gears and a leisurely pace. I was forced to slow by the narrow lane and riders descending on the right. Slowing down increased the pain. I needed to attack the climb and keep my cadence high, but congestion prevented this.

Climbing slowly on a singlespeed is purgatory. It stretches and strains the leg muscles until they sing, a silent melody that screams loud in the brain of whom they are attached. Pedal faster is the only remedy, but when there's traffic ahead you've no option but live with the song. I managed to pass a few riders early on the climb but downhill traffic increased and we were forced to single out as we climbed. Pain pain pain, I wanted the cycling to stop. I yearned for a walk but the track was too shallow and I'd lose too many places. Everyone else was riding and so shall I, slowly grinding my way up the hill.

There were comments from aside, encouragement, disbelief, "dig deep, dig deep". I am fucking digging deep, can't you see that? A rocky corner forced us off for a brief walk, up ahead I saw the carriers, halleebloodyuya a carry. I can't believe I was looking forward to a carry. This is why you don't do the three peaks on a singlespeed. It's these few kilometres near the end that will disassemble your legs into component parts and hand them back to you neatly displayed on mother's best china.

A bit more climbing, gurning, thrutching and finally I'm allowed to get off and sling the bike over my shoulder. The walk up Pen-y-Ghent has begun and not a moment too soon. We solemnly march silently up the steepening path, picking our way over to the rocky traverse. The cloud is still down and I have no idea as the distance to the top, but I don't care. I'm free of the pedals. I listen to the metronomic clatter of my cleats upon the stones. Click click another metre, click click another metre. How I envy the riders bouncing down to my right. They're nearly done, I still have god-only-knows-what of this climb ahead of me. The traverse melds into the hill and begins to flatten. I'm able to drop the bike and push it a while and then I hear the voices in the clouds.

"Cooomonthaleetleboogerthasnarlydooonit", I think it's Yorkshire for "Well done old chap the summit is in sight" and it was. Four men holding timing devices have never looked so beautiful. I'm on my own and spoilt for choice. I ask them which is the better looking, they point at the big guy with a hat. He gets my dib and nearly got a kiss, but his eyes ward me off as I turn, mount and ride my bike down the hill.

It starts boggy, then steepens as I ride above the rocky traverse. Like some perverse cliched movie ending the sun has come out as I make my way down. Round a steep corner and onto the rocky track, I'm picking up speed now and loving the trail I previously learnt to hate. But I say to myself, "concentrate, concentrate, concentrate". This is not the time for a puncture, this is not the time for an off. Keep it together and enjoy the way down. Others pass, I'm tempted, but listen to the voice. I'm not sure whether I'm controlled or mincing. All I know is that I want to finish now, I've done all the bloody hard work so deserve my reward. A last steep nervous bounce down the track then it's the road.

I check with the engine room to see if it's OK to engage the legs. The message comes back to give them a try, four stiff pushes and the news is good, we'll probably make it home. I spin up the single gear and set the rider in front in my sights. A young lad screams past then sits up wreathed in pain. He clutches his right calve, teeth bared eyes wild. Cramp. No time for sympathy from me I'm afraid as we're nearly home and he'll make it. But the lad in my sights is getting away. The final three kilometres prove to be cruel. They stretch into what feels like ten and I'm passed a few more times as the gradient favours the big ring.

Finally the bridge, I sense a rider behind and give it full gas. I've given up enough to geared riders already let me finish at least one position higher and I do. Five metres of loose shale and it's my final dib. I ask for my time but the holder hasn't a clue. We're shepherded into a tent and robbed of our timing devices and numbers. A small piece of paper is thrust into my hands.

TOTAL: 04:24:27

It looks like a shopping receipt. But for once I'm elated with the number at the bottom. Four two four two seven. You can write that number on my grave, soon you'll probably be able to rob my bank account with it. I'll never forget it. I set out to finish the ride and hopefully get in under 6. This time was never even contemplated. I want to run round punching the air and giving out high fives, but this is Yorkshire, so I eek out a wry smile and feign indifference as I exit the tent. The celebrations come as I meet up with friends. Two of them are hurt, Andy's hurt badly and smashed up his face, but he gaffer taped himself up and got back on his bike. We all marvel at the brutality of the event and smile the smiles of plane crash survivors who've walked out alive. I share a beer then get back on the bike and grind up the hill back to the van.

The sun's out and it's time to reflect.

Firstly the race. It's best described as "properly northern", hard as nails and ridden by riders who are equally tough. Nick Craig won it in 3 hours 8 minutes. He could have showered, dressed, cooked dinner, hoovered and laid the table in the time it took for me to catch him up. There are no fatty sportive riders on incongruous carbon bikes here. I was passed by big fellas and whippets alike. The grim air of determination pervades, it's a race and everyone I rode with was determined to show me their arse.

Next the singlespeed decision. If I had a geared cross bike, I'd ride it. Riding singlespeed simply turns the hardness wheel up a couple of notches. For sure, the bike is easier to clean and you get the odd admiring glance but a large number of riders will finish before you. I'd never attempt it unless properly fit. Self depreciation aside, I climb like a goat at the moment and I suffered on the track to Pen-y-Ghent. There's no grace in a grimace (actually there is) and I'm dreading the photos that feature rider number 473.

Would I do it again? Writing this with sore knees, bruises, chainring scars on my legs and the aftermath of dehydration, probably not. But next year I'll be idly browsing Twitter, *that* tweet will pop up and I'll have to fight a very strong urge. A little blue bike in the garage will be whining like a dog needing a walk.

Chapter 22

Nemesis

As soon as you make the transition into slightly competitive cycling you will inevitably meet your nemesis. This rider will be that little bit better than you no matter what. They will arrive at the top of climbs a wheel before you, they'll arrive at the cafe a few seconds earlier and they'll be there to greet you at the end of every village sign sprint. The frustration is compounded by the fact that your nemesis will appear to train less than you do and consume far more cake and chocolate with no apparent weight gain at all.

I met my nemesis in Rob. He was always at the front of our road club peleton merrily chatting away whilst the rider next to him gasped in the throes of lactate threshold. Rob's body rejected all fat and surrounded itself with leanness, he was first to the top of every climb and annoyingly could sprint as well. To make things worse his manner was cheery and friendly. He'd always flash a welcoming grin as he destroyed the riders attempting to hold his wheel up a long hard climb.

As I became fitter and started competing I'd get closer to Rob. I found that I could almost keep up with him on the hills, almost stay with him on the sprints and almost chat to him as we sat on the front of the group dragging it fast into the wind. The key word is "almost". No matter how hard I trained, how seriously I dieted, how well I looked after my bike, Rob would always be a wheel length ahead and I'd silently mutter to myself that I'd almost beaten him. Eventually we began to collude and my nemesis became my partner in crime.

As good climbers we would sit on the front and chat loudly knowing that the fatties behind were unable to speak at the ridiculous pace we were setting. It got to the point where the two of us gained a bad reputation. "Oh no! Barter and Jackson together on the front". We became renowned after making the only successful breakaway in history from the Tuesday night chain gang. Thirty miles as a pair averaging 25+ miles an hour and agreeing not to sprint at the end.

Then came our ultimate crime. On holiday in Italy we were riding together up towards the ski station at Prato Nevoso. Ahead we espied a group of older riders gasping their way round the steep corners. The two of us hatched an awful plan. We worked silently to get within twenty metres of the group, then pedalled hard side-by-side to overtake them on a bend. As we passed we used saved breaths to chat nonchalantly about the weather and then offer a cheery "Buongiorno!". We were both at heart rate max, but maintained the facade of pedalling with ease as we stormed past the group and round the corner ahead.

The two of us then worked together to stay away until the top of the mountain and sanctuary in a ski station coffee shop. We rushed our coffee orders and sat at a table ready for a cheery wave to the group who would surely believe they'd encountered two pros. They spun past and ignored us. I think there may have been the odd grunt in german which would have translated along the lines of "Those tossers are just like the two idiots we have in our club at home who think they're clever making us all suffer but really are despised by all".

Rob's married now and I haven't seen him on the bike for a while. But I do know that if I did, no matter how little riding he'd done, he'd make me suffer in some unspeakable way.

The Virtual Commuter

We are surrounded by sanctimony. From our parents to our TV screens, from school to college to work to old people's homes, newspaper headlines subliminally dictate to us and you will look long and hard to find a religion that doesn't give you at least a mild ticking off for daring to exist. Everywhere we turn there is someone or something telling us that we could and should be doing things differently ... and in my case they are usually right. However, of all the sanctimonious, self-righteous "do-gooders" that harp in my ear, there is one group I especially detest. Cycle commuters.

Yes, that's right, those who tell me that I should get rid of my car and cycle to work everyday. To be fair, they have a point. We all have a duty to contribute towards the well being of our planet and also to dodge the hospital for as long as is physically possible. There is no arguing with the fact that cycling to work saves money, improves health and clears the roads for the school run. But I have a massive problem with cycle commuting - I work from home. About the best I could possibly manage would be a 60 foot mountain bike ride to the shed at the bottom of the garden that has become my office.

Maybe to add interest I could ride from the bedroom, "huck" down the stairs and hone my trials skills as I dodge kids and cereal in the kitchen en route to the backdoor. Now you can see why the commuting zealots get on my nerves. I completely agree with them but I can't join in. It's like worshipping God but being too fat to make it through the church doors. Things worsened when my regular lunchtime riding buddy, Rob, calmly announced that our sessions were to be cancelled for the near future, as he had decided to cycle to work instead.

Through gritted teeth I congratulated him on his brave new step, particularly given that he had taken it in the depths of winter. It was the final straw when I calculated that his 36-mile round trip would push his weekly training mileage way beyond mine. Not only was he to join the ranks of the sanctimonious, but he'd be kicking my arse in the summer as well. I thought he was joking when he said, "Dave, you could always join me. Why not become a virtual commuter?". I dismissively mumbled an excuse only to receive a reminder from him by email a day later. And that's when I decided to become a virtual commuter. The plan was hatched.

I would awaken early, mount the bike and cycle in the direction of Rob's place, a meagre 18 miles from mine. Meanwhile, he would wait for me till 8am, at which time he would set out, heading in the opposite direction. Hopefully we would meet, I would turn round, and together we would cycle on, separating a quarter of a mile from my house, where Rob would continue on to his office and I, the virtual commuter, would roll up at my own front door and report for duty. What could be simpler? Well, a lot actually. The night before saw my frantic preparations. I started by strapping lights to my bike and siting it next to the front door.

The virtual commuter would soon lose the support of his wife if the young children were awoken before the very last minute necessary to clothe, feed and herd them to school. I collected a mound of cycle clothing and placed it strategically. Underwear and base layers by the bed, middle layers on the kitchen table and helmet, gloves, shoes, coat and overshoes next to the bike. Pump, tube, tools, mobile phone and house keys were placed alongside the middle layers ready to be stuffed into pockets. Energy powder was carefully measured and mixed into my bottle, then mounted to the bike.

Then, it started to get anal. I laid out my toothbrush, toothpaste and contact lenses, I put a cereal bowl and spoon on the side and stood a packet of Frosties next to it. I resisted the temptation to tear off lengths of toilet roll. The final step, I set my alarm clock for 6.30am. It made a funny noise - I think it was the digital equivalent of "Are you sure?". It certainly hadn't seen such an early hour in three years of home working. And so to bed, and a hacking cough that saw me finally drift off at about 1am. A perfect start to my life as a virtual commuter. Morning came and I leapt out of bed, driven by the excitement of a pending new adventure.

Resplendent in my lycra underwear I tiptoed down the stairs and rendezvoused with my breakfast apparatus. Swift calculating movements saw breakfast disappear, then my semi-nakedness followed by my contact lenses down the back of a radiator. I rapidly disintegrated into a maelstrom of picking up, putting down, clothing and unclothing. As I zipped up my final layer I caught a glance of my heart rate monitor strap. I had half a mind to leave it, but couldn't face the small gap in my near perfect training log. So off and on came the clothes for the final time. I left the house five minutes later than planned. I had an hour to do the 18 miles to Rob's house. I flicked on the lights and headed into the dark of a winter morning.

The virtual commute was on. Cool fresh morning air rushed through my lungs straight to my senses. As I skulked through my home town I became aware of the indigenous creatures that populate the early morning. A postman struggling with a full bag of mail, a milk float casually blocking a car-laden street, dustmen slinging black sacks and a spattering of early morning dog walkers trying to ignore the defecating canines attached to them by leads. Orange lamplight and mist had repainted the streets and my regular escape route from town became suddenly unfamiliar.

Gradually I slipped from suburbia and followed a steep hill under a railway bridge and into the dark. Here, I learned the first lesson of the cycle commuter: my front light was entirely inadequate. A thin pool of light in front of me failed to pick out the potholes and lumps in the road. I veered from left to right as hedgerows and corners rushed at me, and I desperately fought to keep control in the dazzling flood of full beam lights that streamed from approaching cars and only dipping at what seemed the last possible moment. I could not see and nor could I be seen. Lesson one: attach decent lights.

A motorway roundabout provided temporary respite as I was stopped by a traffic light and lit by a street lamp. I glanced down at my cycle computer: 7 miles in 30 minutes. I was slow this morning, which surprised me, the dark had clearly altered my perception of speed. At 7.30am the motorway was surprisingly busy and as a virtual commuter I indulged in a whiff of sanctimony. The lights changed and I rekindled my fight with the headwind, on into another town. Slowly the dark around me became grey. The groans of a poorly serviced bike were interspersed with bird song. Daylight sneaked up on me as the spectacular sunrise hid maliciously behind cloud.

The bike and I creaked towards our halfway point. And at last I reached a queue of traffic stopped at lights and mocked by unattended roadworks. I afforded each driver a cheery smile and glided to the front of the queue. A mocking (but short) sprint saw me cross the roadworks first and take the race, in which I was probably the only conscious participant. A few miles further and my halfway point was reached. Rob had left on the dot and I met him a few miles from his house. The first half of my virtual commute was truncated as I turned in the road and took a deep suck on Rob's rear wheel.

As is always the case with any rider I meet up with, Rob was better prepared than me. His bike sported a set of powerful lights, it was well oiled and looked clean. I spotted no holes in his kit and he'd even had a shave. I maintained the facade of some friendly banter as I secretly willed pieces to peel off his bike. We retraced my route at what felt like double the speed, driven by the wind behind us and that unspoken agreement that spurs two riders to increase their pace faster than that of one. The traffic jams had become more profound but easily skirted by the confident cyclist.

All too soon I was close to home and waving Rob "goodbye" as he peeled off towards his office. I have to confess that it felt strange to turn the key in my own front door at nine o'clock in the morning. The house was quiet, devoid of children and smelling of breakfast. I changed, showered and then sat with a coffee to reflect upon my virtual commute. I'd covered 32 miles and the clock said "quarter past nine". I had a complete day ahead of me, without the interruption of a lunchtime ride or evening turbo training session. I felt tired, but a motivated kind of tired. No, I'll be honest, I felt the fatigue of the sanctimonious. I was tired, but I'd earned the right to be tired, and that sort of tired felt good.

So I wasn't tired really, I was ready for the day ahead. If you understand that, then you probably cycle-commute already. Following my virtual commute I had one of the most productive days' work in a long while. And so my virtual commute is going to continue. Not every day, mind: 32 miles is a fair distance and I'm sure that a percentage of my motivation was delivered by novelty. But I'm definitely doing it at least once next week, and maybe the week after, and we'll see about the week after that. So now, I'm back friends with the cycle commuters.

I feel I've nearly joined their club. I've been inducted into their strange preparations and practices and after a few more goes I reckon I can apply for full membership. Of course, my commute may seem entirely pointless, it doesn't save a car journey and I would have ridden the miles at lunchtime anyway. But, it's definitely done something for me and I'm planning on keeping at it until I perfect my own unique brand of sanctimony.

Chapter 23

Blank Canvas

A blank canvas, for some artists and writers the hardest thing to face. Most of my articles are sketched out during a ride or event and it's rare that I sit down and try to write something. But a posting on the internet caught my eye, a cycling journal was looking for writers to submit articles for their quarterly publication. I dropped them a line and the requirements came back. Something short (800 words), something soulful, personal, passionate. I thought it would be interesting to have a go.

A few weeks later I fired up the word processor and stared at the blank canvas. I was in France on holiday and the rest of the family had abandoned me for the day to go shopping. I'm not very good at shopping, I tend to march straight up to the thing I want, sprint to the counter, hand over money and then take it home and break it shortly after. Browsing is not really my thing.

Anyway, there I was with an empty screen, surely the words would soon tumble from my mind and a new masterpiece would be created ready to submit. But nothing happened. I typed a few tentative linking words hoping that they would kickstart the creative process, but all I was left with was some "the"s and a complete lack of content. So this is what writer's block feels like. The only answer was to get up and make a cup of tea.

As I dunked the bag into the boiling water I tried reflecting back over ten years worth of cycling for an event that I hadn't already written about. Mountain bike orienteering came to mind, but I'd find it hard to make that "soulful" given that the vast majority of participants are perceived to wear beards and ride Marins. Which is not strictly true by the way as I've never grown a beard, but can confess to previously having three Marins in the fleet.

Then I thought about Moab, I've been there four times now and had various different incidents but not yet written anything about any of them. Trouble is, Moab is boring, everyone and their dog has been there and there are countless articles doing the rounds. Just as I was about to sink into proper despair a young lad kicked a football against our campervan. "Bloody little hooligan", I thought to myself, "Wouldn't have happened if he'd been riding a bike".

Then my mind began to wander a little further, the resentment concerning football grew a little bit more. I began to postulate that football's a little more crap than cycling but the mental process was interrupted by golf. I can't stand golf. Mark Twain labels it as "a good walk spoiled". I think he didn't go far enough. How about; "A complete and utter waste of perfectly good lawnmower time that could be better utilised in overgrown back gardens".

Many years previously I had been thrown out of the Beehive pub in Swindon for professing my hatred of golf. I'd been loudly discussing the potential for golf saboteurs who would hide in bushes stealing balls or using blow pipes to divert perfectly good putts. The landlord, Noel, was an ardent golf fan and immediately threw me out banning me for life. Luckily he had a short memory as well and greeted me with a pint a week later.

Golf and football bad, cycling good. How could I work that into an article. Well you'll find out in a few sentences time. I quite liked the end result, the journal didn't though as I was overlooked in favour of some more soulful, passionate, personal stuff.

The Curiosity Cortex

Football players don't drag their friends onto their favourite pitch enthusing about the centre spot and the challenges it presents. I doubt that golfers slog for miles across barren country on a promise of the perfect sixteenth hole and I am certain that no surprises await darts players as they step up to the oche. Their sports are rooted in numeracy. Time limits within which to score goals, subtraction permutations in order to reach zero or a quest to return home with the minimal set of swings carried out. Numerics are increasingly incidental to my mountain biking. Instead, I find myself driven by hearsay, legend, anecdote and bravado.

"A bloke in the bike shop was telling me that there's some wicked new singletrack been built in the Forest of Dean"

"Jacob's Ladder, it's the hardest off-road UK climb, only five have cleaned it"

"Everyone reckons that Beinn A'Ghlo is THE classic Scottish loop"

"He tried three times before he completed the South Downs Way solo, I think you'd struggle Dave"

Statements like these feed the area of my brain that I've named the "curiosity cortex". It's connected directly to my legs, driving them on to locations where I pit myself against such statements. Often the legend turns out to be fact, the anecdote contains a modicum of truth, hearsay melds into public information but bravado usually remains just that.

"This descent contains seventy highly technical switchbacks worthy of the Alps"

That sentence leapt straight from our Sardinian host Peter's list of mountain bike routes directly into the curiosity cortex. "Highly technical" stoked up the bravado engine, "worthy of the Alps" added fuel to the fire of hearsay, legend and anecdote. I'd never ridden in the Alps, but I read enough stories and heard enough tales to build a picture in my mind of breath-taking scenery embedded with challenge. Previous experience leaked into the cortex as well. We'd ridden in the area before. The rides were harsh and unforgiving, defined by shepherd tracks cut through arid scrub and loose granite. Falls hurt, flow was often hard to find and post ride discussion contained verbs such as " thrutch", "scratch" and "push".

Nevertheless, the cortex filled and spilled into the legs. Peter delivered us high above the village of Talana where we feasted upon trepidation as protective gear was applied, banter quelled to murmur. As we rode towards the singletrack Peter pointed out features, hilltops, ridges and flora. I didn't listen to a word. I'd set a counter in my head, dialed to "seventy highly technical switchbacks". They might be worthy of the Alps, but was I?

Self doubt ran out of time as our track ran out of width and reached the steep valley side. We halted and dropped saddles, morphing well proportioned full suspension bikes into weird looking trials-like machines. Peter led the way, slowly easing us over the valley edge onto the tiniest sliver of shepherd made singletrack, swathed in foliage and littered with rocks. Within fifty metres he halted, stood high on the pedals, fixed his stare over his left shoulder, gently rotated the bars then "whoosh", he was gone.

I thought we'd lost him to the cliff, until Malcolm in front of me followed his line and the switchback was revealed. A full 180 degree turn, steep, narrow and laden with scree, it's intimidation invited me down. I held the brakes and rode wide, my arse hanging as far off the back as my arms would allow. Turning my head I stared down the line, a little more handlebar rotation, a little more courage, off the brakes and then "whoosh", I was round.

Elation was lost in fear, the next switchback trumped the last with it's exposure. A forty foot drop to the left complimented by a steeper exit and an impossibly thin line. The exposure robbed any remaining thoughts of finesse, I placed two feet firmly on the ground and scuffed my way round the corner. On to the next which looked wider and was protected by trees. We added a little more speed, pulled rear brakes and skidded our way round. Forgivable in the granite based terrain that easily won any erosion battle with our tyres.

And so we descended in a staccato rhythm. Fast one, slow one, fail one in any and every order. I quickly lost count as numerics were discarded in favour of experience. Left, right, left, right, laugh, shout, laugh, shout and too soon it was over. We rolled out of the trees and forded the river at valley bottom, my curiosity cortex almost empty.

Were the switchbacks worthy of the Alps? There's only one way to find out, the cortex began to fill again as we pedalled our way back to the van.

Chapter 24

Lost in Technology

How many times have I heard the map and compass brigade witter on about how using a GPS to navigate is foolhardy? They say you can always trust the paper and pointer as long as you have the basic skills. What are those then? Let me fill you in. They are, the ability to be able to practise origami on large sheets of paper in a force ten gale, a keen sense for ferrous objects and an unwillingness to stand next to them, a fear of the Cuillin mountains, a dead steady hand, long distance vision in poor visibility and finally a very deep pocket that can afford £7.99 every time you go someplace new (don't go buying unlaminated maps a single drop of rain and they dissolve).

The GPS liberated me from this world. I'd spent many a happy weekend completely lost with hedges as the only landmark and speeding motorists unwilling to stop and show me on my way. With the advent of the GPS I was able to know exactly where I was at any given time. In the early days this was presented to me as 51.55667, -3.124433, about as useful as the rapidly dissolving map. But then came digital maps and along with them a dirty great arrow on screen that says "You are here".

My cycling was unlocked further by the GPS. I used the electronic maps to plot routes down esoteric looking roads and then the GPS to find them. I rode through and over the darkest corners of Wales on my own, confident that the GPS would look after me and see me safely back to the car. Friends would email me routes and I'd follow them blind trusting their judgement. This did lead to one sticky encounter through a mile wide field of head height corn which clearly wasn't there in winter.

I must confess that it didn't always go to plan. One Sunday I planned a solo epic century ride to Broadway Tower in the Cotswolds. The GPS valiantly delivered me to the coffee shop at its base and then crashed. Nothing I could do would revive it and the woman behind the counter spoke in tongues. As I had foresaken maps my only option was to head in the direction that I thought was south. I rode for hours until I found a sign to Bourton-on-the-Water from where I knew my way home. One hundred and twenty miles later I resolved to always back the GPS up with a map.

Then there is the GPS that I lost. Riding off road in the depths of Wiltshire it detached itself from my bike and was gone. I searched for it for hours, the irony of the situation making itself felt. Here was I looking for something that is supposed to help me find stuff. I never did find it but always hoped that some kind soul would stumble across it and use my trail to return it to its rightful owner.

The GPS even led me into the realms of utter childishness. My friend Andy wrote a complete mapping package for planning and reviewing GPS routes. One night I decided to create a comedy route and carefully rode the shape of a penis into a large field south of Swindon. Such puerile behaviour would not have worked with a map and compass. To be honest it wasn't that successful with the GPS as Andy quickly deleted the penile route that I emailed his way.

No Lights and a Grey Triangle

I've made what in hindsight, is a huge mistake. I've organised to go to the Alps in a few weeks for an end of season road jaunt with my mate Andy. So far, it is hard to see the mistake, a week off work, classic Tour De France climbs and another excuse to dress up in thin stretchy clothing and mince about the place..legally. The mistake is going with Andy, he's a fit, self employed northern Peak District habitating whippet type and when I mean whippet, I'm not talking about his dog. He's been training and he goes up hills quick. My arse will be firmly kicked in the French Alps. Thus in perfect Barter tradition, two weeks before departure I decided that something needed to be done and so I turned to my Garmin 705 GPS.

This has a feature that I'd yet to tangle with, the "virtual training partner", apparently you are able to set a goal time for a ride and the virtual partner will appear on screen, motivating you along at a pace necessary to hit your goal. I planned myself a long hilly ride and set the goal pace at 17.5 mph average, the software I used to do this told me I should be done in about 2hrs 36 minutes.

Interestingly, Andy wrote this software, we'll come back to that later. But I was skeptical of my own ability to remain motivated by a small chunk of technology, and decided that an alternative back-up strategy was required. I'd set off 2 hrs 45 minutes before sunset...with no lights. Therefore becoming motivated not only by my virtual parter, but also by the threat of being run over by a tractor on an unlit Wiltshire lane after dark. It was all looking good. Technology and planetary rotation would work together to get me round a 48 mile ride with 4000 feet of climbing in a respectable time.

Consequently I'd magically become super fit and leave Andy for dust on the Ventoux a few weeks later. And so I set off, switched on my virtual partner and a grey triangle appeared on screen slightly ahead of me. No problem, the road went downhill a bit and I was able to catch up with him and even sneak past a little. I was doing 19mph and it seemed like he was as well, due to the fact that the gap didn't appear to widen as I maintained this pace. I reached the first hill quietly confident, as "Mr grey triangle" was behind me and I'd climbed this slope a thousand times. I doubted very much that he'd be able to match my superior pace.

It was looking good and we began the climb. Suddenly I noticed a change in pace from the triangle. My cadence and speed decreased in line with the gradient, but "Mr cheating bastard grey triangle" shot past me at what seemed suspiciously like 17.5 mph. I gurned and chuntered, spluttered, spat, wibbled and mashed pedals as fast as I could. To no avail, he merrily shot up the hill at a totally unfeasible speed and soon disappeared off the screen and up the road. This wasn't motivation, this was two fingers waved clearly in my face followed by a swift GPS style moony out of the back window. I was tempted to give in there and then 5 miles into the ride.

But somehow I convinced myself it was a glitch. I summited the hill, recovered as best I could and began the chase. A few miles later his grey little arse appeared at the top of the screen. A long spurt of 20mph on the flat saw him caught and an even longer 27mph downhill spat him off the bottom of the screen and saw me right back in charge. I had him sussed. He was riding at a constant 17.5 mph. I just had to keep my pace ahead of this and I'd not see him again. The motivation was back. But so was the next hill. And just like the last, he appeared from nowhere halfway up the climb nonchalantly tapping along at 17.5mph up a 20% gradient.

The ride continued along this theme. Although his cheating got worse. I was stopped at a junction, he just rode across it, through the speeding traffic and off into the distance. I slowed for a horse, he took no notice and zipped neatly by Zara Philips without so much as a doffed cap. He showed no respect for traffic lights, tractors, gradients, roundabouts, rabbits, pedestrians or anything put on this earth to get in the way of personal bests. He just calmly pissed off up the road oblivious to all of them. Our cat and mouse tussle continued for almost 35 miles. Until a long steep hill out of Aldbourne did for me completely.

I'd climbed over 3000 feet by this stage and was utterly wasted, mainly due to poor route planning or winds in the wrong direction, whichever you choose to believe. He pissed past me on this hill, and I let him go. His involvement in this ride was over, I decided to solely concentrate on completing it before dark. There was definitely resentment on my part and I became slightly pissed off that he was simply pixels on a screen. I'd liked to have been able to "have words" about his reckless style of riding and scant regard for the road hazards that affect the rest of us. So, my head went down and I bashed on with the ride, only glancing at the GPS for route directions, until it said 42 miles completed and he sneaked back onto the top of the screen.

I felt a burst of elation as I realised that he was only half a mile in front and there weren't any major hills left. With 6 miles to go I reckon I could catch him, especially seeing as he was stuck at 17.5mph even on the fast bits. I guzzled the rest of my Lucozade Sport, pushed my sunglasses up my nose and headed off after the little grey bastard, motivated as hell! The next few miles were a bit twisty and the gap didn't seem to be coming down by much. I sat further forward on the saddle, got lower down the bars and pushed harder and harder. It was really really starting to hurt, but I was powered by resentment, he may be equilateral, but I was going to show him that geometry was no match for puerile desperation.

We got closer and closer to home and the gap between us was narrowing, at one point I was right on top of him. But a small hill gave him the advantage and he led on screen by almost a centimetre. However, the last few miles played to my strengths, mainly flat, fast and with a tailwind. I fought and fought and fought, literally 500 yards before my house I passed him and then the cheating bugger pulled out his final trump card. The GPS unit decided that I was "off course" and my grey virtual twatting partner disappeared off the screen. He knew I was going to win, he knew I'd sail into my drive hands aloft with him trailing in my dust, so he decided to just give up. Apparently the Garmin 705 plays a little tune when you beat your virtual partner. Mine just told me I was home.

I gingerly dismounted the bike and checked that I was capable of walking. Then I returned to the GPS and checked my average speed....17.8 mph. The double cheating bastard!! I'd finished the ride a little over two and a half hours, he should have been at least 0.75 miles behind me, not just round the corner. And then I twigged how Andy has got so fit. I'm sure his software has a secret setting that turns the GPS into the worst training partner you can have. A conniving, cheating git who has no regard for you or other users but hammers on relentlessly at their own pace. But aren't those sorts of people the ones you always want to beat? Maybe I'll go out riding with him again.

Chapter 25

For The Hell Of It!

Probably the greatest and often most overlooked aspect of cycling is that in the main it is done outside. I accept that there are small veins of lunatics who practise their art under roof. I myself have trod the boards of the velodrome, riding at stupid speeds and obtuse angles ludicrously close to other cyclists. In fact I once shared Newport Velodrome with the Welsh junior talent team, it was a sobering experience to be told how to ride in no uncertain terms by a thirteen year old girl as she overtook me.

But the outdoors is where the majority of my cycling is done, and given that my outdoors consists in the main of Great Britain, the experience can vary wildly. Some days are just plain hard. Horizontal rain, fog, unrelenting headwind or hail serve to remind me of the reason that the human race evolved to invent roofs and central heating.

On these days there is no celebration of the outdoors. I have to take my mind to a different place and focus on the physical benefit to myself instead. The pleasure is all in the end of the ride, that wonderful feeling of depositing dank clothing in the vicinity of the washing machine and looking pleadingly at your partner. The cup of coffee that you can feel as it descends the oesophagus and spreads warmth throughout your innards. Finally the knowledge that hopefully the vast majority of those you will end up competing against probably stayed indoors. Surely you are now a few fractions of a watt further ahead of them in the power stakes?

Then there are the other days. The days when the sun shines, the wind drops, the flora and fauna all decide that this is showcase weather and come marching out into your view. These are the really special days when being a cyclist is the best person to be. Not only do you get to feast your eyes, you get to feed them unhindered over a much wider spectrum than those who have decided to walk. There are no car window pillars to obscure your view and, unless you are a poor mechanic like me, your journey will be bathed in stealth and silence. These are the days to forget the training plan and embrace the experience instead. There will always be a patch of bad weather round the corner ready to toughen you up and scare your competition away. These rides often end in sadness, returning home is the opposite of what I really want to do.

Therein I have described one of the dichotomies of cycling. The fact that the motivations can contrast wildly even though the rider and the bicycle remain the same. Interestingly this applies to the riders you share it with as well. Turn up at a Tuesday night chain gang session and I can guarantee that there will be no discussion about the fluffy squirrel you passed near the woods. The best you can expect is a shouted instruction to "hold the wheel!" Conversely a group of BMX riders hanging out at the local ramps will look upon you quizzically as you chase round in circles banging out intervals and furiously feeding upon energy gels.

Cycling offers you a door to a remarkable variety of worlds and often you open it never fully understanding into which one you will step. I suppose that's why I come back time and time again for a series of mini-adventures. In fact I'm sure I'll return to the boards and another bollocking from a thirteen year old talented Welsh girl.

Forty Candles, Six Wheels

To date, my mountain biking career has been peppered with milestones. The first bike I rode, the first set of suspension forks, the first ride with clipless pedals, my first race, my first trip abroad, my first serious accident. As my fortieth birthday approached I felt the need to bang in another significant mile marker yet strangely I found myself struggling for inspiration.

Over the years mountain biking friends and internet forums had opened my eyes to a wealth of opportunity. I had been fortunate enough to travel and ride extensively throughout the UK and abroad. I'd ridden most types of bikes and events over most types of distances. I was really struggling to pick a ride to celebrate my impending "vet"ness and open the door into what many would consider to be old age.

I was pondering this fact during the gaps in conversation whilst sat with close friends in a local pub. My finger lazily circled the lip of a half drained pint glass as I contemplated my dilemma. Meanwhile I overheard them enthusing over their preparation for an impending local half marathon.

I've known Neil and Steve for years. Steve and I had competed in Trailquests together ten years previously but his mountain biking career had lapsed into the occasional muddy Sunday morning, dragging his heavy Saracen through rutted Wiltshire byways. Neil was another infrequent biker, but the kind of bloke who was always keen to have a go at something new.

Suddenly the pieces fell into place.

I had been handed a mission by whatever deity directs us as mountain bikers. Here were people with something missing in their life. If they were able to enthuse about two hours of beating their soles against tarmac, imagine their elation having ridden a fine stretch of singletrack. I've tampered with running myself in the past, but I have no memories of relishing the pavements that races took me over, or discussing a particularly tricky curb step with a fellow runner in the café afterwards. In fact, I can't remember ever going for a post run tea stop. All I seem to recall is the elation/disappointment offered by the stopwatch or my position at the end of the event.

I leant over and rudely interrupted their conversation. "Lads, I'm forty next Monday, how do you fancy taking the day off work and having a go at something different? I reckon I might just be able to convert you away from that running lark". They were three pints down the line and it didn't take much convincing to get them to sign up.

And so my watershed mission had been defined. I would drag these poor unfortunates away from the stopwatch and man made paths and introduce them to our suburbia. I'd take them to some man made trails and give them a taster of the kind of mountain biking that we often take for granted, fast, flowing, challenging, accessible trails. In doing this I'd not only become a mountain biking philanthropist but I'd also get some answers to the man made vs natural trails debate. In short, my fortieth birthday ride would be the same, but different. Physically little would change, but I'd be with different riders and hopefully get a completely different glimpse at the sport that had helped define my life for the previous ten years.

A week later, and forty years old, I was unloading mountain bikes in the car park at Afan Argoed. My Santa Cruz Chameleon drifted off the bike rack when compared to Neil and Steve's Saracens, both nearly 10 years old and lacking any lightweight components. I gazed in awe at Neil's toe clips and Suntour forks, his bike was a retro vision fitting with my new retro age.

Within minutes they were both dressed and ready to go. This was very different from the car park messing about that I had grown used to. I still had air pressures to check, shocks to pump and disk brakes to adjust. Neil and Steve put me to shame with their simplicity. A quick slash and a sandwich stuffed into a coat pocket was all that was needed for them. In deference I chose to ignore my pre-flight checks and joined in with the spirit of getting out to the trails as quickly as possible.

We nipped out of the car park and chose the Penhydd trail as a suitable "man made" introduction. This gave me a certain sense of satisfaction, as years previously I had spent a cold winter's morning lugging hardcore up to the top of Hidden Valley and whacking it into the ground. The trail started with a climb on easy fire road. Steve's runners legs took him up it at a fair rate of knots, whilst Neil started to puff and pant a bit. I played yoyo between them as the gap increased, reminding Neil of those sneaky cigarettes in the pub, whilst trying to pretend to Steve that I could manage his pace easily.

Already the benefits of man made trails were becoming clear. Neil had a hard time battling the gradient, but the compacted fire road gave him one less thing to fight against. Had this been a rutted, steep bridleway I think he would have been pushing. However, the consistent, well drained surface allowed him to get a rhythm and grind up the climb, not pretty, but he made it. At the top Steve was still looking fresh. As the more accomplished runner of the two, he seemed to find the climbing easy. It was time to challenge his abilities downhill, so I chivvied the two onwards to the beginning of Hidden Valley.

Hidden Valley defines the Penhydd trail. Its fast sweeping singletrack switchbacks eke out the maximum possible enjoyment as the rider descends into the valley below. It's technical enough to require a degree of concentration but forgiving, so the rider can push the speed up a bit and really give it a go if they are feeling confident.

I took off first and stopped halfway down to take a few photos. It wasn't long before the others came snaking through the trees. Well, I say "snaking" but as snakes don't have vocal cords I think I might need another metaphor. Neil and Steve were whooping their way down the trail, neither of them had ridden terrain like this before and they were relishing every lump and turn.

I looked down at my £1000 hardtail and indulged in a wry smile. Here was living evidence that enjoyment was to be had no matter what bike you stuffed between your legs. I was actually quite envious of the two of them. They were having as much fun as I was, however, their bank balances were probably £700 healthier than mine.

We tipped our hats to the trail builders and set off again for some more. Steve and Neil had taken a bite from the good stuff and were starting to show signs of a hunger for the gnarly. There was a lot less moaning on the next set of climbs as they realised that each ascent was there for a reason. The trail builders were lifting them up as efficiently as possible in order to maximise the time spent twisting down hill.

A few rocky sections created a pause in celebrations. The short travel forks on both of their bikes offered little help and both riders hit the deck, but this did little to abate the enthusiasm. In fact for me it was refreshing to hear a rider own up to their own mistake rather than blame the tyres, suspension set up, brakes etc... These two weren't aware of all of the technical advances available to them. They were simply lost in their own enjoyment of the ride. They had no expectations as to how they would perform, and this lack of expectation freed them to enjoy the ride for what is was, rather than what it should have been.

I found myself caught up in their ride rather than mine. Their enthusiasm was giving me more pleasure than the trail itself. I stopped focusing on how I was performing and simply willed the two of them on. And it got better. Their legs were diminishing but the smiles were noticeably wider after each section of trail. A river crossing bred laughter and we shouted each other on to the final descent and a reluctant walk down the steps to the car park.

Neil and Steve were tired yet elated. I gently suggested another trail but was brushed aside by the essence of baking wafting out from a café door. It wasn't long before the traditional ride post mortem began, triggered by large mugs of tea and freshly made rolls. I casually mentioned that some riders considered man made trails were wrong and that all trails should be ridden from the front door. Neil and Steve were aghast. They had really enjoyed the flow of the Penhydd trail, they'd enjoyed its rideability and the fact that casual mountain bikers such as they felt challenged by it. They had ridden every inch of the trail without a push or a drag. And to top it off the ride ended with instant hot food and drink. It seemed that Afan had done more to drag them back into mountain biking than any muddy wet winter Wiltshire trail could possibly achieve. Steve began to plot his return with family before we were even a mile from the car park on our way home.

As we sped back towards the Severn bridge I took time to ponder the mission I'd been handed. I'm not sure that I converted two committed runners away from pavement bashing, but I think Afan allowed them to experience the promise a mountain bike makes when sat gleaming in the bike shop window. And that's exactly where it fits in my take on the "man made trails" debate.

In fact the person converted was me. I had become caught up in achievement and forgotten the simple pleasures to be had in riding your bike whilst not giving a toss how fast, how hard or how difficult your riding should be. I'd succumbed to the virtual arms race of equipping my bike with the latest gadgets and gears and forgotten that it's just as much fun to ride when you do it with others and take pleasure from their enjoyment rather than your own.

So when you're sat staring at the blank piece of paper that's destined to become next season's objectives. Think of those friends who haven't ridden for a while, think about what they and you are missing and drag them out for an hour or two of "who cares" mountain biking.

Chapter 26

Extreme Weather

Many years ago a British weatherman named Michael Fish became a little more famous by putting us all at rest. This was achieved by pointing at a weather chart and telling a worried country not to be concerned as there would definitely not be any hurricanes. The next day Brighton was devastated by some of the strongest UK winds ever recorded. Trees were uprooted, windows broken and countless lattes spilled on coffee shop tables. I lived in Brighton at the time but don't expect a tale recounting my experience as when the winds hit I was in an alcoholic stupor many miles away.

A clear piece of emotional cowardice caused me to flee Brighton the previous day after splitting up with my girlfriend. Like a typical man I ran away from the heartbreak and sought solace in a few pints of lager and a doss on my London based friend's floor. My ex-girlfriend had the last laugh as she got to experience the extreme weather, something I actually quite like to do. There's definitely a morbid fascination that runs through many of us, willing us on to take our place as voyeurs at the scene of destruction. I'm the first in the queue for a ringside seat at a good thunderstorm, some wild seas, forest felling winds or a country stopping snowstorm. That is as long as it has no impact whatsoever upon my cycling life.

A few years previously I flew to Denver with a friend for a week's mountain biking in Moab. We landed in clear skies and drove to a hotel to sleep off the flight and prepare for a long drive through the rockies after which warm desert based cycling awaited. The next day we awoke and attempted to get to our car which was parked 10 feet from the hotel entrance. The word "attempted" is the crux of the last sentence. The hotel doors could not be opened, an issue caused by the four feet of snow that had fallen through the night. I've never seen so much of the stuff in my life and I've done a fair bit of skiing on the side.

The two of us retreated to our room and switched on the TV. News reports bore seriously bad tidings. This was record breaking snow, completely out of the blue for the time of year and completely stopping every single show in town. Andy and I were marooned. Separated from our tangle with the sandy desert by an expanse of white snow dunes. All roads to Moab were closed and the highways department were struggling to find their ploughs in the depth of the snow.

We sat in our room for days, fixated upon the TV screen, waiting for any glimmer of hope that the snow would recede and allow us to be on our way. I got so bored I eventually succumbed to swimming and for the first time in my life completed an imperial mile of chlorinated, slightly pissy indoor pool. I looked like a human prune as I emerged vowing that me and swimming were now "done". Finally the roads were announced to be possibly drivable. The two of us nervously ventured out on the highway and crept up into the rockies for the most stressful ten hour's driving of my life. Within a mile I had seen a car gracefully pirouette in my rear view mirror. Fortunately we arrived at the desert unscathed but that did not last long as I fell off a lot.

It's a common theme in cycling. The weather intervening to mess things up before, during and after you have mounted the bike. My children welcome the onset of snow, looking forward to chucking large volumes of it into my face. I'm a little more reticent. It certainly makes the weedy garden look a little bit nicer, but the impact upon my riding will definitely be felt. Here's a little article about an icy ride born from necessity.

The Art of Remaining Upright

I wasn't going to ride my bike today. It was far too cold, the driveway was covered in ice, my left knee was complaining of overuse and a large quantity of unfinished household tasks were beckoning with crooked finger. No, today was going to be a nice domestic Sunday culminating in the addition of slippers to my Amazon Xmas wishlist.

However, this plan was sabotaged the evening before, when lying on the sofa I noticed that my stomach had gained more altitude than my nose. How on earth had that happened? I've ridden nearly 7000 miles this year and it wasn't so many weeks ago that I was whippeting my way up Mont Ventoux. Clearly the past few weeks of work based travel and hotel food had taken their toll, especially when combined with a special set of genetics passed down the Barter line which ensure that all weight distribution begins from the waist.

So, like a self flagellating pious monk, I donned seventeen layers of mismatched lycra and headed out into the wilds of west Wiltshire straddled across my poorly maintained mountain bike. The increased tummy altitude demanded a ride of at least three hours in order to ensure that sufficient calories were burned to cover weight loss and several mounds of roast dinner.

It started badly. Ten metres from the front door and I'd lost the front wheel completely to black ice. Fortunately I hadn't even clipped into my pedals properly and a quick dab corrected the slide and pointed the bike sort of in the planned direction of travel. For once a main road provided brief respite and gave me the luxury of an ice free mile out of town and onto a minor road heading towards some tracks. Or, to give it a more suitable name, the B "linear ice rink".

The road conditions could not have been worse. The previous day's rain hadn't even had the courtesy to drain away before it froze solid. I gingerly pedalled the bike with my shoes clipped out of the pedals and the front wheel locked dead straight and pointing forward. It would have been quicker walking, but I've fallen onto tarmac before and it doesn't seem to have much give.

Three miles, and what felt like three hours later I turned right and headed off road and onto the Ridgeway. Surely, conditions would improve on rougher surfaces. I had visions of getting the bike up to the dizzy speed of ten miles an hour, and even maybe getting a little bit warm, but the Wiltshire glacier put paid to that.

The Ridgeway had accumulated even more ice than the roads. In places it was inches thick and the lack of any temperature was ensuring that it remained solid regardless of the sun that had deigned to make an appearance. My cautious road riding evolved into out and out off road mincing. I gripped the bars like a child learning to ride for the first time and timidly rotated the pedals in a vain attempt to move forward. All I could think of was "keep the bike vertical, keep it upright, don't brake, keep the bike vertical".

A few miles of this and the sense of commitment was huge. The ice was not getting any thinner, but glimpses of walkers certainly were. And as for mountain bikers, I'd only met one, my friend Rick who had mirror image minced towards me and told me that it "only gets worse" as you carry on. I nearly cried off at that point, but a quick hand to belly confirmed that I was still carrying far too much lard for a lad of my supposed thinness.

Rick had taken a tumble a few miles back, I proudly exclaimed that so far I had managed to remain upright, I knew this was a mistake, which manifested itself in a power slide followed by arse braking manoeuvre down the next hill.

Several hours of this got me to Lambourn and I was reunited with backroads. It seemed as if the sun had actually started to work a bit as the road I joined was virtually ice free. I experimented with leaning the bike a little and the wheels remained in traction. It was even possible to change up into slightly harder gears, and feel a little bit of wind through the helmet. Decision made, I was going home on the road.

Ten miles later I reviewed this decision along with the choice of wide knobbly tyres that I had affixed to the bike. I'm not convinced it was entirely wise and mincing and nervousness had been replaced with lack of breath and muscle fatigue. It was a sorry looking Dave that limped home after four hours riding and less than forty miles covered.

Normally cycling articles end here with some cliche about it all being worth it in the end as the rider manfully tears into some pig based meal whilst quaffing beer and sanctimoniously   postulating that his non-cycling friends wouldn't have had half as much fun. Not for me. This was a ride born of necessity, in fact lets go further than that, it was a direct result of my own excesses and lack of self control.

The sun and scenery failed to temper the abject horror of the hours spent simply trying to stay vertical and contrary to the title of this piece, I don't think I've discovered the art. What I think I have discovered is that it's the potentially great rides I put off that lead me to having to suffer the poor ones.

Chapter 27

The Bucket List

Modern times have allowed us to create the concept of a "bucket list". Quite simply a detailing of the things we would like to have done before we kick the bucket. If you're not careful your bucket list can become stuffed with cliches; swimming with dolphins, visit Machu Picchu, drive a Ferrari or successfully open a carton of milk without spilling the contents down your shirt.

We should celebrate the fact that we are able to construct such lists as our ancestors would not have been so fortunate. Their aspirations would have been more along the lines of, survive beyond thirty, not catch the plague that the neighbours are currently dying of, become the proud owner of an outside loo and visit Cleethorpes to see the sand.

Cycling provides ample opportunity for bucket list creation and I have constructed one of my own. Interestingly item one is to write a book about cycling, so if you are reading this on paper or in an electronic device then you can be reassured that I am one tenth of my way towards death.

Next comes the list of things I would like to achieve on the bike, some of these may be a little less feasible as I've always wanted to win a proper race and I don't mean a time trial, I mean crossing the finishing line with hands in the air. My best performance to date is a sixth. Given that I've not ridden many races it's tempting to settle with that, but I can't help imagining that the feeling of winning from a sprint or a long solo break would eclipse the slow hand clap of a top ten place.

There's a list of bikes that I've always wanted to own but probably never will. For example, a full carbon lightweight race machine custom built to my odd shaped frame. There's no point in me having one as I'd break it somehow. Try as I might I just can't ever find the time to bestow the love on my bikes that they deserve. Too often they lie uncleaned resting against each other in a dark damp garage. I've also had yearnings for a unicycle, but my doctor said "no". The National Health Service have refused point blank to increase the budget in Accident and Emergency.

Then there's the places in which I'd like to ride. The Atlas Mountains, the American Rockies, the Italian Dolomites and up that 45% hill in Harlech that is supposed to be the steepest in the UK. In fact the world is my bucket list as there's nowhere that I wouldn't like to ride. Well apart from Cleethorpes that is, I've actually ridden there and all you can see is the sand.

High on any cyclist's bucket list will be a series of classic events. L'Etape du Tour, the Marmotte, the welsh Dragon ride and maybe some off road shenanigans like Mountain Mayhem or the Great Tour Divide. I'm very fortunate in this aspect as my obsession has allowed me to tick off many of these events. To be honest there's not much left on my little list as I find personal adventure into the unknown to be a far greater draw. But one event had stood out over the years, the Dunwich Dynamo. Ever since I saw magazine photos of eclectic riders disappearing into the dusk I was hooked. This event was one that I needed to ride before the grim reaper turned up to liberate my bike fleet from me. And in 2011 I managed to do just that.

Debut in the Darkness - The Dunwich Dynamo

How often have you turned up at a cycle event and thought to yourself "I just don't belong here"? This happens to me all of the time. At road races I stare enviously at the muscles, carbon, determined faces and support crews then realise this is probably not for me. Sportives have a similar effect, I cast my eyes over the plethora of timing instruments attached to bikes and wonder if anyone present is actually going to enjoy the ride rather than use it to measure their own performance.

As I get older I find myself shying away from anything with an expectation concerning my cycling attire, performance or behaviour. Almost a full circle back to the spirit of my youth where we stuffed playing cards into our spokes and worked hard on creating the longest skid mark possible outside of our school. However, I've never felt more at home in a group of cyclists than on Saturday 16th July 2011 as I leant on my bike in the middle of the melee that was the start of the Dunwich Dynamo.

You can't enter the Dunwich Dynamo, there's no entry fee. There's no list of riders. There's no timing, in fact there's not even a start time. There's no signed route and for the vast majority of the ride there's no support. You're on your own, but you're not. Those that ride with you are your soigneurs. Fall, they'll pick you up. Break something, help will be offered. No agenda, no expectation, no competition, just a single objective. Ride through the night to the seaside.

Apparently it all began in 1993, initiated by bike couriers who decided to flee London for the coast inviting all and sundry to come along for the ride. Eighteen years later the formula is unchanged. Turn up on whatever bike you feel like riding. Meet at the "Pub on the Park" in London Fields at around about 8pm. Get hold of a route sheet if you feel the need. Hang around for a while, maybe have a pint. Take in the eclectic mix of riders and bikes that surround you. Talk to others, dispel the myths you've heard, gain reassurance that no matter what, you'll make it eventually. At some indeterminate time, decide you're going to leave. Ride past the pub, under the bridge and continue for 112 miles until you reach the cafe on the beach at Dunwich.

2011 was my first Dunwich Dynamo. I'd read a little bit about it but didn't really know what to expect and bike choice presented me with a quandary. I stood in the garage and interrogated each in turn. The lightweight titanium geared road bike put forward a compelling case including speed, comfort and previous performance on other distance rides. However, she slipped up in failing to convey any passion for the event. All she wanted to do was get the thing over with as fast as possible so that she could preen herself upon the beach. So I turned to the mountain bike, but it was currently off sick, squeaking and groaning in the brake area and struggling to hold air in the forks. My son's Islabike was keen and enthusiastic, but sadly too young for a long night on the road.

This left the Pompino, a fixed geared do-most-things type of bike that only ever seems to come out when the weather is terrible. She raised her eyebrows when I told her of the distance and pointed at her current footwear, knobbly cyclocross tyres. I nodded at the four season slicks adorning the road bike and our pact was formed, Cinderella shall go to the ball.

Bike quandary untangled, I focused on logistics. I live miles from London and had to get to the start. After the ride I had to get home. There is an organised coach service back to London from Dunwich. I'd left it too late to book and needed an alternative. Simple, use the train. Well, it could have been simple but bikes appear to be about as welcome as a stray curry fuelled fart on our modern locomotive network. "Without reservation, carriage of bicycles cannot be guaranteed". I took on reservation websites, call centres, timetables and internet forums in an attempt to make this journey happen. I came out of the other end with a single reservation from Diss in Norfolk to Liverpool Street. Now the car would have to get involved. Long drive to Diss, train to London, long ride to Dunwich, ride to Diss, long drive home. I left a sleeping bag in the car.

Frustrations faded as the hour hand clicked closer to 8 on my watch. I stood twenty yards from the pub in the park, bike leant against my legs, eyes pulled in all directions by the menagerie of cyclists that surrounded me. I've never seen so many different people on different bikes. Every cycling creed was represented as was every race, gender, body shape, haircut and apparel. It was as if the organisers had made a clear attempt to cross match the two in every combination.

- "Rasta guy in jeans on fixed".
- "Fat bloke spilling from lycra on tandem"
- "Chic middle aged lady in woollens on shopper bike"
- "Racing snake, pro-team kit on carbon TT bike"
- "Bearded fellow, total clothing mismatch on recumbent"

The list would be as long as the riders attending. I've never seen such diversity at the start line of a cycle event before. I'm sure it happens elsewhere, but this was new to me. All sorts of thoughts traversed my mind.

"How is she going to keep that skirt out of her chain over the length of the ride?"

"Aren't you supposed to have at least a front brake?"

"Surely that light's going to be as much use as a cake candle when it gets properly dark?"

"Why the potted plant on the back?"

Thing is, the diversity made me feel properly at home. Any subconscious niggles about incorrect attire were dismissed by the smiling faces radiant above kit that pushed new levels of inappropriateness. My bike choice seemed sensible when compared to the bloke who was preparing to borrow a Boris bike for a little longer than the terms and conditions dictated. These weren't racers, or tourists or fakengers or sportive baggers or clubmen or mountain bikers. They were a bunch of cyclists caught up in the event. I could have stood there all evening, chatting, laughing, admiring and earwigging. In fact I probably would have until I realised that nobody was going to fire a gun and set us all off. You leave, when you're ready. At about half past eight I decided I was feeling pretty ready and gently pushed my way through the crowd to begin my bike ride. Others were ready too. A line of flashing red light stretched away from the Pub in the Park. I took my place within the line and followed the light under the bridge away from the start.

The first few miles were about urban survival. Traffic seemed surprised to see us and our line was disrupted by buses, cars and taxis all piloted by quizzical looks. We stopped and started and halted and began and trackstood and weaved our way through the network of lights, junctions and city hazards. Our quest was punctuated by horns, shouts, occasional claps and questions.

"Eeer, what you lot doing then? This some sort of charity ride?"

"We're heading for Dunwich"

"Where?"

"Dunwich"

"No idea where that is mate, farking good luck to yer anyway."

The line held fast though, I had no need to navigate as the flashing red lights showed me the way. I was thankful of this, as urban riding saps the concentration from a country boy like me. Other riders seemed less concerned, a lady on a Hudson engrossed in her headphones tunefully singing along, two old friends catching up after a year apart, the recumbent rider at exhaust level holding his place in the traffic. At Walthamstow the atmosphere dipped. I saw riders abused in the name of Saturday evening entertainment. Newspapers thrown from a bus at the cyclists, a car passenger spraying a rider with drink from a can, verbal abuse and pedestrian threats. But the line took it all in its stride, we rode on as the sun set behind us.

As the city began to fade from my back wheel, I began to establish a rhythm. Ride, chat, look up, swerve a bit, pass other riders, chat some more, ride, pass other riders. The fixed gear kept me at a fairly constant speed, I appeared to pass more than be passed. But who cares, nobody around me did. There was a complete absence of any kind of competitive urge, it seemed accepted that the elements of the flashing red line moved at a variety of speeds. Soon it was late. Darkness enfolded the line and we'd shaken off most of the traffic. It was often hard to tell whose light beams I was riding in, or what I was riding past. I think there might have been some forest, or houses, a bus shelter or a phone box. Shadows rose and died in front of us until we coursed into Epping and my hunger made itself known.

I'd completely forgotten to eat! My body had prioritised sensory overload in front of hunger. It took miles for my stomach to properly find its voice and remind the rest of the system that it hadn't seen food since 5pm. Jersey pockets revealed sparse pickings a result of poor planning, so I left the line and dragged my bike through the door of a 24 hour garage. I emptied their shelves of flapjacks and filled my face with egg sandwich. Leaving the garage I was amazed to see the line intact. Looking up and down the high street it became clear that it went on for miles. I bet we riders dream of flashing rear lights for days beyond the completion of the ride.

Egg sandwiches clearly make singlespeeds go. Rejuvenated I moved from grinding to windmilling, catching riders, sitting on their tail then passing to get to a comfortable pace. The weather system had delivered us a tailwind and with a route devoid of major hills good progress was available for those who wanted it. Past Epping we were out in the country and the line had fragmented into clusters of flashing red as groups formed to co-operate their way through the night.

I rode a few miles on my own, then with a group, then just me after a short climb fragmented us. One thing constant. My smile. I was in love with this ride. Two emotions banged a drum within my head. Adventure, we were out in the night, on our own, riding a hell of a long way on silly bikes for no purpose or reward. Belonging, I genuinely felt part of something, yet I'd never met these people before. Also, this was how I loved to ride, at my pace not a forced pace, riding and feeling great, a winning combination.

I lost myself for miles and miles. I struggle to recall the places I rode through, the riders I rode with or the terrain. The darkness focused my vision onto a small patch in front of my wheel, thoughts narrowed accordingly, I spent long distances with earworms. Forty miles and I was singularly lost in thought when a group of six come hammering by. I join it for company, but the pace is really fast. Really really fast. Windmilling becomes egg beating as I up the cadence to hang on. After a few minutes I adapt to the rhythm and I look at the riders around me.

Sinewy legs, lean torsos, Marmotte jerseys, carbon bikes, concentration and speed. These guys aren't out for a chat, they've got an objective and they're working hard together to get to the sea as fast as they can. I ride with them further, it's exciting. We pass small groups, we hammer through villages, we take turns on the front and regroup at the top of hills. Five miles pass, then eight, then ten. I look at my watch, twenty five minutes! I look at my speedo, we're doing twenty three miles an hour! This isn't really singlespeed pace. Forward projections tell me that seventy more miles of this will hurt too much. I make excuses and slip silently off the back into the darkness and solitude.

Sixty miles and Sudbury. I'm past my bedtime now and feeling the urge to sleep. The last ten miles have been ridden solo with few distractions. My pedalling and breathing are rhythmic, a lullaby effect. Drunken shapes stagger home either side of the road and I attract a wolf whistle. She blew it in irony, but it spurs me forward as I imagine myself a sleek co-ordinated riding sex object parting the night in front of me. In the dark even I can dream.

Sixty four, sixty eight, seventy three, seventy nine, wasn't there a feed station on this ride? Bollocks I've missed it, bollocks bollocks and more bollocks I'm low on water. Plenty of flapjack, but no sodding water. Every streetlight offers some hope as I yearn for an open garage or 24 hour supermarket, but they're all tucked up in bed. I consider ringing a doorbell and pleading for water and am steeling myself to the task when at eighty miles I spy a lit sign.

"Tea. Coffee. Bacon Rolls"

Surely this is a hallucination? I cannot quite believe that the lit tented serving area in the quiet cottage garden really exists. I test the mirage by getting off the bike and feeling for the gate. It's real, as are the family who've done it before and understand the need. They get cash, I get a bacon roll and some tea. There's water here as well with a suggested donation to the Air Ambulance. I drop the change in the bucket and my water problem has gone.

There are other riders here, it's the fast boys. Two of them are Italian, they stare in bemusement at my bike and its logo "Il Pompino", look it up in an Italian dictionary. We joke for a while as only the fatigued can do but the cold is starting to nibble around my edges and I feel the need to ride. I make my excuses and leave. They'll catch me soon and maybe I can ride with them to the end.

It's tight country lanes again, concentrate, concentrate. Fatigue has a real grip and I'm starting to make mistakes. I pep talk myself. "You've come this far Dave, don't f**k it up". Something's not right at the back, please no .. not on the fixed! It's a puncture. All my warmth, rhythm and a small portion of my sanity is lost as I stop and get out the spanners. I have to pep talk again. "Dave, slow down, do it right, you DON'T want to have to repeat the process up the road". I really struggle for patience as the back wheel is fumbled off a reluctant chain. Thankfully the culprit is a thorn. Slowly, deliberately I reverse the process. The fast boys, speed past, offering assistance. I wave them on up the road, gutted, there goes my lift to the end!

Morale is re-inflated along with my tyre which stays up. It's really bloody quiet, where are all the other riders? I get back on the bike and look at my watch. 1:44am and thirty miles to go. It's possible, I could watch the sun rise from the beach. I'd gone to this ride with no objectives other than to finish, but a sunrise. Irresistible.

I spin up the legs and take full advantage of the new vigour. More miles disappear as I'm occupied by calculations. When do I think the sun will rise? How fast must I average? Bloody hell look at that moon!

A striking silhouette forces me to stop. A moonlit church looks benevolently down on the road. The moon hangs in clear skies and aches to be photographed. I park the objective for a few minutes and try desperately to do justice to the scene with a compact camera. I fail, this fatigue is not conducive to complex night photography. Simple tasks like pedalling a fixed gear bike are all that my brain can cope with, so I return to that. More riding, more concentration then from nowhere a flash! I have no idea where but someone has taken my photograph and shouted something at me. I haven't a clue who, or what, surely not a speed camera?

Less than ten miles to go and the roads have narrowed. Singletrack country lanes lead me closer and closer to the sea. I have to slow a bit as the surfaces vary, a pot hole here, some stray hedge there and a section of wet sand that the slick tyres are not at all happy about. Still no other riders? I'm concerned that I've gone wrong but tracks in the sand offer some reassurance.

Darsham, less than five miles to the sea. I'm overtaken by excitement. I can bloody walk five miles if I have to but there's no question, I'm going to finish the ride. My systems have coped with over one hundred miles and they don't shy from telling me. The objective wins the shouting match though. "Dave, get there before the sun, only five miles, I reckon you have it in you mate".

Pedal pedal pedal pedal, Westleton, pedal pedal pedal pedal, Dunwich Heath sign, pedal pedal, Dunwich beach sign, pedal pedal, round a corner and there it is. A car park. Hang on, it's still dark, I squint and can see a beach. I look to my right and can see a huge great cafe, that's open and has bikes leaning against it. I've ridden the Dunwich Dynamo, it's still dark and I've achieved my secondary objective of watching the sunrise. In fact I've been a bit of a pillock really as there's at least another hour to go until it comes up and I could have ambled along instead of riding like a loon.

The cafe is full of smiles, which is pretty unique seeing as it's half past three in the morning. There's a scattering of riders hunched over coffee and breakfast, they're currently outnumbered by staff in preparation for the rest of the "line" who'll all pay a visit in due course. I'm one of the first to arrive, purely down to the fast bunch who picked me up and dropped me off at a point that I would never have reached under my own steam. We sit and reflect. There's no talk of times, speeds, performance or averages. Instead we trade views of the moon, bat stories, traffic incidents, sandy road frustrations and interesting bikes spotted.

I'm feeling more at home than ever. This ride has changed me and my outlook on the bike. I realise that my performance logs need a review. The columns with numbers in must be removed and replaced with "experiences", because that is what the Dunwich Dynamo is. The ride is simply one huge great experience. The gathering of eclectic cyclists at the start, the twilight fight with the city, the line of flashing red lights, the quiet lanes in the dead of night, the distance and the way you decide to attack it and the early morning seaside ending replete with breakfast.

I left the cafe as the sun rose above the beach. I reached for my camera then pushed it back into my pocket. This experience was for the memory bank alone, the lens would capture the light, but leave the emotion outside. It could have been a long hard ride back to Diss, bit it wasn't, I was giggling all the way.

Chapter 28

Motivation

In the 1990's a terrible thing happened to British Television. This decade proved to be the advent of mainstream breakfast TV. Television can be dire at the best of times as reality TV programmes suck the creative lifeblood from a nation and soap operas add interest by exploding airplanes above idyllic northern villages that were interesting enough as they were.

In my view breakfast TV was the start of the invasion of moronity into the UK household. These programmes were supposed to cover current affairs but after they'd run out of proper news they would turn their attention to other aspects of British life in the same way that Esther Rantzen used to relish carrots shaped like men's willies.

Some bright spark came up with the idea of a daily fitness regime for their viewers and my generation suffered hugely as we'd turn on our TV to be greeted by Mad Lizzie or even worse Mr Motivator. These two cheery souls would dance up and down in front of us screaming into the camera for all to take part. The thought that certain households partook still haunts my mind. I can't contemplate the horror of coming down the stairs to my cornflakes only to spot my Mum and Dad in green leotards grinding away in unison to some lunatic on the TV.

Mr Motivator would illicit you to lose some weight by dressing in skin tight lycra and implying that if you jiggled in time you too could look like him. Personally I think this strategy is flawed. These days I am as lean as a sprat and regularly dress in skin tight lycra then jiggle round the block on my bike. I have yet to receive any feedback from local residents that they would like to look like me. No DVD has been made of my workout series and a nation of women have decided they prefer six packs instead.

Mr Motivator could have cut his five minute workout sessions to thirty seconds. All that would have been required is for the viewer to fetch a mirror and then undress. They would have stood in front of it, and the lycra clad presenter would collapse laughing on screen at their folds. Then after 29 seconds of laughing he would stand up and show them a picture of a bike.

I know that this works, trust me! Having lost the weight the simple reoccurrence of any love handle inference sends me flying out the door and onto the road. Strangely I find fat hugely motivating and have noticed that as soon as I reach an ideal weight the hand will enter the cookie jar and the riding frequency will drop. I don't need Mr Motivator to tell me to ride, my waistline does it instead and as a result I regularly yoyo between famine victim and skinny bloke with a gut.

Thankfully the Breakfast TV workouts are now a thing of the past. They have been replaced with dour forecasts of stock market crashes or extreme weather fronts that will bring the country to a stop. It's almost as if the TV producers have turned full circle and their strategy is to convince us to end it all now while we can. Mr Motivator has moved back to Jamaica where he still ardently follows Bristol Rovers from afar. It appears that he also has a masochistic streak.

Not Being Arsed

I've just had another one of "those" days, all of us cyclists have them. It's a day when you know you "should" go riding, but the motivation is just not quite there. Your will to "get out and turn pedals" is sapped away by a number of malignant influences; the brooding dark cloud base, the unfinished work task list, the slow puncture you have been meaning to fix, the confectionary fix tempting you from the store-cupboard and quite often the simple fact that you just cannot be arsed.

I found myself in exactly this position last night, six o'clock in the evening staring out of the window at brooding clouds and pondering decimating the large slab of Dairy Milk cowering in the larder downstairs. Eventually, after flicking through the excuse list, I arrived at "can't be arsed" and felt a sense of liberation that I'd decided upon the worst possible excuse of all. I leaned back in my chair, clasped hands behind my head and stared out of the window whilst considering what to expend the next few hours upon given that I couldn't be arsed to go cycling. I thought of all of the unfinished work projects, but it was late and I couldn't be arsed to think about them any more.

I wondered if it would be worth cleaning the road bike, but I'd get all wet doing that, and couldn't be arsed to change my clothes. I pondered making a cake or something, but I'd have to go to Co-op and the women with smelly pits would be on the basket checkout, and I couldn't be arsed getting another whiff of them. So, my mind flicked to the chocolate, I'd eat that, but then I'd feel fat and guilty and I'd have to go for a ride and as you are now painfully aware, I couldn't be arsed to do that.

Suddenly it was all getting a bit too much, not being arsed to go for a ride meant that I also couldn't be arsed to do anything else, and this caused it's own set of problems, in that I'd end up watching the One Show or desperately trying to find something of real interest on Facebook.

Panic set in and suddenly the whole reason for not going for a ride, was the reason I shot out of my chair and decided to go for a ride. Decision made, I went to my bedroom and fought my wardrobe into submission when it finally gave up my mountain biking clobber. Then it was downstairs to take the Camelback bladder out of the freezer, then back upstairs to put in some contact lenses. I set off down the stairs and out of the front door to get the bike out of the garage. Then back in, and upstairs to get my garage keys out of my office. A quick trip back to the garage revealed the bike was locked, so back in and upstairs again to get the lock keys.

Finally the bike was liberated from the garage, along with my Camelback. But a cursory inspection revealed that there was nothing in it. I remembered putting the tools, pump and tube in a daysack last holiday. So, back up the stairs into the attic to retrieve the sack. Downstairs a search of the sack came up with a complete lack of cycling gear. I then remembered that, I had thought about this on return from holiday and the offending items were in my kayak dry bag (why?). Off to the kitchen where this had been dumped and back out to the garage. Things were now looking good as I had most of the requirements for a bike ride assembled in front of me. Apart from some sunglasses. Back upstairs, into the office and these were retrieved. The fourth trip to the garage was almost the last, until I remembered my Camelback, defrosting in the kitchen sink, and my mobile phone, and my gps and a waterproof (dark brooding cloud remember).

Luckily, I was home alone. But I'm sure the neighbours were wondering why on earth the bloke next door kept going into his garage, shouting "for fucks sake", returning to the house and slamming doors. Twenty minutes after deciding that "not being arsed" was a poor option. I pedalled off up the road in an unbelievably bad mood, totally resentful of my bike, the lot of a disorganised cyclist, and the genes that expand my waist drastically without extreme levels of exercise.

But you know what? Within ten minutes of leaving, it had all evaporated away, left behind in the twisty corners of the Croft mountain bike trails. In the fading sun I had the place to myself. The ground was dry and the trail builders had been busy ensuring that even a talentless, jey, lightweight like me could feel adequate riding a mountain bike. I left Croft and headed up onto the Wiltshire Ridgeway, it was windy and my legs hurt, but I couldn't be arsed to stop and rest them. I just couldn't be arsed to do anything other than ride my bike in solitude and beautiful countryside.

So, yes, I've had another one of those days. Where initially I couldn't be arsed to ride my bike but did. And it all ended well. I'm sure I've had days like that before and in fact I'm sure they always ended well, as well.

The evidence seems to suggest that not being arsed to ride should actually be the catalyst that springs me onto the bike, as somehow the not being arsed'ness adds an extra dimension to the ride.

Chapter 29

The Great British Bike Ride (2001)

20 years ago at the age of fifteen my parents bought me my first "proper" road bike for my birthday. A Raleigh Carlton, I'll never forget it, red, light, fast ... I loved that bike. It was stolen from my Halls of Residence in London five years later and if I'd felt like I feel about cycling today I would have remembered the sense of loss. Truth is, 15 years ago I didn't care. However, 20 years ago I was an avid reader of "Bicycle" magazine, I loved the articles about cycle touring, new bike components and all of the latest gear. Most of all I remember reading about the "Great British Bicycle Ride - Land's End to John O'Groats" I always wondered whether I could make that ride.

I left my youthful love of cycling to follow a more conventional route of growing up, the curriculum included plenty of smoking, drinking, laying about and general apathy far removed from the back roads of Wiltshire where I had formally cut my cycling wings. I went from cycling to school, to hitching to the pub, Sundays in the hills to a game of pool in The Mallard.

It catches up with you in the end. University, job, marriage, kids, led to 30 years old,.. I played squash and football, but the gut grew larger, at 12.5 stone, I discovered running,.. I couldn't get enough of it. 4k races led to 10k's led to 10 miles, led to half marathons, led to 22 mile cross country races up and down Devon hillsides and across shingle beaches, until a bad tackle in a game of five a side football led to the surgeons table, and my retirement from distance running, sans 1/3 of the cartilage in my right knee. Finally I rediscovered cycling, Mountain biking to be exact, and in true character I threw myself at the Wiltshire downs, rapidly purchasing and upgrading bikes and pushing my own fitness and performance as hard as I could.

Cue midlife crisis, two kids, a comfortable job and a holiday in the USA on my own, biking across the slickrock of Utah. 5 days into the holiday I hiked on my own into "Negro Bill Canyon" on a beautiful sunny day, and listened to the buzzing of the insects as the canyon brook lazily ambled beside me. The insect's voices were loud, they spoke in unison,"Dave, go home, give up your comfortable job, do something different, you won't regret it". So I did. On April 17th 2001 I resigned from a well paid job and decided that my next objective was to ride from Land's End to John O'Groats, a dream I'd pushed to the back of my mind since the age of 15. This is the story of my ride.

Preparation

Deciding to do the ride in April is all well and good, but the warning lights in the fatigue nodules of my brain were telling me that I hadn't cycled more than 30 miles in a day for over a year, and the "End to End" is at least 870 miles long. So I'd better think about some training. I stuck some road tyres on (one of) my mountain bike(s) and started getting used to riding on the roads, the exercise was good and it made a change to get home not covered head to toe in mud, but something wasn't right, I needed a road bike. After months of careful research I decided that the bike for me was a Dawes Galaxy, a classic tourer.

So typically with a rational head on I allowed a local cycle retailer to talk me into a Dawes Giro 500 race bike, aluminium frame, close gear ratios, no small front chain rings, no rack hangers, no mudguards. About as suitable for 1000 miles cycling as a Raleigh Chopper, but what the hell, this was my End to End. Fortunately the Giro was an excellent training machine, and May to July saw me hammering up and down the Marlborough Downs looking for the steepest hills and most scenic training routes. I found villages a few miles from where I grew up, who'd spent years hiding from me. OS Landranger 173 became my personal friend as I sought variety and diversity from my regular weekend rides. My cycling log shows that every week I rode at least 100 miles, some weeks I rode 150 and in the last week in July I rode 55 miles every day, each ride taking less than 3.5 hours.

That's training covered, but there was a whole host of other activities required to get Dave's show on the road. I planned to do the ride supported up until the "Scottish legs", meaning that my wife (Helen) and kids would follow me in our camper van, setting up at pre-booked campsites every night and helping out in the event of any mechanicals. At Scotland, Helen would leave me for a few days to visit an old friend. I would then continue using bed and breakfast accommodation until Inverness, where we had planned to meet up and finish the ride.

So, I sat down and started to figure out a route, immediately discounting the standard "A road" dash up the A30, A38, A6, A7, A9. I joined the CTC and received a copy of their scenic/B&B routes, but remained un-inspired. Finally, I found "Land's End to John O'Groats The

Great British Bike Adventure" by Phil Horsley, a tenner was despatched to Amazon and I had my route. Phil's book describes a backroads route broadly as follows:- Cornish North Coast Devon/Somerset by backroads Bristol, cross Severn Bridge to Monmouth Welsh Borders/Shropshire West Coast, North country Lake District Carlisle/Dumfries/Ayshire Aran, Mull of Kintyre Oban - Great Glen East Coast to John O'Groats

The route looked interesting, many points of interest were documented and most of all it took me to parts of the country I hadn't seen before .... Sold ! However, the maps were appalling so I decided to rectify the situation with Ordnance Survey maps, pre-marked as a backup. That was until I realised I would need nearly 40 maps, at a cost of well over 200 quid. I ended up making my own route maps by downloading "clips" from a mapping website and pasting them together to make my own maps, printing them out using my trusty HP Deskjet colour printer.

I found that at a scale of 1:50000, 10 sides of A4 would cover about 100 miles worth of cycling, I printed each map single sided, stuck two sides together and laminated the map using clear self adhesive plastic covering bought from an office supplies store. This took nearly 2 solid days of cutting/pasting/printing/annotating/laminating ... and of course, I left it until the last minute. My ride was planned to last 10 days, and each day would see me carrying no more than 6 A4 maps, each pre-marked with my route, much better than 2-4 folded un-laminated OS maps. In hindsight it would have been sensible to also carry a 1:250000 scale map, just in case I needed to vary the route for any reason. Now for the bike, as I stated earlier I did all of my training on a Dawes Giro 500 road racing bike, with a 52, 44 front chainset and 11-28 rear. Having done the maps and looked at some of the Cornish/Devon gradients, I became a bit concerned about my poor legs given the lack of "granny" gears available to me.

So the day before the ride, in a moment of pure Barter bodge brilliance, I lifted the front and rear gears from my mountain bike and installed them upon the Giro. The local bike shop assured me that this wouldn't work, I was told that I would need (at least) a new front mech, a new bottom bracket, new shifters, and a new chain ... rubbish, with a bit of tinkering it all worked (until the Lake District that is). Finally I started to look at luggage, the stages with my wife in support would not be a problem, all I needed was a bar bag big enough to carry food, tools, maps and a waterproof. My Altura Bar Bag fitted the bill perfectly (until Devon).

My Dawes does not have any pannier fixings, so I purchased a Carradice TRS saddlebag for the B&B leg, I can't tell how well it performed as I never used it. On an incredibly hectic Tuesday August 7th the Camper Van was stuffed full of clothes, food, bike bits, toys, kids, maps and duvets and we dashed off to Land's End arriving at our campsite somewhere near 5pm.

Prelude to Day 1

At 11am the day before, I told Helen that I didn't feel that well, "Nerves" she said, I knew it was something else. I had some sort of stomach virus and felt tired, ill, bloated and generally not up to getting on a "Heath Robinson" tourer and caning the hills of Cornwall the next day. I think my moaning started at about 1pm and reached a crescendo at 8-9pm that evening, with talk of delaying the ride, reducing the distance, packing it all in, and other assorted negativity and general self centred self pity. I didn't sleep very well that night and woke up feeling just as bad, the moaning and whinging started with a new vigour, quickly quelled by the swift reaction of two young children (Jake and Holly) who assessed the situation and decided to distract Dad by being as naughty as possible.

Day 1 - Land's End to Camelford

The plan was to get up early and set off at 9am, ... At 9.45am our camper van pulled into Land's End and we lined Peter de Savary's pockets with another £3. I carried out the final checks on the bike and suddenly realised I did not know how to reset my bike odometer, how would I track my daily mileage. More shouting, swearing, moaning and frantic button pressing finally culminated in 5 zeros showing on the trip meter. The computer was plugged in and I was ready to go.

I took my CTC record sheet to the hotel reception and gained my first "stamp", the receptionist hardly batted an eyelid, but I knew she was secretly applauding the fitness and gallantry of the handsome young cyclist stood before her, preparing to throw himself at everything Britain had to offer. Then it was time for the "leaving" photo. I couldn't be bothered to find the corny multi-limbed signpost, so Helen took an equally corny shot of me crossing the START line. The sun was out,... I was off. I started up the A30, but soon departed for the back roads of the north Cornish Coast, a beautifully scenic ride through St Just, Pendeen and up to St Ives.

I stopped to take a self portrait at Zennor and was embarrassed to be caught posing by a lone pedestrian who appeared from nowhere. To make matters worse the end result was out of focus and poorly framed. St. Ives proved interesting as I managed to get myself a bit lost in the town centre, but was soon put back on track by a grizzled old local lady waiting for a bus. Just before Hayle I stopped to look at the map. "Is that one of the new aluminium Dawes bikes" I heard from behind a tree, and out stepped the most eccentric looking road cyclist I have ever seen, his hair defying gravity and any form of style. He enthused about my bike for a few minutes and then proceeded to warn me of the perils of street furniture in Hayle. I set off on my merry way with his warnings front of mind, and was not surprised to travel through Hayle without sighting a single bollard or speed bump.

I enjoyed the climb up to Portreath and relished a banana break whilst sat on a typically Cornish stone wall. The rollercoaster ride of hills and troughs continued as I made steady progress towards St. Agnes. At Towan Cross my home made maps let me down as I realised that a couple of miles of the route had not made it onto the paper. An incredibly helpful gardener soon put me right, and then for some reason informed me of his stint working in Israel for El Al. Perranporth came and went as did Goonhaven and I soon found myself sat down for lunch in a supermarket café just outside of Newquay. Entertainment was laid on by the two "skateboardy" youths at the table next to me who spent hours perfecting their roll up cigarettes only to set fire to them when finished.

I still felt a bit ropey and decided to take a direct route to Padstow along the "A" roads, soon I was gliding past my old school (Padstow junior school, now a series of offices) and onto the harbour side, which was absolutely heaving with tourists. At Padstow I decided to take the ferry over to Rock, rather than risk the Camelford trail cycle track, which whilst scenic is also a bit rough and rocky providing me with visions of buckled wheels and pinch flats. I waited 45 minutes for the tide to rise enough for the ferry and swiftly crossed the Camel estuary, chatting to a pleasant couple from London on the way. He asked me how many years training I had put into the ride!

I think he was a bit surprised when I replied "3 months"... suddenly I was a bit worried. At Rock I quickly accelerated away from all of the "poshos" hanging round the sailing dinghies and headed up the hill towards Camelford. An enjoyable B road took me all the way to the campsite for the night, where I found the crew just about ready for me. The first day had been 85 miles in total, I felt pretty good and had averaged over 14 miles per hour.

Day 2 - Camelford to Taunton

I remember the morning of Day 2 being one of the strangest psychological moments of the ride, the reason being that I had no idea how my body would feel after the previous day's exertions. As I climbed out of bed the news was good, legs a little stiff but otherwise I felt like I wanted to get back on the bike. The weather certainly didn't seem to promise much and it had rained fairly heavily during the night, so I wolfed down 3 bowls of cereal, 2 bananas, packed my bar bag with food and set off into the drizzle. The journey towards Launceston was fairly boring, consisting of main roads up until Egloskerry, then the fun started with an excellent diversion down (and up and down and up!) a single track backroad into Launceston.

Halfway along I paid the price of my gear tampering and snapped my chain. However, I was fully prepared (and practised) and only lost 10 minutes to the roadside repair. After Launceston the heavens opened, and unrelenting rain accompanied me along absorbing minor roads to Bratton Clovelly, after which I followed the A3079 to Okehampton, where disaster struck. I noticed that my bar bag had sagged a little and was rubbing on the front wheel. Stupidly I tried to forcibly correct this with the bag mounted in its bracket, forgetting that the bracket was plastic. Of course the bracket snapped under the strain, and passing motorists wondered why the lone wet cyclist was jumping up and down on the verge making frantic "V" signs at a black object lying useless on the ground.

The problem with breaking the bracket was that I had to find some way of attaching the bag to the bike. It weighed a couple of kilos and would not sit well on my back. I managed to "sort of" strap it to the handlebars which would last about 10 miles or so before requiring readjustment. On reaching Okehampton I telephoned a local cycle shop, who patiently listened to my ramblings before calmly advising that there was no way at all that they could help. I think they built up a mental picture of this mad, wet, incoherent lunatic brandishing a heavy black sack....and simply decided they didn't want him anywhere near their shop. A panic call to Helen established that she was too far away to help, and thus was despatched to Halfords to purchase a new bag for the remainder of the trip.

I continued my sodden way up through Devon, arriving in Crediton hungry. Sandwiches were purchased from the local "Spar" who will regret making me wait 10 minutes (lunchtime, one cashier, when will they ever learn) as I created my own mini Atlantic in their aisle. It was at this point that I noticed how badly I smelled! The exertions had taken their toll and armpit and other odours made their way from under my waterproofs to the outside world. "Cyclists and winos unite!", I thought to myself, "Pigpen is our leader".

I repaired to a local bus shelter to eat my lunch, accompanied by a trio of teenage "text messenger" babes, who sat frantically manipulating their Nokias in search of last night's gossip. With perfect timing I slipped right on my arse chucking my sandwich wrappers in the bin. Stifled giggles melted into howls of laughter as I picked up my bike, pride and toddled off towards Cullompton. The rain abated for a while and I almost enjoyed the next section of minor roads and steep hills passing through Thorverton, Stumpy Cross and Worth.

At Silverton Mill I came across "white van man" at a junction, stereo on full blast, mobile phone glued to left ear and one hand gently stroking the steering wheel. Luckily he missed me, but I'm convinced I heard a skid followed by a crash as he sped round the corner. Having no sympathy whatsoever, I convinced myself I had imagined it and carried on. The backroads unfortunately gave way to the A38, and I suffered 18 miles of wind, rain and speeding motorists before the centre of Taunton was gained. I got there at about 5.40pm ... rush hour and learnt new cycle courier skills as I weaved my way through the impatient commuters.

Eventually the "Tanpits Cider Farm" came into view and I rode up to the van to receive an enthusiastic welcome from Jake and Holly. Ten minutes later I was pushing them both on swings at the local play park whilst Helen cooked tea. It had been a long day, 95 miles in total, I'd been on the road from 9am till 6pm, my backside hurt and I was very very wet. To make matters worse, the bar bag Helen had bought from Halfords was missing parts. So tomorrow I had to travel with a rucksack on my back. However, tomorrow promised Somerset, which is flat.

Day 3 - Taunton to Monmouth

The weather promised a bit more this morning as the previous day's clouds had given way to warm sunshine and hardly any cloud. I managed another relatively early start (9.30am) and soon got shot of the Taunton metropolis, easing myself along the flat roads of North Curry. The scenery was delightful as I rode past canals, rivers and elderly folk washing their cars (I reckon the average Honda Civic is scrapped not from engine wear but "overwashing" by elderly people). Unbelievably flat roads took me all the way to Pedwell, however, two days in the hills had sapped my legs a little and I didn't feel that I was making the progress the terrain deserved. Things became worse towards Shapwick as contrary to my predictions I encountered some hills.

Climbing to the top, I stopped for a drink and got out the camera to take a photo, perfectly on cue six Hercules aircraft appeared above my head and dipped their wings towards me. I'd like to believe that they were saluting the courage of a solitary "End to Ender" but actually think they

185

were practising some sort of top secret airforce manoeuvre designed to confuse enemy cyclists in times of war. The weather stayed with me to Cheddar and I enjoyed a grand view of the Somerset moors from Winscombe hill. From then on it was backroads battling on to Gordano where (typically) I struggled to find the cycle path over the Avon bridge.

The ride over the bridge was an experience in its own right, I couldn't believe just how much road bridges move and shudder under the stress of the traffic hammering over them. I have to confess that I was relieved to get off it, it felt like at any moment the huge structure would shake itself to pieces and come crashing to the ground. A skirt round (or more accurately up and down) Bristol took me to Hallen where I popped into a small newsagents to buy a sandwich.

In conversation with the shop owner, I established that he was the nephew of (insert name of venerable record holder here) the record holder for the Land's End to John O'Groats walk. I think he said it took 48 days walking 20 hours a day and that his Uncle disputed any improvements upon his time as they'd cheated and taken a shorter route, or they hadn't walked continuously

I dragged myself from the fascinating conversation and sat in the most miserable lunch spot ever, a derelict driveway, with a view of a factory smelling of sulphur and silage. The old Severn bridge was conquered next, and I noted much to my displeasure that it moved even more than its cousin over the Avon. Additionally the wind flew across its spans adding to ground friction and gravity's attempts to heed my progress. Next came Chepstow and the racecourse followed by a foolish decision to climb up to Trellech, which involved a whole load of very steep hills designed especially to depress the cyclist about to end a long day's grind. One further hour of swearing later I descended into our glorious campsite at Mitchell Troy.

Day 4 - Mitchell Troy to Ellesmere

The night before I confided in Helen that tomorrow might be difficult as it looked like I had to cover 110 miles or so to get to our next campsite. Additionally I was not too sure of the terrain and equally unsure of my legs and stamina. I was subliminally warning her that I would be substantially late for supper. Consequently I woke at 7.15 ingested 3 bowls of cereal and dashed away from the campsite before Helen or the kids had a chance to stir. I managed to get a full mile down the road before the bike needed adjusting (loose pedal clips) and a further 10 miles to Skenfrith before the front derailleur completely refused to cooperate in any manner whatsoever.

I can't remember the name of the pub in Skenfrith, but I'm sure the residents will not forget the idiot cyclist weaving round and round their car park frantically fiddling with his gear levers. Eventually I managed to get them "sort of" working and continued on into the persistent Welsh drizzle. The Landscape whimpered rather then screamed out as I eked my way up the Welsh borders through Grosmont, Pontrilas, Abbey Dore, Peterchurch and Eardisley. I stopped for an energy bar at a pub on a cross roads with a trio of bikers for company. They adjusted racing leathers, tweaked helmets and compared tank shine whilst I squelched across the car park in soggy lycra and a grease streaked Altus jacket.

From my pocket I defiantly flicked two fingers at the bikers and departed just as the drizzle gave way to everso slightly brighter weather and even a little sun. At Brampton Bryan I came across the strangest village fete, which seemed to consist of locals running round with clipboards searching for things whilst poorly crafted mannequins looked on. Typically I picked the one American tourist to ask what was going on, and equally typically it took her about a novel to tell me that she didn't know.

The improved weather heightened my pace and I quickly despatched Bucknell, Lydbury North and Church Stoke and stuck the head firmly down for the grind onto Ellesmere. Stopping only to chat with a farmer at Argoed (little choice actually as he blocked the road with his cows). I made Ellesmere by 6.30pm.

I must admit that this was one of the high points of the whole ride, I'd ridden 122 miles and actually felt good at the end of the day, I'd averaged over 15 miles an hour when on the bike and only got lost once. The campsite was dreadful, a scrap of land stuffed behind a grotty pub, additionally, it started to rain again. Later that evening, Helen's sister Sara joined us bolstering the support crew to 4, little did we know that her services would prove indispensable over the next couple of days.

Day 5 - Ellesmere to Yealand

Another furtive breakfast shoved down in the van whilst trying not to wake Helen or the kids and the earliest start of the campaign saw me leaving at 8am sharp. I left the campsite for Pentire to rejoin the "book route" but dithered for over 30 minutes trying to chose one of three junctions to set me on my way proper. The ride through Threapwood,

Beeston, Tarporley, Delamere and Hatchmere was uneventful and I ventured into Frodsham looking for the cycle path that would take me through Runcorn, Widnes and Warrington.

I finally found it after several further moments of indecision and hoiked the bike up onto it only to ride through the deepest cycle path puddle in the country. I don't know what was in the puddle, or whether it was just the worst ever case of "pinch flat" but I managed to burst both of my inner tubes and rip the front tyre. The entire New English Dictionary of curses was orated under a sodden railway bridge after 3 failed attempts to fix the punctures in driving rain. Eventually I managed to get both tyres inflated (I hadn't spotted the ripped front tyre) and continued along the cycle path clutching Phil Horsley's increasingly sodden book in my left hand.

It was at this point that I discovered that Phil's skills clearly lay in route finding and description whilst he was severely lacking in the cartography department. The directions were impossible to follow (for a gibbon like me) and I became increasingly more frustrated and lost. Phil, if you ever manage to read this, I would be more than happy to spend another summer adding some descriptive text to your maps, that phrase about a picture and a thousand words does not apply to town centre navigation.

Eventually I stumbled over the Runcorn bridge and had my bacon saved by a passing mountain biker who stopped me heading away from Warrington rather than towards it. But still I got further confused/lost/panicked until the moment was saved by my front inner tube exploding once more. Tired and frustrated I pulled it from the tyre, but the situation was hopeless as a half inch gash stared back at me, I had no other spares and finally I noticed the corresponding half inch gash in the tyre.

To make matters worse, it was Sunday and all of the bike shops would definitely be closed. At my lowest ebb yet, I called Helen, she was over 2 ½ hours away in Charnock Richard Service Station on the M6. Thankfully she agreed to come back along with spare tyres and inner tubes. This still left me in a bit of a pickle as the time was 1pm, it got dark at 8.30pm, I was at least 70 miles away from that evening's destination, however we decided to make the attempt.

The kids were unceremoniously dumped upon Auntie Sara and Helen dived into the van and gave it all she had. I sat beside the A574 for nearly 3 hours waiting for Helen (who had been caught in traffic), in steadily worsening rain with only a cycling jacket for protection. Whilst waiting for her I carried out all sorts of mental arithmetical gymnastics, calculating average speeds required in order to be done before dark. Helen eventually arrived and I broke the North English record for tube/tyre changes and light bodging onto bike.

A quick kiss and I was off again at 3.45pm, the scenic route was torn up and I decide to head for the A6 and make the best time I possibly could. I headed towards Warrington and was immediately cut up on a roundabout by an over zealous motorist. The hours of waiting and frustration caught up with me and I'm afraid the middle finger was extended, not a good move as he came back. With sheeting rain and terrible driving conditions, he pulled up alongside me and deftly flicked the switch to lower the passenger side window.

I heard some muffled northern expletives and then turned my face towards him. I had not shaved for 4 days, I was covered in oil, my eyes were red from fatigue and tinged with the sort of "devil may care" madness that comes with 3 punctures. Basically I didn't have to say a word, he looked at me, deftly pressed his button again and beat a hasty retreat ahead of me. Luckily he wasn't able to smell me as well. I took the direct route to Preston, trying to avoid the major towns, and punctured once again at Garswood.

This time I was prepared and the repair held through the unrelenting rain up towards Preston. A climb at Appley Bridge dented progress a bit, but otherwise I was flying along at an average speed in excess of 15 miles per hour. Eventually Preston was gained, as were the dual carriageways that make up the ring road, Phil Horsley had detailed a cycle path route across the town, but I didn't trust him any more so I simply followed the signs to the A6.

This caused a number of hairy moments, particularly when the dual carriageway I was following met another, and I found myself trying to filter left across traffic merging at 70 miles per hour, in the pouring rain! The centre of Preston dragged on and on until, voila! I found the left turning onto the A6, along with the sign informing me of another 34 miles to go until Lancaster.

I phoned Helen, "How far on from Lancaster is the campsite?", I casually enquired, "About 10-15 miles", she equally casually replied, "Oh f****ng b*ll**ksing h*ll", I wittily replied and threw myself back onto the bike. The reader may be interested to note the I had recently finished a book on cycling training that talked about "visualisation" as a powerful mental tool for improving ones performance, additionally I was part way through Lance Armstrong's autobiography including his graphic descriptions of how he bounced back from cancer to win 3 Tour de France's.

So the head went down and I became Lance. That ride up the A6 was easily the fastest and hardest of my cycling career to date, I didn't stop once and powered the bike in the lowest gears concentrating on eating miles and beating the dark. I completely forgot the rain, the traffic and the uncomfortable sensation breeding in my right knee, I pedalled like mad. At about 8.20pm I got to the top of a steep hill very close to the campsite, my energy completely spent.

I was so tired that I called Helen to make ABSOLUTELY sure the campsite was at the bottom of it, as I had no intention of retracing my steps (or revolutions) were they to be incorrect. At 8.30pm I fell into the van, cold, wet tired, hungry, yet strangely elated that we had managed to overcome the difficulties and kept on schedule. I ate, showered and collapsed into bed proudly wearing my "most fatigued cyclist in England today" medal. We had decided that tomorrow would be a short ride and I consequently didn't bother to set any mental alarms.

Day 6 - Yealand to Carlisle

I awoke to the usual rain, but none of the usual haste as I had decided to take it easy for the day (I must admit I was even considering not cycling at all). After the usual fight for space at the van breakfast table, I wandered up to the farm for a wash and got speaking to the campsite proprietor, Mrs Clarke. She was an absolute gem, very interested in the ride and when she heard I was doing it for charity refused to accept payment for the night's camping (bear in mind they were farmers in the middle of the foot and mouth crisis). A few minutes later she tracked me down after listening to the local radio, a presenter had been boasting about his training efforts for a 30 mile sponsored ride. Mrs Clarke would have none of it. "30 miles !

I'm ringing him to tell him about the young lad camped in my back yard who does 100 every day" Later on I passed by her front door to thank her once again and say "goodbye", I didn't get a chance as I heard her on the phone ..." B A R T E R" she bellowed, "yes, 100 miles a DAY ! He'll be in yellow,......yes yellow Y E L L O W .. it's for CHARITY....". I had terrible visions of being stopped halfway though the Lake District by a local radio outside broadcast crew desperate for the hottest story of the day. As it happened nobody even waved.

I decided to push on, and the support crew were instructed to meet me at Ambleside for lunch and a quick review of my legs. I set off into the drizzle and immediately my right knee began to complain, very loudly. The previous day's exertions had taken their toll and I had done something nasty to the ligaments below my right knee. I'd had this before when cross country running, and unfortunately the only cure had been a couple of weeks rest. I stopped and adjusted the saddle height in an attempt to ease the pain, no good. Stupidly I did some mental arithmetic, I stood to raise over £800 if I finished this ride, in hindsight a terrible mistake as I now had a real sense of commitment to the charity.

I thought to myself, "keep going,.. it may be one of those injuries that simply goes away", and with that thought I trundled on. Until Levens

Bridge that is, where my over stressed front derailleur finally gave into the rigours of stretching out to my mountain bike chainring, and bent. No matter how much I fiddled and tweaked (and swore) I could not fix it, so I removed it completely and changed gear by hand, stopping at the top and bottom of hills to manually shift the chain from small to big rings. My only hope was Ambleside, the Lake District sees a lot of mountain bikers and I knew there would be a couple of bike shops, hopefully containing mechanics with a sense of humour.

Despite the weather and the knee, I really enjoyed the ride into the Lake District, as the scenery became ever more rugged and the gradients began to meander again. The Windermere ferry provided a welcome break as I crossed the water and headed up the hill to Hawkshead. A quick dash into an Off License replenished my energy drink stocks and before I knew it I was outside Biketreks in a rain sodden Ambleside. I dragged the bike into the shop and launched into a blubbering spiel containing; charity, Land's End, making Carlisle by nightfall and hybrid road bike gears. The kind but confused mechanics agreed to help, but after looking at the Mountain Bike chainset stuffed onto the road racing bike, informed me that it would take a couple of hours at least to fix.

I made contact with the support crew and we agreed to meet for lunch, meanwhile I spent the best portion of £60 on new tyres, inner tubes and various other bike bits and bobs. Helen, Sara and the kids turned up and we repaired to a local tea shop for toasted sandwiches and tea. A few hours later, in trepidation, I walked into the bike shop. They had fixed it, but the repair was slightly "Heath Robinson" with "not quite the right, but they'll do" gears attached to the bike. The support crew were despatched to Carlisle to find accommodation, and a weary, wet, smelly, dirty cycling type thing pushed off out of Ambleside. With ever descending clouds I came to Dunmail Raise, a relentless climb alongside Helvellyn, which I'm sure offers spectacular views to those not enshrouded in H20 vapours. Past Thirlmere I dived off the main roads and enjoyed a few miles of country riding until rudely interrupted by the A66.

The interruption lasted a mile or two before I turned off at the White Horse Inn heading for Mungrisdale,.....big mistake. The book route was taking me up a singletrack road signed as part of the Trans Penine Coast to Coast trail. One of the roadsigns had some plastic sellotaped to it, stupidly I failed to investigate. My suspicions should have been aroused by the disinfectant mat covering the road, along with the gates across the road itself, ever more ignorant I carried on. Finally after about 2 ½ miles of mostly climbing I came to an abrupt halt ... faced with a large and very clear sign stating "Foot and Mouth -Access strictly forbidden beyond this point". Despair!

I didn't have any other maps and my planned route was closed, I retraced my steps back to the A66 and called Helen. The poor girl was on the other end of another 5 minute moaning session as I lamented my woes, talked about giving up and snapped at her to provide me with alternative directions. Calmly she directed me to Mungisdale via a quick dash up the A66, I saddled up and painfully ground on. A good series of fingerposts saw me back on track and just as I left the scenery of the Lakes. The cloud rose and out came the sun.

At this point my knee was very painful indeed, and I was having real doubts that I would be able to complete the ride. Every hill strained the knee further and I soon discovered that when pushing off I was using my right leg to get started, adding further strain to the knee. Some relief was gained by re-training myself to push off with the left leg, not as easy as it sounds after years of automatically unclipping left from the pedals at every stop. Helen called with good news, they had found a reasonable motel close to my planned route, at Durdar I turned towards the M6 and meet the crew at the Terracotta Restaurant and Hotel, our first night under a proper roof. The first priority was a good hot bath, followed by an excellent meal of chicken in the restaurant along with medicinal glass of wine.

I'd covered 72 miles in all, my shortest day yet, however, the lack of distance was mitigated by the knee pain and a long wait for repairs in the Lake District. Again, I considered a complete rest the following day, but eventually decided to press on and see how far I could get.

Day 7 - Carlisle to New Cumnock

Enviously side glancing at Helen and Sara's full English platters, I force fed myself the usual muesli, bread and orange juice breakfast (for some reason the hotel refused to charge us for breakfast?). I decided to head for somewhere in the Dumfries area and we agreed to meet up somewhere near Greta to review my knee and potential for progress. It wasn't raining, but the wind had picked up (15mph at a guess) so progress would be variable as at certain points I would turn into it. I picked my way through Carlisle in search of the A7, eventually found after interrogating a "baggied up" BMXer at a set of traffic lights. The road to Gretna via Longtown was pretty bleak and my knee was still hurting, but I was starting to get used to the pain. The injury didn't affect my ability to pedal, it just reminded me at every stroke that something down there was not quite right.

I resolved that the ride would be finished, the challenge from now on was to ignore the messages from down below as long as they remained constant. Additionally I decided that the scenic route would be slightly compromised in favour of reduced distance. The "Welcome to Scotland" sign at Gretna certainly raised my spirits, even though there was a long way to go.

Cycling from Land's End to Scotland was an achievement in itself and I mentally brushed aside the remaining 400 miles, convincing myself the ride was nearly done! I met up with the crew at Rigg and we decided that I could make Sanquar, 40 miles or so up the road, they went off in search of children's entertainment and I fought the wind towards Dumfries. At Annan I made a terrible decision and decided to head for the A75, a more direct route into Dumfries, what a nightmare.

The A75 proved to be an uninteresting, poorly surfaced, well used trunk route completely devoid of any sane cyclists. I loathed the 15 miles to Dumfries, as insult was teamed up with injury by the downpour that accompanied me. Finally, spitting slightly acidic precipitation, the outskirts of Dumfries appeared and in atrocious rain I navigated the ring road in search of the A76. A big "thank you" to the lorry driver who took pity on me at a particularly vicious roundabout and appeared to block traffic behind me allowing a traffic free circuit onto the A76.

Helen and Sara overtook me a few miles down the road, after a section of cyclist revenge at roadworks. There's nothing more satisfying than scooting past stationary traffic on your bike, especially when the cars contain the dastardly motorists who'd paid more attention to their tourist maps than the drenched pedaller they were overtaking. My smile hid a virtual "two fingers" as I quickly made the front of the queue and took the traffic through the roadworks at my leisure.

The A76 improved its scenery outside of Dumfries and gave way to absorbing curves and hills as it tracked the River Nith northwards. I'm not sure whether it was the wind, the road surface or a new brand of fatigue, but I endured the peculiar sensation of having to pedal downhill in order to make progress. One hour ahead of schedule I crested the hill at Sanquar and rode up and down the main street in search of Tea Shop... gutted, couldn't find one.

The local Spar came to my rescue and I spent a miserable 20 minutes squatting in a bus shelter feeding myself macaroni cheese pie and fresh milk. I can't fathom why I did this as the shop assistant had informed me of a Tea Shop 1 mile up the road. Finally common sense kicked in and with a pot of tea and cake by my side (and pretty soon inside me) I awaited my support crew. Slowly the water, sweat and other liquids massed within my cycling shorts made its way onto the seat below me. Eventually, shamefaced, I confessed to the staff, they weren't bothered.

It was then I noticed the CTC sticker in the window, they were obviously used to it. 45 minutes later the crew arrived, more tea and cake was had and we debated the evening's accommodation. Sanquar seemed a bit bleak, and a poster in the Tearoom came to our rescue, advertising Farmhouse Bed and Breakfast. A quick call confirmed availability and we were reliably informed it was only a few miles down the road. Ten miles later I came to the junction heading for the farm, fortuitously someone was expecting me as a young lady in a Fiesta rolled down her window shouting "You must be the cyclist", (well done love), "the bed and breakfast's down this road". ½ a mile later I found the van parked outside of Low Polqueys farm, the bike was shoved into it and the day's cycling was done.

I'd covered 82 miles in total, the knee still hurt but my average speed had not dropped (consistently above 14 mph for every day so far). Helen cooked us a meal in the van and served it up in Mrs Caldwell's dining room, a few hours later she joined us for a pleasant chat, after which I flaked out, tired, but feeling better progress had been made than expected. As head hit pillow, a cockerel crowed in the farmyard below, "If I hear a peep out of the little bugger before 8am", I thought to myself, " there'll be one more Fricassee in Scotland tomorrow." He got the message and kept his gob shut until well after we'd gone.

Day 8 - New Cumnock to Tarbert

Tearfully we waved "goodbye" to Sara, who reluctantly had to return to England and a proper job. Helen's challenge increased as the kids main source of entertainment departed. I was really looking forward to today, most of the riding was on minor roads, and included the Isle of Arran with its mountain passes and spectacular scenery. The ride from New Cumnock to Irvine was perfect, almost totally traffic free, not too hilly and easy to navigate. The weather was reasonably kind, with little rain, but almost no wind to impede me.

The experience was tarnished somewhat at Irvine, where yet again Mr Horsley's maps proved impossible to fathom and a combination of luck and guesswork eventually got me across town and into Ardrossan, where the camper van sat awaiting the Arran ferry. We waited for an hour or so, during which I changed the worn rear tyre and attempted to clear the chain of as much accumulated clag as possible. Helen told me that the last ferry off Arran left at 6.30pm, this put the pressure on. I had exactly 1 hour and 15 minutes to get round the Island or we would be stuck there for the night. So in preparation, I stripped the bike of all unnecessary weight and prepared for the route's first time trial.

This really was turning into a mini Tour de France. One uneventful crossing later, I whipped the bike off the back of the van and perched eagerly in the bowels of the ferry awaiting the opening doors. A chink of daylight appeared and I was off, hacking through Brodick and out of town at 20 mph plus. I was feeling pretty good, until another roadie passed me a mile up the road, the competitive juices were stirred and I hauled up to his back wheel ready for a challenge in the hills. It never came, as we ended up chatting. He was an Arran based triathelete and a veteran "End to Ender" having taken a route similar to mine, he accompanied me for seven miles or so and kept the average speed well up above the 20mph.

Just before the hills he departed (suspicious eh?) and wished me well. The climb over the mountains past Sannox was breathtaking, the sun was out, the clouds had gone and mountains towered above. At this point the ride really came back to life and any doubts about the diversion onto Arran were banished. The knee pain was there, but forgotten as I sweated my way to the top relishing the promise of a downhill coast into Lochranza.

The ride was over too soon, 20 miles had been covered in 55 minutes and we were going to make the ferry. In glorious fading sunlight we played with the kids on the beach and left for the Mull of Kintyre bang on 6.30pm. Another beautiful climb later I hit the A83 and at a leisurely pace cruised into Tarbet where Helen awaited ensconced within a "designer" bed and breakfast (Ikea furniture, pastel coloured bedclothes, chocolates on pillows etc....). Deep rooted anarchist tendencies surfaced as I washed my cruddy cycling shorts in the perfectly clean porcelain sink. The bike computer showed 70 miles in total, the shortest day of the whole trip, but one of the best.

Day 9 - Tarbert to Fort William

I was up before the rest of the crew and ate hot rolls and fruit in the breakfast room accompanied only by a Bodum of tea. The oft practised manoeuvre of wrestling on damp cycling kit was completed and I groaned out of Tarbert somewhere near 8.15am. It was a beautiful Scottish morning as mist hung over the Mull of Kintyre and only the early bird workers brushed past me on the A83. Knee pain was still very much in evidence and I keenly awaited the 45 minute point at which the pain killers started to numb the sharpness. The ride from Tarbert to Lochgilphead was enticing with snatches of Loch Fyne keeping moral at a reasonable high.

At Lochgiliped the Mull was lost and I turned inland towards Oban on the A816. Gravity started to call as well and the "huffing" and "puffing" started in real earnest around Kilmartin with a long pull accompanied by staring tourists entombed within their coaches. The weather held reasonably well and every threat of rain failed to materialise once I had deftly flung on the waterproof. Slowly but surely I traversed the west coast and beat my way up to Oban, pausing only to offer a wry grin and infinitely sarcastic "Hello" to the two overburdened American cycle tourists sweating their way past Kilmelford.

It may have been the pain killers, but I'm convinced that road surfaces got increasingly worse the further north I rode. With local council budgets scrimping on smooth tarmac, instead providing me with a carpet of mixed aggregates to jar my muscles and bones. I was now seriously regretting the decision to buy a road bike, and also developing a new discomfort, scientifically labelled "bloodisorearseicus".

Oban came and went in a few turns of the chainset (with help from the hill just before it) and I climbed steeply out of the town towards Connel and a planned rendezvous with the support crew at the Sea Life Centre. Helen had told me it was just outside of Oban, some 10 miles later I found it. The kids were (apparently) having a whale of a time within, so I found the van in the car park, helped myself to lunch and sped off without even a cursory "Hello".

The target for the day was Fort William and I still had some 40 miles or so to go. Fifteen minutes later the rain started again, not showers, but that relentless Scottish drizzle as unrelenting and annoying as a single bagpipe note held too long. With sore arse, painful knee and soggy everything the day lost its magic and faded into a simple struggle to decrease the distance between myself and Fort William. The support crew caught me at Ballachulish with more bad news, the van had started to fart like a sumo wrestler on a rice purge and obviously needed some serious exhaust attention.

Helen was despatched to Fort William to purchase Gun Gum and a campsite pitch, whilst I was left to the rain and the pain. The final stretch of the A82 into Fort William offered nothing of interest, apart from the fat foreign motorbiker, who stopped at a layby completely without view, got off his bike, looked around, smiled, mounted again and rode off. It left me wondering whether he could actually see whilst on the road hence this being his "sight" break, or maybe he savoured some nostalgic memory from years gone by spent stopping at the world's most boring layby.

At Fort William, I rushed into Nevis Sport, completely soaked and purchased a pair of semi-waterproof tights. An impulse I was later to regret as they were too small and I had lost the receipt. A few miles more saw me at the campsite with a view of Ben Nevis to boot. The knee hurt like hell and my arse was starting to compete for neurones with its own particular set of complaints.

That evening I made the big mistake of calculating the distance left, nearly 200 miles. I wasn't sure I could face many more long days and it looked like I might still have 3 more to go. Today's mileage said 95 miles in total along with the second highest average speed of the trip (15.3 mph), my face in the campsite toilet mirror said a whole lot more. At this point only Helen's encouragement and the promise of sponsorship money was keeping me going, I thought tomorrow was going to be tough, it was worse.

Day 10 - Fort William to Dornoch

Another stifled breakfast in the van trying not to wake the kids, followed by another misty start following the A82 out of Fort William. All thoughts of minor roads were banished today, prostituted to the goal of distance, Inverness or bust! The first hour or two proved quite pleasant once the painkillers had numbed the knee pain and reasonable progress was made along Loch Lochy. However the road was miserable, built for coaches and maximal wear resistance with no quarter given to cyclists comfort whatsoever. After 10 o'clock the traffic started to increase, compounding the misery as every passing motorist competed with each other to remove my right hand side brake levers.

After Invergarry I came across the Caledonian Canal towpath seemingly offering some respite, but 100 yards of bone shattering cobbles forced me back onto the main roads. At Fort Augustus I stared longingly at my planned diversion to the right hand side of Loch Ness and up into the hills around Foyers. However, the knee dictated terms and sternly forbade any attempt at serious climbing if distance were to be gained today.

The A82 alongside Loch Ness was as worse a road as any encountered upon the whole trip. Endless streams of coaches buzzed past, whilst trees deprived me of any view whatsoever and the road surface sent my arse into symphonies Mozart would have put his name to. Halfway along I passed a Nordic couple, smiling on their tandem and dragging their two year old behind on a trailer, I soon found out why they were smiling, they were only going to Inverness. Drumnadroicht provided some short relief with a hill, but the pain continued as Inverness got closer.

Fifteen miles outside of Drumnadroicht the 3 litres of energy drink made themselves known and I stopped by a copse for a little tinkle. Layers of lycra were peeled back to free John Thomas and he was dutifully pointed at a bush well out of sight of any passing motorist. True to the nature of my luck so far, two female antipodean hikers emerged giggling from the side of the bush, giggled even louder and set off in the opposite direction.

Please remember dear reader,... it was cold,... the shorts were tight etc.. etc.. A familiar farting noise caught me up at the outskirts of Inverness and the support crew re-filled my bottles and provided energy bars. Poor old Helen took another ear bashing as I whinged about my arse, knee and any other appendage remotely connected to cycling. We agreed to aim for Tain, and dutifully she set off, farting slightly less than the previous day as a kindly mechanic at ATS had botched up a temporary repair for us.

Finally I gained Inverness and hated it. Horrible traffic and roundabouts spat me across town and onto the Kessock bridge, with a sign of relief I left the A9 and followed back roads towards Munlochy. After a couple of miles I was accompanied by a stray dog, a beautiful spaniel apparently parted from his walkers. Having saved him from a couple of near fatal road accidents I stopped and read his collar, I then called the phone number attached but got no reply.

I sat there for 10 minutes trying to decide what to do and eventually made up my mind to drag the poor bugger up the nearest drive and beg their assistance, however Rover or Spot or whatever he was called would have none of it, and buggered off sharpish across the nearest field. I called the owners several times later that day, but got no reply, I hope the poor dog is still okay.

The rise towards Fortrose was uneventful, until two teenage mountain bikers pulled out in front of me and sped off in granny ring heaven. A final prayer was said to the God of leg muscles and I set off in pursuit catching them at the bottom of a very long hill. The whippersnappers were passed and I rested easy that my 10 day legs would soon see their youth off. But No. 400 yards later they were gaining on me, I gave it everything I had and reached the 471 foot summit some 200 yards ahead. I didn't look back all the way to Cromarty and pride was restored as they failed to pass me (or they simply turned off). Cromarty provided a mild panic as I couldn't find the ferry, eventually one 45 minute wait later I was on the strange beast and crossing to Nigg.

At Nigg I phoned the crew and suggested I could make Dornoch, off they went in search of a campsite and I continued on with gritted teeth ignoring every message received in the pain reception centre of my brain. At Dornoch bridge I watched an eagle sat on a fencepost looking for some scran, and finally rolled into campsite at 10 to 6. I'd done 110 miles in total and felt pretty bad, I had 80 or so miles to do the next day but somehow felt a long way from finishing. Today was our wedding anniversary, we celebrated it with a bowl of pasta and some orange juice in a camper van. Who said romance is dead?

Day 11 - Dornoch to John O'Groats

Anticipation got the better of me and instead of lying in as planned, I got up pretty early hacked down breakfast and shot off up the A9, leaving the campsite somewhere close to 8.40am. The initial horrors of the A9 road surface soon subsided and around about Golspie I was even starting to enjoy the cycling, although with a degree of trepidation. The night before I made the mistake of reading the book and came across the following quote about Helmsdale:- "The reputation of the next section has caused quivering knees among a century of "End to End" cyclists. The road climbs and twists ...." What! I thought I had done all of the hills, the bloke on Arran told me it was flat from Oban onwards, my knee hurt and my arse was killing me. I couldn't be doing with hills as well.

Somehow this chivied me up and I made extremely good progress that morning with only a brief stop at Brora for a banana and energy bar. Eventually I fought the way up and around the Ord of Caithness, a terrible climb that seems endless, until all height is abruptly lost and then regained at Berridale. The worst feature of the climb was the ability to see what is ahead of you, no false summits here, only 30 minutes of sweating, swearing and hard bloody work. I waited at Dunbeath for the support crew and was passed by a couple of oldish blokes on a tandem.

They were obviously in the same boat and I wished them luck (they looked completely and utterly shagged out, increasing my morale no end!). Eventually the crew arrived, we agreed all was looking good for a finish and they set off for John O'Groats with my ETA set and somewhere around 4-5pm. Things smoothed out at Lybster, but that didn't stop my arse going into near labour contractions. At Ulbster I stopped and stripped naked in a piss stinking bus shelter. Underwear was rearranged and a pact signed with my buttocks that if they let me make it that day, I wouldn't cycle for a week afterwards.

The road to Wick seemed to take an age and suddenly I wasn't enjoying it again, the knee pain stepped up a gear and fatigue slowly dragged my speed down to near stationary,.. that is until I entered Wick and saw a piece of magic..... It read "John O'Groats 16 miles",.... 16 miles ... I had done that in 40 minutes before, if I got moving it could all be over within the hour. It was 1.45pm, I called Helen. "Are you at the end ?" "No" she said "we're on a beach" "Well bloody get off it" I swore "I'll be there in an hour" The phone was stuffed back into my pocket and the hammer went down, I shot out of Wick greedily eating yards and visualising a flat downhill finish with the wind behind me. Until I got to Reiss that is.

The bloody roadbuilders were taking the piss when they created the first track out to John O'Groats. They knew how tired the "end to ender" would be and subsequently decided to go up and down a few more hills for good measure. I was averaging 20mph plus until Reiss but rapidly dropped to a much more realistic 9-12mph. The last hill really hurt, the knee screamed, the arse even hurt when off the saddle and the thighs and other assorted muscles let it be known that they'd had enough, and then I saw it. The final few hundred yards should have been the best of my cycling career, somehow they were strangely anti-climatic.

I'd been to John O'Groats before and it's a dump. I was greeted by a full car park and my wife desperately trying to control two hyperactive young children. I stopped for a brief hug and then we sidled over to the finish line for our "official photo". At the signpost another end to ender stood, post photo session. It seemed to me that he was waiting (like I was) for the fanfare that never came, he was still in his cycling gear and his gaze started to turn in my direction, I avoided his eyes and quickly decamped to the van to change. His wife held a video camera and started to film the hotel, I get the feeling she'd run out of angles for her husband and was as keen as I was for him to get in the car and go home.

It did feel good to finish, there was a sense of achievement, but somehow it was filtered off along the ride with every stage, rather than some momentous rush at the end. I changed in the van and went for a quiet pint on my own whilst the kids played on the beach. As I ordered my beer, the landlord asked "Are you Dave Barter?" and then handed me a note of congratulation from my parents. That note somehow meant much more than any self congratulatory photo session next to a signpost, but then again I'm a cynical...etc.etc.

Two more finishers entered the bar after me and signed the book held under the bar for all those that have made the journey. I scribbled something myself. I can't remember what. Shortly afterwards the tandem boys followed, they'd done it in 12 days and (I think) the guy on the back was blind .... Fair play! Drinking my Guinness I started to line up my thoughts. The ride had been worthwhile, I'd pushed myself harder than ever before and equally raised a lot of money for charity. Somehow something was missing, and I decided that the mechanical problems and knee injuries were a major contributor. I had set out to ride the "scenic" route, but after Preston this objective had been compromised in favour of shortest distance and ease of access to support crew.

Additionally, I realised that this "green and pleasant" land is not as green or pleasant as we're led to believe, I envied the cyclists in the earlier years who didn't have to contend with lorries or roundabouts or traffic lanes. I especially despised the tourist highways that cut their way through the Highlands, I felt a special kind of resentment for those achieving the scenery without any kind of effort whatsoever. So truth be told the finish was a relief, but an anticlimax, after one pint, we packed up and headed off towards Dornoch in the van. The sensation of speed was unreal! The cycle computer said 80 miles, 1,019 in total for the whole trip.

Chapter 30

Could Do Better?

If you managed to read through the previous chapter you may be tempted to conclude that my Land's End John O'Groats experience lacked a certain "Je ne sais quoi?" and you'd be right. The ride itched away at me over the years as I remained convinced that it could be much more than it was. In particular I had issues with the route. It had been enjoyable in places, but there were sections that made me want to ditch the bike and hitchhike instead.

In particular I felt that Scotland had been hard done by. It's my favourite place in the world, yet a lot of the riding had been traffic ridden and tedious. Like a mountain climber I stared at maps looking for the perfect line until one day it came to me, the Hebrides, they were the key to the perfect route.

However, I had to bide my time as I'd slipped into another period of proper employ. I had a job with responsibilities and little time available to spend dallying about on the bike. Yet this itch was in need of a scratch and on almost the tenth anniversary of my previous LEJOG I was at the starting line ready to tackle it again.

The writing bug had spread like a virulent virus through my mind distracting me from work and calling me out onto the road. I had spotted an aspect of British cycling that needed to be written about before it was too late. Thus in October 2010 I handed in my notice and spent a year on the road writing full time about the country and the cycling I love. This book is still in the making as I write these words. It's taken many long days and sleepless nights to beat into the shape it deserves.

When planning this year I pencilled in October as my return to LEJOG, or as I prefer it "redux" which implies that something is brought back and restored. I felt I needed to restore the ride to true classic status within my mind. This next article is the last in the book, it's a blog post that I wrote at the end of the ride and I've added to inject some balance.

In a previous chapter I mooted cycling pilgrimages. Whilst Ventoux is certainly high on the list, every British cyclist should aspire to complete a LEJOG. It's a journey that will underpin the reasons why you ride. It's a journey that will deliver you into the heart of this country and understand that we still have reason to suffix it with the word "Great". It's a journey that will make you realise that us cyclists are not universally despised, quite the opposite.

You will be humbled with the awe that still greets your endeavours from those who have not made the journey themselves. You'll be amazed at the friendliness and helpfulness that still exists right in the heart of our society despite the best efforts of the media to convince you otherwise. But most of all you will find yourself somewhere along the way and have a jolly good chat. As a result you'll discover what makes you tick, why you do things and where you want to go next. That is unless you're one of these time trially types who simply sets out to ride it as fast as you can. In that case you'll be disappointed, as you'll never beat Gethin Butler. He did it in one day 40 hours.

LEJOG Redux is a long term writing project for me. I hope to publish a guide to my route in the next year or so. In the meantime, here's a little taster.

Land's End John O'Groats Redux (2012)

Sat on my office desk I have two photos. They contain pictures of two very different people. At first sight this may not seem so obvious as both pictures depict me holding my bike near signposts. But I can assure you that the individual in the second picture has undergone some considerable change both physically and mentally. I've spent the past twelve days riding from Land's End to John O'Groats. This wasn't for charity, wasn't for personal whim, it was a quest to vindicate my belief that a perfect cycling route exists between the two points. It had to be ridden in October for logistical and family reasons and it had to be done unsupported to prove that my route would "go" without the need to camp or sleep in bus shelters.

When planning the ride I set myself a tough schedule, 90-100 miles most days. I visualised myself riding in an untroubled manner through sunshine on perfectly surfaced roads. I imagined the idyllic tea shop stops and leisurely evenings spent kicking back in bed and breakfasts. What could go wrong? This is the UK we're talking about and October is always sunny isn't it? Our Indian summer was due and I'd be having a whale of a time with twelve continuous days of the most scenic cycling ever.

Things began to go awry as I travelled down to Penzance on the train. The heating in my carriage was not working well so I donned all of my cycling gear. I was still freezing. I whiled away the time looking at weather forecasts on my smartphone. It was going to be sunny in Kent, everywhere else could expect wind and drizzle. Disembarking I spotted another fellow pushing a laden bike. We chatted briefly, and discovered that both of us shared a destination in John O'Groats. In fact we were due to arrive on the same day via different routes. The steady rain falling on the station route curtailed our conversation. We both faffed with waterproofs and bade each other a hasty "Good Luck".

And so I set off. Twelve days later I finished.

When I did English 'O' Level at school, the précis was a major part of the test. Mr Nesbitt would hound us until we had got the plot of Macbeth down to 200 words. So he'd be very proud of the last paragraph given that the drama contained within my twelve days equates to a Macbeth, two King Lears with a dash of Hamlet and some Merchant of Venice thrown in for good measure.

The full story will be saved for another day as I need to do proper justice to the ride but I'll give you a few edited highlights.

Accommodation

First let's start with the Devon pub under new management who gave me a room that clearly hadn't been slept in for years. Flies and bugs crawled out of cracks in the wall, the smell of damp pervaded everything and the only tea available was Earl Grey. I could have coped if the jukebox in the bar below hadn't malfunctioned and randomly played hits of the seventies throughout the night. I will never ever be able to listen to the Doors without smashing something to smithereens.

Then there's the posh hotel in the Hebrides with the room door that jammed after I closed it. I was blissfully unaware of this as I slept through the night and only found out once dressed and ready to ride to a ferry. It was 7.30am, my ferry left at 9.15 and reception would not answer the phone. My window looked out onto a glass conservatory, there was no alternative means of escape. I eventually broke out of the room using two spoons to unjam the lock only to find that the room containing my bike was locked as well. Like a scene from the Shining I ran through hotel corridors in search of help, eventually scaring the shit out of a Polish chambermaid who I found in the kitchens. My crazed eyes and furious watch based gesticulations persuaded her to free my bike and unleash the country's most scenic time trial as I sprinted for the ferry through a beautiful Scottish glen.

I mustn't forget all of the lovely B&B owners as well. Karen from the Farr Bay Inn who let me a room even though they'd returned from holiday at midnight the night before. The owners of the Crown Inn in Tarbolton who dried my clothes, offered to cook me dinner (even though they don't do food) and tried to undercharge me. Kath from the Clark Farm House in Lancashire who attempted to give me money back and made me the most wonderful breakfast. Also the lovely owners of Troutbeck Cottage near Carlisle and Maeve and Weavel from Dingwall who took a real interest in my ride and drove me to dinner in the evening.

I have grown a real affection for UK Bed and Breakfast accommodation. All of the owners I met were fantastic and especially keen to aid the cyclist. It may be coincidence, but the further north I came, the lower the price and greater the welcome.

The Weather

Up until the Lake District it was mostly going well. Devon had been full of drizzle, but the other days had been mostly dry with a following wind. Then I set out from Carlisle, crossed into Scotland and rode into the worst weather I have ever encountered in all my years of cycling. The pain began with a gale force northwesterly head wind. I'd used up all of my gears on the flat and saw my average speed drop to "armadillo".

Progress was measured by counting fence posts and praying for farm buildings to get in the way of the wind. Then it rained. Actually it didn't rain, some mysterious entity followed me pouring full buckets of water down my neck at thirty second intervals. At one point I stopped pedalling and travelled a section of road by osmosis alone. The water entered everything, me, my clothes, my luggage, my protective plastic bags and finally my expensive compact camera killing it quickly.

I somehow became accustomed to this mode of suffering and managed to plod onwards towards that day's destination. But Scotland wasn't having that, it turned down the temperature scale and switched the rain to hail. This was the absolute low point of my ride. I crouched beside the A79 desperately trying to hide from the falling ice. The agony and despair is something I hope never to suffer again.

If there had been an option to pack and go home I would have taken it without question. Unfortunately I was on my own and forced to struggle on. Lorries and cars honked horns in disbelief at this idiot cyclist struggling along a flooded main road in the near dark. And this was proper flooding, at one point I rode into water that flowed over my bottom bracket which will now need to be replaced.

That day was 103 miles of riding without a single moment of pleasure. Writing this it still does not seem real that I made it and I'm sure the nightmares will replace the usual recurring theme of having to take my maths degree again.

The wind and rain continued for days with a terrible pattern emerging of a soaking at the beginning and ending of rides with sunshine only appearing as I stopped for lunch or a trip on the ferry. I properly lost it on a number of occasions. I've realised that I need to find religion so I can have someone to blame for my predicament. As it was, I shook my fist at Scotland and pleaded with it to make it stop. I cursed at the injustice of the headwinds and shouted at nothing to make the rain go away. I even tried to cry a few times but the tears would not come.

Eventually I developed a mantra that went "At some point today, all of this will stop". I used it to get through the bad spells but at times felt like the mythological Greek bloke who pushes that rock up a hill.

The bike and equipment

You'll be surprised to know that most of my gear choices were sound and the bike survived relatively unscathed. Well, it is covered in shit, has no brake pads left at all and is in desperate need of some lube and much adjustment. I suffered three punctures and some annoying brake rub which is pretty damned good given the terrible state of many of the roads and it also being hedge cutting season.

The one set of clothes I carried now stinks. Twelve days in the same set of pants is not ideal and my single shirt is covered in food and splatters of drink. I'm so glad I carried the Kindle to while away nights lain on a bed with nothing but crap on the telly. Sadly it died on day eleven with a failed screen, probably due to a poorly packed bar bag or nasty bump in the road.

Me

Physically I seemed to hold up quite well. I found the heavier laden bike a frustration and constantly wondered why I was riding so slow. Climbing was a chore as well. It was like I'd suddenly become fat as I huffed and gurned my way up the slightest of hills. Cornwall and Devon destroyed my climbing legs further and I never seemed to recover properly from the damage done. But each day I was able to bang out the miles at a seemingly constant rate. Eating and drinking well aided this and I stuck to a regime of nosebag every twenty miles which seemed to do the job.

I've eaten such crap though. A full fry up each day, four bottles of Lucozade sport, three to four flapjacks, crappy sandwiches for lunch, a Snickers bar, cans of coke and inevitably something+chips for tea. It's not stopped me losing weight, 3-4 pounds I reckon, weight I just didn't have to lose in the first place.

Mentally, I've learnt a lot about myself. The main thing being that when I'm on my own I moan like a baby. Constantly feeling sorry for myself and asking "why, why me?". Several times I came close to cracking and packing it all in. Luckily the options weren't there as these occasions usually coincided with wilderness and a lack of phone signal. I'm nowhere near as strong mentally as I thought I would be. I now have myself down as a "self-indulgent-whiny-plodder" and have to clearly recognise the moment where I start to slide in to personal despair and distract myself away.

It's no mean feat to ride 1100 miles in 12 days through spells of disastrous weather. The real achievement is to free yourself to enjoy it instead of adding to the burden with unnecessary stress.

The route

This is why I set out in the first place and to be frank this is where I feel the greatest sense of achievement. The route is sublime. From the north coast of Cornwall through the back roads of Devon and over the Severn into the best bits of the Welsh borders. Over the Long Mynd, into the Lancastrian hills and onto a major Lake District pass. Some of the best of Ayrshire followed by the Hebrides then Sutherland, it's a cyclist's dream. I can only remember a few miles of tedium in the thousands ridden. In fact there are only two really shit bits of the route, one's Land's End and the other is John O'Groats, two pieces of Great Britain that need ripping up and starting again.

I'm really proud of the route I've designed. I'm sure that out there someone will have ridden it before and will claim a first ascent. I couldn't give a toss. I genuinely sat at a computer for a week and followed the most interesting lines on the map. This needed ferries to achieve in Scotland. Have I cheated? I couldn't care less.

Without the ferries the route just wouldn't work and to me it felt like a well planned orchestral movement leading to the crescendo of the day riding in Sutherland. This is the day that I slowed down for fear of it passing too quickly. The day that laughter replaced guttural despair as I thanked circumstance for placing me on two wheels in this wonderful wild wilderness. I even forgave the idiot encased in the latest German engineering who passed too close on the road round Loch Naven.

Anyway it's done now and I'm safely ensconced in the van enjoying my birthday with Helen, Jake and Holly. They did a magnificent job in driving a huge distance to scoop me up from Wick, hose me down and coax me back to normality. I must also doff a grateful cap to friends and family who supported me along the way. Chris, your text was a powerful piece of medicine on a day when things weren't looking so good. The twitter messages helped enormously but the top motivational prize goes to the cafe owner in Kyle of Lochalsh who offered to give me cash there and then for a copy of the book. I didn't take the money, I just banked the sentiment instead. Lady, I'm getting this drivel published just so that I can rock up at your door and take you to your word.

Chapter 31

A Goodbye

Firstly, my hearty congratulations for reading this far, unless you have cheated and dived straight to the end in frustration at the verbosity that intervened. I sincerely hope that you've enjoyed the journey required to arrive at these final few sentences. Even if you haven't you can sit in smug satisfaction that at least one person on this earth has derived pleasure in the creation of these words, namely me.

Last time I did a proper count there were over 83,000 of the little bleeders sandwiched between these pages. Believe you me they are not alone. Scattered across my various computers and network drives are hundreds of thousands more, all of them lined up ready to offend, inform, bore or antagonise the reader depending upon their point of view. Of course they're all about cycling. There's a simple reason for that.

Cycling is without question one of the richest elements of my life. I find it impossible to not write about it. Every single incident or outing on two wheels triggers a new emotion or conclusion that I sadly feel the need to document. My family life is the only greater source of inspiration but there are some things that really should remain behind closed doors. I don't just do cycling either, I'm a failed climber, keen but lax scuba diver and make the odd perilous trip out on my barnacle encrusted sea kayak. But cycling, like the mafia, draws me back time and time again to chunter on about it through the medium of my keyboard.

I owe cycling a huge debt for the years of happiness it has thrown my way. Cycling owes me a huge debt for the large amounts of money it coerced out of my pocket and into all sorts of cycling related tills. But the happiness tips the balance right to the floor when compared to the fiscal loss. That explains the reason why I write about cycling in the way I do.

I'm not and never will be a cycling "James Joyce". I've tried to sit down and write some deep meaningful cathartic prose that describes one of my rides. In fact I sent it to Dan Joyce at the CTC and asked for his thoughts. "It reads like bad poetry" was his response. What did he know? So in a huff I sent it to my friend Rob instead. "Dave, it's shit, stick to writing in your own voice matey".

In a sulk I went out for a ride on my bike and spotted an abandoned pornography magazine by the side of the road. It was a pretty foul day but the soggy breasts staring up from the tarmac inspired me. I began to construct a piece in my mind about the recent lack of discarded hedgerow porn disturbingly aligned with the disappearance of white dog shit.

They were right, that's the kind of writer I am. I should stick to pointing out the things that occur to me and not try to embellish the words to suit a higher audience. And that is what you have just hauled your eyes through. Eighty three thousand words that illustrate what cycling means to Dave. There's no campaigning in there, I'm not very good at that. There's a distinct lack of firm advice as I'm probably the worst person to offer it. But what hopefully emerges is a tinge of passion from a fairly ordinary British guy who loves his sport, the people who partake in it and the places and experiences it takes him to.

Now it is entirely possible that this was only part achieved. As mentioned right from the start this is a conglomeration of stuff that I've written over a period of time and glued together with bridging text. I can appreciate there may be a certain staccato nature as articles are not ordered by genre or timeline. I tried to mix them up a bit to keep the interest there. I also appreciate that they vary in quality, but so does my writing and I wanted to portray a proper picture of me.

Let's discuss the element of vanity. This is a book about Dave, it's written by Dave and it concerns bike rides that were ridden by Dave. A tinge of egotism cannot be escaped and I can properly understand if you dragged your way to the end willing the author to shut up about himself and write about someone else instead. I've tried it before and admit that I find it hard to do. The emotions you read within are genuine. I have no idea what others think when they're out on the bike, apart from the bloke who called me a tosser in a fourth cat's race, he made his emotions perfectly clear.

So I'll shut up now and leave you to consign this text to the charity box or eReader trash icon. If you do, maybe take a second or two to drop me a line. dave@phased.co.uk. I'm always there and mustard keen to know what people think even if it's not what I was hoping for. If you liked it you can drop me a line as well. Apart from Mum, as I detect a subtle tone of bias no matter how impartial you say you will be. The table I made at school that you so proudly display is wonky and really a bit crap. I've known it for years.

Forthcoming Publications

I've spent 2011 riding all over Great Britain and a book celebrating this journey will be published in 2012.

I am working on an insight into the Year Record Mileage holders such as Tommy Godwin and Walter Greaves. Possibly 2012, more likely 2013

My Land's End John O'Groats guide is work in progress, maybe I'll use it as an excuse to ride the whole thing once again, but I've promised Helen it will be done in 2012.

All of these and my regular blog are available at:-

www.phased.co.uk

The End Bit

Thanks and Acknowledgements

No man is an island and I feel like a continent. There is no way on earth that this book would have come into existence without the following people. Depending upon your outlook you can either thank or blame them.

Firstly there are those who inspired me to write in the first place.

Mr Nesbitt who taught English at Wootton Bassett Comprehensive in the 1970-80's was a leading influence. He didn't just prepare us for exams, he showed us depths that existed in literature. His wit, sarcasm but genuine enthusiasm for words have always been a strong influence on me. I can just about forgive the thwaks around the head with his reinforced ruler and my nickname "Billy" as it was he who introduced me to John Carpenter films, George Orwell and accepted my hypothesis that Banquo was gay.

My uncle James Loader who is a published author in his own right and spent time helping me edit and rephrase my early writings. James taught me about structure, voice, consistency and flair. If you didn't find any of these within then it is my fault not his. James must also take some responsibility for the sense of humour. Our childhoods were peppered with hilarious conversations with James. I'm still laughing about the seagull.

And of course, my Mum and Dad, Jenny and Colin. Both have been incredibly supportive and encouraging over the years. Dad's collection of Spike Milligan literature and Goon show records have done irreversible damage to any sense of decorum that I may have once had. Our house was full of books, we always had books when we wanted them and we were always encouraged to read. Also, we always had bikes.

Then there are those who have published my stuff over the years.

Dan Joyce, Editor of the CTC Cycle magazine who published the first piece I managed to get into print. Dan has published further articles over the years, but more importantly offered sage advice on my writing that has always been correct. I wish all editors were as conscientious as Dan in providing feedback to ideas and articles provided. I was tempted to include the article he marked as "bad poetry" to exhibit his brilliant advice, but he'd tell me to just bin it instead.

I must also thank Chipps Chippendale at Singletrack magazine and

Tony Farrelly formerly of Cycling Plus who have also put me in print in various forms. Chipps, I'm sorry about the parrot trolling incident, actually, I'm not, it was one of the funniest online moments of my life, but I'd have done the same in your position. Mike Davies also needs a salute for publishing a number of my witterings upon the Bikemagic web portal which is nowhere near as good now he's left.

Onto those who helped me with this book.

Kath Allan for your encouragement along with the legion of internet forum dwellers for their publishing and printing advice. Alex Leigh for listening to me drone on about my various writing projects and Andy Shelley for telling me to focus on a few important tasks. Andy, I promise that all of this was written out of hours in underpants or dressing gowns.

A huge clap must go to the riders who've put up with me over the years.

Steve Forrester and Steve Green for the early days on the mountain bikes. Russell Pinder, my racing partner and huge influence on my mountain biking. He's now taken to the skies as a microlight pilot which worries me a bit as he was always pretty quick heading downhill. Swindon Road Club riders and the Sunday crew, in particular Jeff and John Smith, Alan Semple, Pete Jeans, Rob Jackson and my Club Captain Malcolm Bates. The Chilterns riders, Mike Beckley, Peter Wallace, Nick Cummins, Jay Tejani and Jon Hall. My neighbour Malcolm Toop-Rose whose time round Croft Trail defeats me even after weeks of training. Peter and Annie Herold, Cronan and Donna Ó Doibhlin lifelong friends after a surreal night annoying butterfly spotters halfway up the Col D' Tourmalet. Ryan O'Neill for his Captain Oates speech and Mark Fidler for nearly getting me divorced in Moab.

Those who read my blogs and internet articles and offer the occasional "Like", Jen Haken, Chris Covell, Roger Cooper, Jon Wyatt, John West, Anthony Firth, Duncan Gilbert, Hugh Carroll, Bev Plaxton, Peter Catherwood, my sister Sally Cornwell and the in laws (hatchet) Barry and Joy Compton.

But the final mention and biggest thanks must go to my long suffering wife Helen who appears in many of these tales mostly with her head in her hands. No man could have greater support than I from one who accepts my addiction with active support and encouragement. You have always been there to help and encourage and without you none of the words within would be possible. I'll mention my children Jake and Holly as well who bring further light into an already enriched life, but that still doesn't mean that they can leave their bedrooms in the state that they are.

Flippin 'eck that lot read like an Oscar speech. This is only a poxy set of articles assembled by an idiot. Anyone would think the author is preparing for the arrival of a Booker.

Printed in Great Britain
by Amazon.co.uk, Ltd.,
Marston Gate.